THE ULTIMATE
Home
Office

TIME
LIFE
BOOKS

Time-Life Books, Alexandria, Virginia

CONTENTS

CHAPTER 1

PLANNING YOUR HOME OFFICE

MILLIONS OF AMERICANS HAVE FOUND A WAY TO BYPASS

traffic jams on the way to the office each morning. For them, the morn-

ing commute is nothing more than a short walk across the hall, down

the stairs, or out the back door to what used to be the garage. By the

mid-1990s, there were more than 41 million home-based businesses in

the United States. For people who feel that starting their own business

from home is a little too risky, there are still ways to work from home.

Working for an employer outside of the corporate office—a practice

known as telecommuting—is rapidly gaining acceptance with both

employees and management, as it often benefits both parties.

The types of businesses that can be run from home are almost as

limitless as your imagination. All you need is to find the space in your

house, draw up a plan to create a customized office area, then fill it

with the necessary furniture and accessories.

*RIGHT: The versatility of laptop computers—
most of which are equipped with fax, modem,
and e-mail capabilities—makes it possible to
set up an office anywhere, even in an out-of-
the way corner of a room.*

WORKING AT HOME

There are many good reasons to work from home: creative freedom, flexible hours, casual dress, cutting out commuting time, and other less tangible rewards such as being close to your children. There are often tax advantages; you may be able to deduct part of the rent or mortgage and household expenses for your home office.

You'll also need to consider the following questions: Do you like to be challenged? Can you take initiative? Do you need regular feedback from colleagues to do your best work? Does being alone free you from distractions or make you feel isolated? Can you keep regular hours even if you are accountable to no one but yourself? Do you know when to stop working? Can you ask for help when you need it?

If you know you are ready to work from home, choose an activity that is marketable as well as one that you will find rewarding and enjoyable. If you lack start-up ideas, consider your technical skills, what you like to do with your time, your hobbies and interests, and volunteer activities or jobs you've enjoyed in the past.

Determine whether any of your interests or skills can be transformed into services or products. For example, if you have a nose for antiques and you love to shop, you might try offering your services as an antique locator. Have you remodeled your house yourself? You may have a career in home renovation or restoration. What about giving seminars on your favorite hobby or skill? Write down all the possibilities,

HOME OFFICE OCCUPATIONS

- Bookkeeper
- Broker (real estate, business)
- Computer instructor
- Computer repair and maintenance
- Consultant (variety of fields)
- Copywriter
- Database designer
- Desktop publisher
- Fund-raiser
- Graphic designer
- Interior designer
- Medical transcriptionist
- News-clipping service
- Paralegal
- Professional services
- Researcher
- Software developer
- Technical writer
- Translator
- Web site developer

then narrow the list down to the ideas that are practical, taking into account whether there is a market for the service or product, who the customers would be, how your business could be better than the competition, how much time and start-up money the business will demand—and how this will affect your home life.

Bylaws in many communities across North America either forbid or restrict the operation of businesses in residential neighborhoods. Many of these laws were enacted before the age of computer technology and were designed to preserve residential neighborhoods and protect employees from unsuitable or unsafe working conditions. In general, the bylaws regulate the type of business, parking, traffic and noise levels, fire or health hazards, and outdoor lighting and signs. To find out about such zoning regulations in your area, contact your municipal or county government.

If you run into obstacles at City Hall, it may be possible to apply for a zoning variance or to have your area rezoned. Organizations such as the Home Office Association of America (HOAA) can advise you on working with local lawmakers.

- Home Business Insurance: As well as insuring equipment, include items like inventory, supplies, and data.
- Insurance for cars and other vehicles: If the family car is used for business, check your policy; your present coverage may not be enough.
- Business Interruption Insurance: If disaster strikes, this will enable you to pay the bills until you are back in business.
- Disability Insurance: This replaces your earnings if you can't work due to accident or illness.
- Liability Insurance: This is necessary in the event of injuries to clients or other visitors to your home office, or to cover employees making deliveries.

Other laws may affect the operation of home-based businesses, including building codes, health permits for certain businesses, and various business licenses. Furthermore, if you rent or live in a condominium, you may require permission from your landlord or condo association.

INSURANCE

Most homeowner's policies do not cover a home business. When looking for coverage, start with the agent who handles your present insurance needs, but don't be afraid to ask questions and shop around, as prices vary considerably. Make sure you understand the policy you are buying and any restrictions that apply. Be honest with your agent—you can't expect to get good coverage advice if you don't divulge all the facts. Keep the following in mind: Buy only the insurance you need, but do not undervalue your technology or data. If you travel for business, make sure your policy covers off-premises equipment.

Accurate records will make filing a claim much simpler. Keep receipts of all purchases and a list of equipment, inventory, and supplies. Take pictures of everything—stills or video—and keep a copy off-site in a safe-deposit box or with a friend or relative. Update your records as needed.

Health insurance is another, potentially costly consideration. As with other types of insurance, be realistic when assessing your needs, and shop around, as insurance plans vary widely. Membership in a professional or business association may entitle you to insurance at group rates.

Whether you plan to section off a corner of your kitchen or will remodel a whole room, dedicating a permanent space for your home office will make you feel more professional and help keep you organized. A special work area will also create a psychological separation between home and work. Choosing to do the job yourself or hire outside help depends on your abilities and the time you have available. If you decide to do all or some of the work on your home office yourself *(Chapters 2 and 3)*, you may benefit from bringing in a professional at the planning stage. If you are remodeling an area of your home or building an addition, an architect could help you decide on the design, make sure your home's structure is not compromised by the new work, guide you through the maze of building codes and zoning bylaws, and help you find a good contractor. For a smaller job, a home-office designer or a professional decorator can assess your needs and ideas as well as offer suggestions.

When choosing a professional, find someone you can work with comfortably. Start your search with firms who have designed projects that you like. Friends and neighbors are good sources of information. Before you set up an interview, find out if the professional has experience working on home offices. Ask lots of questions, and make sure you understand the answers. When everything is settled to your satisfaction, put it all in writing.

HIRING A CONTRACTOR

- Get more than one estimate and make certain they are for the same procedures and materials.
- Make sure the contractor is licensed, insured for worker's compensation, public liability, and property damage.
- Check with the Better Business Bureau or other consumer agencies to see if there are any complaints filed against the company.
- Ask for references. If possible, visit former clients and check out the work.
- Get everything in writing. Include the contractor's name, phone number, address, and license number; time schedule; materials to be used; work to be done; cleanup agreements; and terms of payment.
- Never advance full payment for any work.

Often, the biggest stumbling block to setting up a home office is finding the space. If you already have a spare room in your house, that may be the most obvious solution. If not, you will need either to adapt an existing room to accommodate the office, or create a new room by converting an unfinished space. Before making a choice, take the time to carefully determine your space requirements. In choosing between possible locations, you may want to develop a detailed floor plan for each *(pages 16-25)*. Other considerations, such as how separate the space feels from the rest of the house, are equally important *(below)*.

Adapting an Existing Room: Almost any room in the house can serve double duty as an office. However, locating an office in a living room or bedroom, for example, can create a conflict between your need for a private working area and the needs of family members. In addition, setting up the office in a corner of an existing room may not provide enough psychological separation between your working and living spaces. A simple solution is to divide off the area, at least visually, with some kind of screen or divider *(pages 44-47)*. If the room is large enough, building a permanent wall between the working and living areas may be more satisfactory *(pages 38-41)*.

Hidden Space: An examination of your home may yield some surprises. A small office can often be tucked into an unused corner such as the space under a stairway *(pages 13-15)*, or perhaps you can free a large closet.

Creating a New Space: Converting an unfinished attic, basement, or garage *(opposite and pages 12-13)* is generally a more expensive option than adapting an existing room. However, such a renovation may be the best way to gain privacy for your office. Creating a new room also allows you to tailor the space to meet your needs. If your budget allows, building an addition may be the best way to create the ideal office space.

Choosing a Space

Any space in your house will likely require at least minor renovations in order to meet all the requirements listed below. However, the following points will help you choose a space that can be transformed into a satisfactory working area with the least trouble and expense.

✔ Is your space large enough to accommodate all office activities? Is there storage space at hand?

✔ Is the area adequately isolated from noise and odors from elsewhere in the house? Will the sound of office equipment be bothersome to other family members?

✔ Does the space feel psychologically separate from the rest of the house? Is it a space where you feel both alert and relaxed?

✔ If you expect visitors, will they have to walk through or past private areas of the house to reach the office? Would it be possible to install a separate entrance?

✔ Does the room have sufficient electrical outlets and phone jacks for an office? Will you need to add new electrical circuits?

✔ Is there adequate lighting? Are there windows?

✔ Is the space well ventilated, heated, and cooled? Is it dry?

RAFTER

SKYLIGHT

GABLE VENT

COLLAR TIES

KNEE WALL

JOISTS

PLYWOOD SUBFLOOR

Converting an attic.

An unfinished attic can be transformed into an attractive and spacious work area, but a number of adaptations are necessary. Before installing a floor, check whether the floor joists can adequately bear the load of people and furniture. Joists made from 2-by-6s on 16-inch centers can span up to 8 feet, while 2-by-8 joists can span 11 feet. If the joists exceed these spans, double them by fastening a second joist to each. (If the floor is not insulated, you may want to add insulation for its soundproofing qualities.) A plywood subfloor can then be installed over the joists to support the new flooring materials.

The sloping walls of the attic can be a problem for placing furniture. To square off the walls, install short partitions called knee walls running from the floor to the rafters. About 5 feet is a convenient height. In some cases, knee walls are required by code.

To make the ceiling easier to insulate, square it off with collar ties, attaching one tie to each pair of rafters. *(In the above illustration, some collar ties have been removed for clarity.)* A good ceiling height is $7\frac{1}{2}$ feet. Make sure the area above the new ceiling is adequately ventilated, with a gable vent or fan. If there is inadequate headroom in the attic, consider building in a gable dormer. A skylight is another attractive addition.

Insulate the attic knee walls, the ceiling, the floor area behind the knee walls, and the exposed rafters with fiberglass batts so the vapor barrier faces toward the room. When insulating rafters, create a 1-inch gap between the insulation and the roof sheathing with cardboard baffles. Between floor joists, do not jam the insulation against the eaves—this will block the airflow. After the insulation is in place, finish the walls and ceiling with wallboard.

Provide access to your attic office with a stairway at least 36 inches wide, with steps no less than $8\frac{1}{4}$ inches high and 9 inches deep.

The simplest way to heat the attic office is to install heating registers to allow warm air to rise from below, but cold winters may call for electric baseboard heaters.

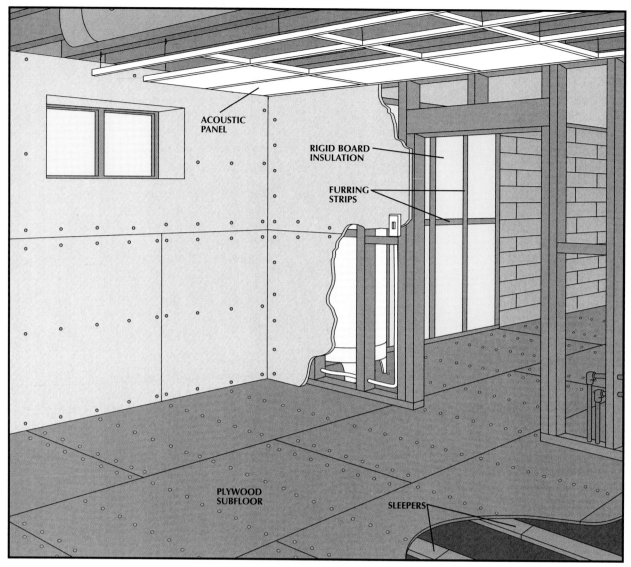

ACOUSTIC PANEL

RIGID BOARD INSULATION

FURRING STRIPS

PLYWOOD SUBFLOOR

SLEEPERS

Finishing a basement.

The first step in finishing a basement is to correct any moisture problem. Seepage from outside can be prevented by roof gutters and downspouts, soil grading, and proper drainage to direct water away from the foundation. Condensation from inside can be controlled by using a dehumidifier, venting clothes dryers to the outside, and wrapping water pipes with insulation.

As a foundation for a floor, first lay down building paper, then fasten pressure-treated sleepers to the concrete and top them with a plywood subfloor. In cold climates, you can insulate the floor with rigid board insulation laid between the sleepers.

The extruded polystyrene type is best, requiring no vapor barrier. Fasten the plywood to the sleepers.

To finish masonry walls, construct a stud wall insulated with fiberglass batts. Or, you can add polystyrene boards, securing them with furring strips nailed to the wall through the insulation.

If you decide to wall off basement appliances such as a furnace or water heater, leave 3 feet of space around the equipment and provide for adequate ventilation.

Many building codes require 7 feet, 6 inches of headroom for a finished room. If you're short on space, you can leave the ceiling

unfinished and paint everything overhead—including pipes and ducts—a light color.

A wallboard ceiling takes little room and can be installed on resilient channels to dampen noise from above *(page 60)*. However, you will have to reroute or raise ducts and pipes that extend below joists. If you can spare the headroom, a suspended ceiling *(above)* can be built below ducts and pipes, while leaving them easily accessible *(page 57)*.

A finished basement can be heated by tapping into a forced-air heating system. Or baseboard heaters can be installed to provide an independent heat source.

UNCOVERING HIDDEN SPACE

An office in a closet.

If you're really pressed for space, a large closet can accommodate a small office—20 inches deep is a bare minimum. If you don't have enough room to fit a standard desk *(right)*, you can hang a work surface from cleats on the closet walls, and install shelves above the surface for storage *(pages 158-161)*. If the doorway is too small to make the space accessible, consider widening the opening and adding bi-fold doors.

If your office will house electronic equipment that must run continuously, ventilation may be inadequate when the doors are closed. Louvered doors, or a vent into the next room, are two possible solutions.

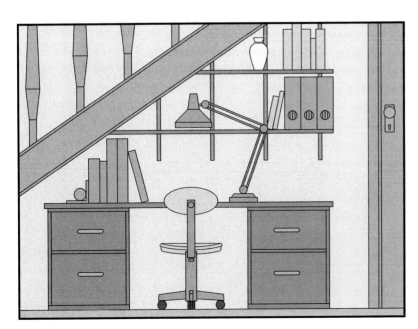

Under the stairs.

The unused space under a stairway may be just enough for a small work space. Shelves can be attached to the wall under the stairs. To blend the work area into its surroundings, finish the desk and shelving to match the stairway. To save on space, you can attach a lamp to the back wall, or to the back of a stair riser.

RIGHT: One end of this large bedroom does double duty as an office. The color and style of the office furniture blend well with the bedroom furnishings. A comfortable chair, a good task light, and a portable computer transform this neat corner into an efficient work space.

BELOW: A plain wood desk and hutch complement the uncluttered style of this home office. The simple window treatment and rag rug complete the picture. A tall paneled screen provides a sense of privacy by visually dividing the work area from the living space. An extra-wide pullout keyboard tray with room for a mouse combines traditional styling with a modern touch.

ABOVE: This elegant wooden cabinet and bookcase hides a compact workstation. At the end of the working day, the pullout keyboard tray and printer shelf slide into the unit and are completely concealed by hinged doors.

Designing sample floor plans of your proposed new office will help you choose and arrange office furniture, and will also serve as a guide for any renovations required to adapt the space to your needs.

Base Map: First, draw a base map—a detailed scale plan—of the existing space *(below)*. A workable scale is $\frac{1}{2}$ inch to 1 foot. Use graph paper with $\frac{1}{4}$-inch squares, or photocopy the grid on page 23.

Adding Furniture: The next step is to determine the dimensions of the furniture and equipment you will need. To sketch potential layouts, make a number of copies of the base map and draw in the furniture, or design each layout on a piece of tracing paper placed over the base map. Alternatively, photocopy the silhouettes of typical furniture and equipment on pages 24 and 25, cut them out, and arrange them on the base map. Several examples of home-office layouts are illustrated on pages 18 to 21; specialized computer programs are also available that can help you develop a floor plan *(page 22)*.

Don't stop at a desk and chair—try to anticipate other furniture that your activities will require, such as a stand for a photocopier, a conference table, a second desk for a co-worker, or perhaps a large cutting table for a sewing business. Be sure to leave adequate room around each piece of furniture *(opposite)*.

Refining the Plan: As you arrange the furniture, note any changes you would like to make to the space. You may want to add dividers or walls to separate different work activities *(pages 38-47)*; you may even consider removing a wall to create a more open area *(pages 48-50)*. Once the sketch is finished, you will also be able to plan any modifications needed to the lighting and wiring *(Chapter 3)*.

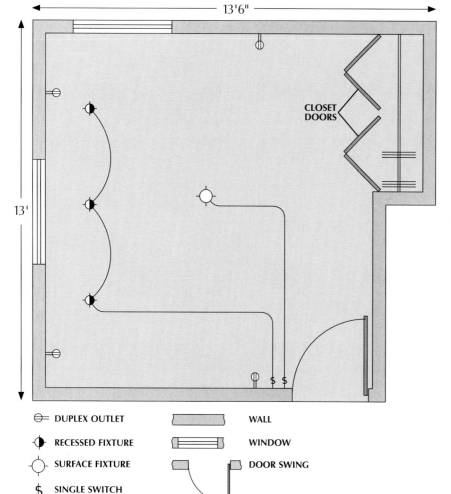

CLOSET DOORS

13'6"

13'

⊖— DUPLEX OUTLET

◐ RECESSED FIXTURE

○ SURFACE FIXTURE

$ SINGLE SWITCH

▭ WALL

▭ WINDOW

▭ DOOR SWING

Preparing a base map.
First, carefully measure your space. After determining the overall dimensions of the room, draw the perimeter of the room to scale. Then, determine the size and location of any openings such as windows, doors, and closets, and add them to the drawing. (You might also want to record the height of the windows to help with the placement of cabinets.) Note which direction each door opens and, with a compass, draw in an arc representing the space taken up by the swing of the door. Finally, add to your plan locations of any existing electrical features such as switches, outlets, and lighting fixtures. Standard symbols used by designers for these elements are shown in the legend below.

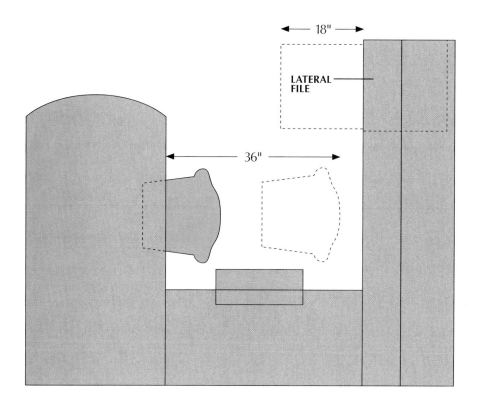

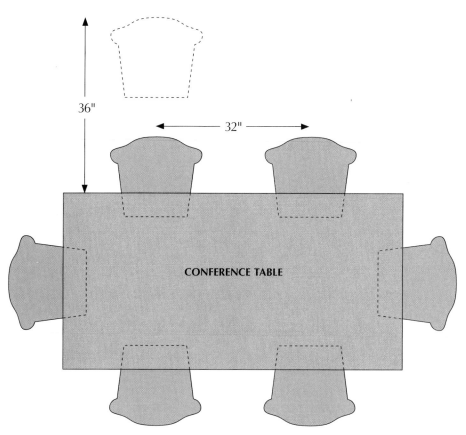

Space requirements.

As you arrange furniture on your base map, be sure to leave enough room for chairs and open file cabinets. For example, allow at least 36 inches for a chair to be pushed away from a desk (left, top). Measure this distance from the edge of the desk to the back of the chair when it is pulled out). Lateral files require 18 inches to open fully. If you are setting up a conference area (left, bottom), allow 36 inches behind each chair and 32 inches between chair centers for elbow room.

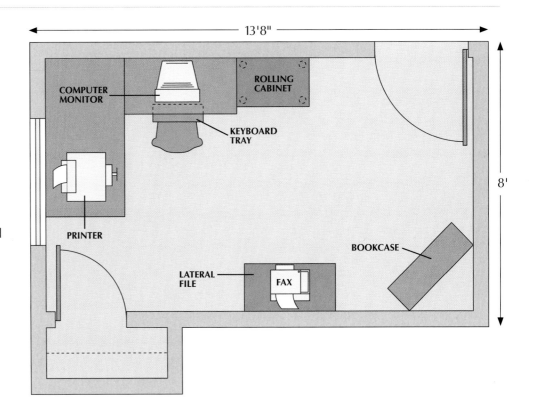

A small office.

An L-shaped computer work-station makes the best use of space in this small one-person office. A rolling cabinet can be pulled around to serve as an additional work surface. A fax machine sits on a lateral file, and a bookcase spans the corner.

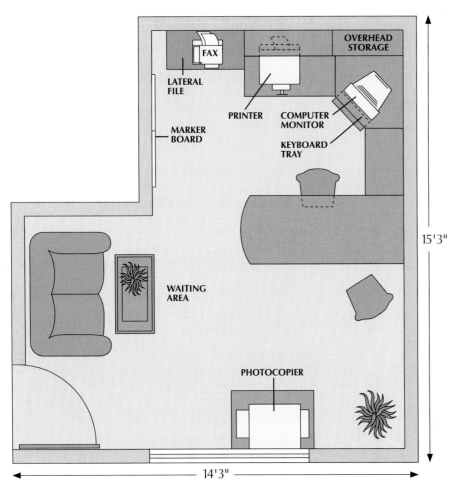

A medium-size office.

This one-person office features a generous U-shaped workstation with ample desk space for a computer monitor, a printer, and paperwork, as well as overhead storage. A marker board—for erasable felt pens—is hung on the wall behind the workstation. The space on top of the lateral file is occupied by a fax machine, while a separate table houses a photocopier. To accommodate visitors, an extra chair can be pulled up to one wing of the desk or, for less formal meetings, moved toward the coffee table in a waiting area set up near the office entrance.

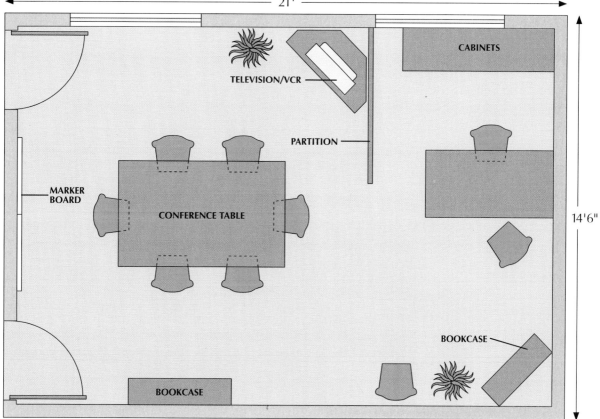

Office with a conference area.

If your business involves meetings and you have sufficient space to host them, consider including a conference area in your office plan. This one has a corner unit with a television for video presentations. One wall is devoted to a white marker board. The work area is screened by a partition—a commercial screen would do the job, or a half-height wall could be built. Additional chairs accommodate one-on-one meetings, and low cabinets along one wall store promotional or reference materials. A laptop computer is stowed away when not in use.

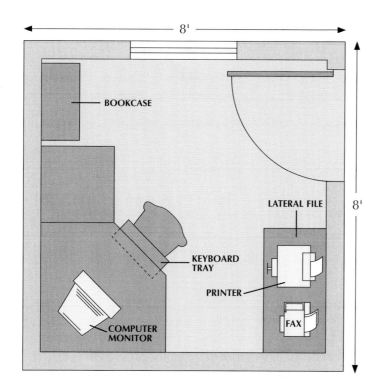

An alcove office.

A functional office can fit into even a small area like this one. Locating the computer workstation in a corner saves on space. There is even room for a small bookcase and a lateral file with enough surface area to hold a fax machine and printer.

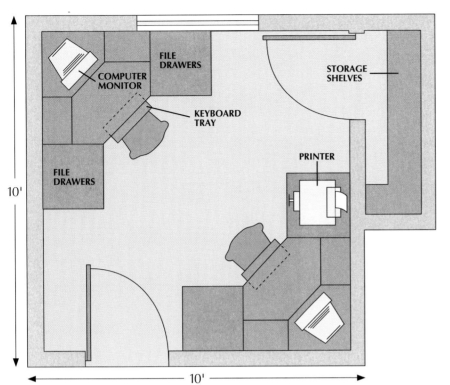

Two-person office.

Two people can work comfortably in even a relatively small office. In this one, two identical corner workstations, each with file drawers, make efficient use of the space—and placing the two stations back to back gives the individuals a sense of privacy. A large closet is equipped with storage shelves.

Work area for a graphic artist.

This spacious studio accommodates both the desk and drafting table needed for a graphic-design business. The U-shaped workstation includes a circular table for meetings. A counter with a file drawer along the wall accommodates a plotter. The drafting table is placed near a window, and a large cabinet in one corner stores artwork flat in large drawers and holds supplies vertically; a small table supports a color scanner.

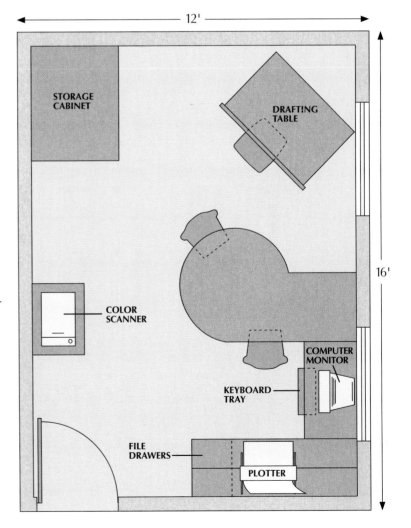

A sewing space.

This generous office houses everything needed for a sewing business. The sewing machine table sits near the window, and a small cabinet alongside accommodates supplies. A large storage unit in one corner can be used for bolts of fabric. Recessed into the wall, the ironing board can be folded down when needed, and the large cutting table on wheels can be pulled out from the wall to allow access on all sides. A small desk tucked into a corner holds a computer used for accounting purposes, and a bookcase for reference material fits behind the door.

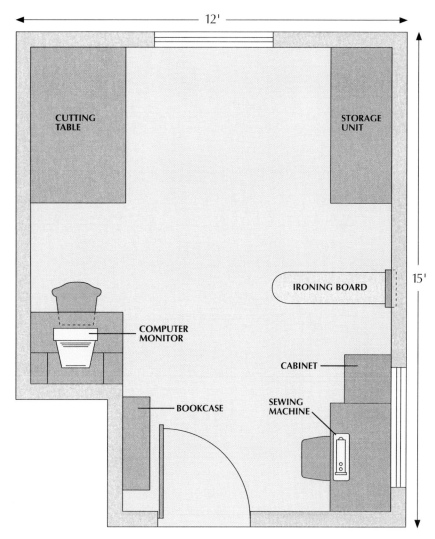

A walk-in closet.

Even a walk-in closet can house a minimal office. In addition to a desk with file drawers, there is room for a lateral file with a fax machine. Devoting one wall to a marker board or an organizing calendar helps keep clutter off the desk.

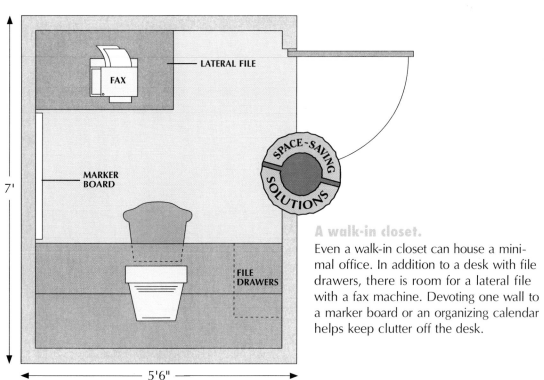

LAYING OUT THE OFFICE

The blank grid *(opposite)* will help you plan your office. Each $\frac{1}{2}$-inch division represents 1 foot, the same scale as the furniture and equipment silhouettes on pages 24 and 25. Make several photocopies of the grid and silhouettes, create a base map by drawing your room to scale on the grid *(page 16)*, then cut out the silhouettes that correspond to your furnishings. Rearrange the cutouts on the map until you have a layout you like; then trace around the cutouts. Compare several different layouts to decide which one best fits your needs. Or, use a computer design program *(box, below)*.

COMPUTER DESIGN PROGRAMS

There is a variety of computer programs available to help you design your new office. These programs typically provide three-dimensional views of a proposed working space, enabling you to "walk" around it before you even pick up a hammer to remodel.

Professional CADD (computer-assisted drafting and design) software is expensive and can be difficult to use. It is much easier to experiment with different layouts using graphics-based drawing and planning programs designed for the average computer user. Most of these software packages have symbol libraries containing a full selection of office furniture that can be resized to fit your requirements, and some even include human figures and plants. Look for programs with a "drag-and-drop" feature that lets you move items around easily until you are satisfied with your layout. Some software packages allow you to either view the room and its furnishings in a wire-frame form or turn the objects into solids *(below)*. Most programs come with a variety of sample plans.

Whichever kind of program you choose, start by drawing the walls, add the windows and doors, then fill in the available space with the furniture and equipment you think you will need for your office.

A program featuring solid objects allows you to visualize the final results of a plan.

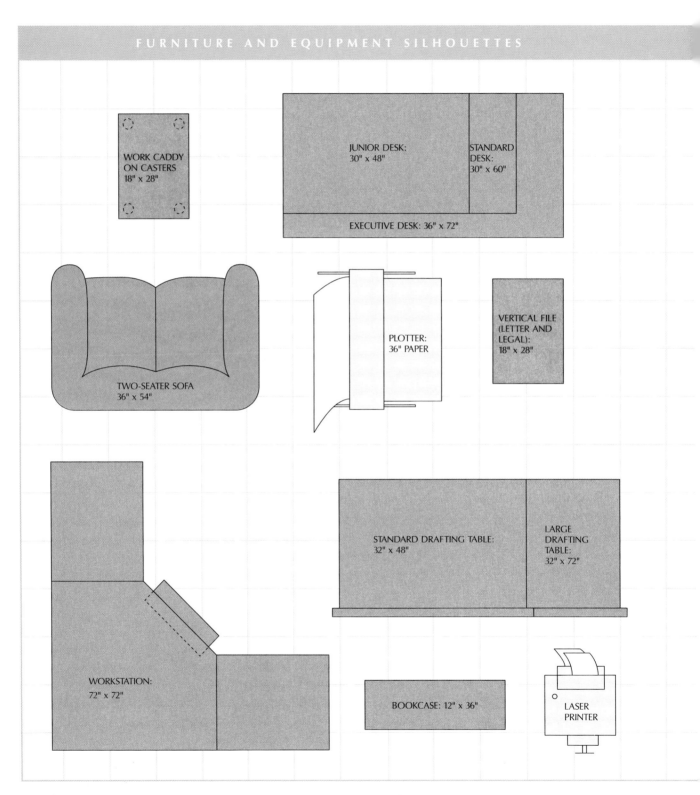

WORK CADDY
ON CASTERS
18" x 28"

JUNIOR DESK:
30" x 48"

STANDARD
DESK:
30" x 60"

EXECUTIVE DESK: 36" x 72"

TWO-SEATER SOFA
36" x 54"

PLOTTER:
36" PAPER

VERTICAL FILE
(LETTER AND
LEGAL):
18" x 28"

STANDARD DRAFTING TABLE:
32" x 48"

LARGE
DRAFTING
TABLE:
32" x 72"

WORKSTATION:
72" x 72"

BOOKCASE: 12" x 36"

LASER
PRINTER

SCALE: $\frac{1}{2}$" = 1'

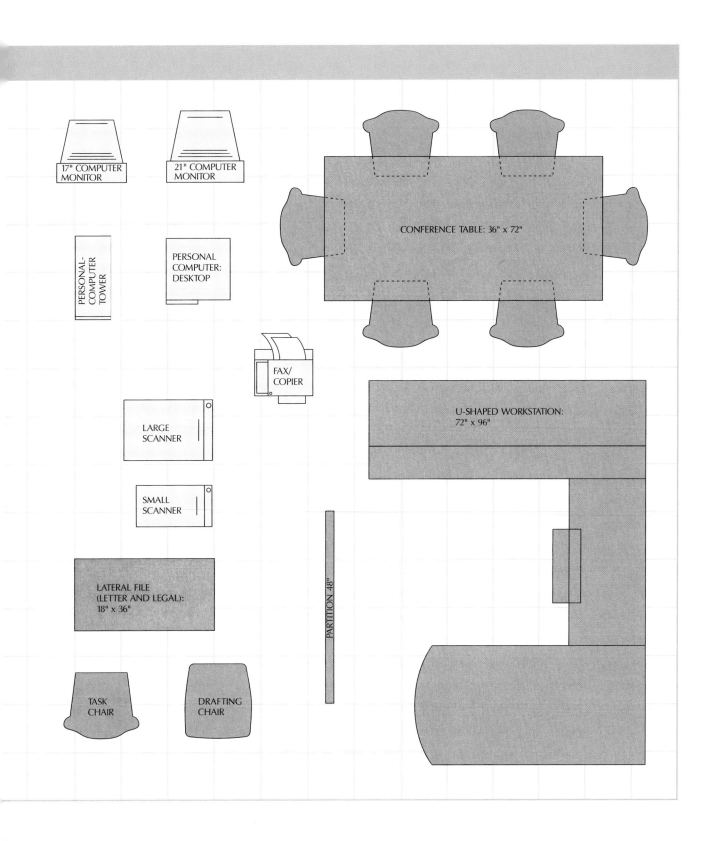

17" COMPUTER MONITOR

21" COMPUTER MONITOR

PERSONAL-COMPUTER TOWER

PERSONAL COMPUTER: DESKTOP

CONFERENCE TABLE: 36" x 72"

FAX/COPIER

LARGE SCANNER

SMALL SCANNER

U-SHAPED WORKSTATION: 72" x 96"

LATERAL FILE (LETTER AND LEGAL): 18" x 36"

PARTITION 48"

TASK CHAIR

DRAFTING CHAIR

LEFT: This no-nonsense modular arrangement makes efficient use of a limited amount of space. The work surface extension is perfect for meetings; the computer monitor is positioned to swivel easily so it can face visitors when it is being used for a multimedia presentation.

ABOVE: A little bit of ingenuity is often all that is needed to turn "lost" space into work space. A half wall provides some privacy from the rest of the house. The work surface, with a file cabinet tucked neatly underneath, has been built to maximize available space. Wicker baskets and colorful boxes on the shelves provide storage for stationery and other small items.

LEFT: When privacy is not an issue, there may be no need to conceal a work space. A corner of this one-room loft is set aside strictly for business. Still, the effect is not jarring. The clean, spare lines of the modular arrangement echo the simple elegance of the arched window, while the honey-colored wood of the work surface reflects the warm, rich tones of the hardwood floor. Decorative touches in the work space—dried flower arrangements, photographs, and a wicker tray to hold correspondence—help to harmonize home and office.

LEFT: Light, bright, and airy, this corner office features a built-in desk. The wraparound counter provides plenty of space for a telephone, a task light, a notebook computer, and other desktop equipment, while the cupboards underneath take care of storage needs.

LEFT: Sometimes all you need is a wall: This arrangement of work surface and storage units puts every inch of space to work. A lightweight freestanding table provides additional working space.

RIGHT: A converted attic houses this luxurious modern office. The light-colored walls and the track lighting build on the limited amount of light from the single window, creating the illusion of a naturally bright room.

An under-utilized dining room can be the perfect spot for a home office. Here, an antique pedestal dining table does double duty as a desk. Its large surface easily accommodates a notebook computer, a small printer, and a correspondence basket. A fax machine sits on a delicate antique sideboard. When company arrives, the table is cleared of business paraphernalia and the chairs are brought back around the table.

This modern variation of a partners' desk has plenty of room for two people working together. The rounded end makes it easy to confer over files or include visitors in the discussion. The shelves and a hutch with glass doors provide attractive storage space.

BELOW: A built-in desk for two can be both attractive and functional. Shelves at the far end of this desk provide storage for current files; the long work surface has ample room for a phone, two portable computers, and a shared printer; cubbyholes under the top shelf store desktop accessories.

LEFT: This attractive and compact work area blends unobtrusively into the living space around it. Conveniently located to take advantage of the illumination from two skylights and a window, the desk matches the style of the coffee table.

ABOVE: Built into the end of a run of kitchen cabinets, this mini workstation provides room for the essentials: a phone and answering machine, notepads, and pens and markers. The surrounding shelving holds books and files.

ABOVE: This spacious modern office has an abundance of natural light. The angled walls behind the desk ensure that everything is within arm's reach. Built-in cupboards under the window provide adequate storage, helping to give the room its uncluttered look.

BELOW: The traditional style and furnishings of this office belie its modern efficiency. The work surface curves gently around, putting most of the desktop within easy reach; a pull-out tray holds the keyboard at a comfortable height. Current files can be positioned on a low table beside the desk.

ABOVE: More than merely efficient and practical, this office is very much part of the home surrounding it. The whimsical in-tray and the wicker filing basket combine nicely with the other furnishings in the room. The eclectic style ensures that even the modern electronic equipment does not seem out of place.

CHAPTER 2

ADAPTING THE SPACE

IN A PERFECT WORLD, YOUR LIVING SPACE WOULD ALREADY contain a spare room just waiting for you to call it an office and get to work. Realistically, however, you may have to make do with a situation that at first seems less than ideal. But even a closet can become a small, efficient home workstation with careful planning and some fairly straightforward renovations.

Consider your present living space carefully. Is there a large room that could be divided—either by a partition or a half wall? Is there a small room that could be opened up by removing a wall? Could you create a work space with a simple solution such as a decorative screen or divider? Or does your family situation and the kind of work you will be doing dictate that you need a soundproofed area that can be closed off to family members? With thought, imagination, and some elbow grease, there is virtually no limit to what you can achieve.

RIGHT: Almost any space is enough space when you use imagination and good organization. Here a half wall defines the work area and provides a usable surface as well.

Dividing an existing room may be the only option you have to create space for a home office. Or, if you will be setting up a large office, you may want to partition the space further, creating separate working and conference areas, for example.

New Walls: A floor-to-ceiling partition, with or without a door, is the most permanent divider *(opposite)*, one which gives you the opportunity to build in soundproofing *(page 42)*. Another option is to build a half-height wall *(page 43, top)*, thereby allowing air and light to pass through. If space permits, consider adding a built-in closet to your new office *(page 43, bottom)*.

New partition walls can run parallel to or perpendicular to the ceiling joists; however, if the wall will run parallel to the ceiling framing, build it directly under a joist.

Screens and Dividers: Less permanent than a partition wall, a screen can effectively fence off your office.

You can choose from among a variety of commercial screens or dividers *(pages 46-47)*. You can also create your own by building a frame to hold a panel of lightweight material such as opaque plastic or latticework *(pages 44-45)*.

Providing for Power: If you plan to install electrical outlets or switches in a new wall, run the wire through the studs and install the electrical boxes *(page 85)* before covering the walls with wallboard.

TOOLS

Tape measure
Circular saw
Combination square
Plumb bob
Hammer
Electronic stud finder
Pry bar
Utility knife
Handsaw
Staple gun
Corner clamps
Miter box and
   backsaw

MATERIALS

1 x 3s
2 x 4s, 2 x 6s
Common nails ($2\frac{1}{2}$", $3\frac{1}{2}$")
Finishing nails (2")
Brads ($\frac{3}{4}$")
Staples ($\frac{1}{2}$")
Cedar shims
Fiberglass insulation batts
Wood glue
Material for screen panels
Lattice strips ($1\frac{3}{4}$")
Quarter-round molding ($\frac{1}{2}$")
Decorative molding

SAFETY TIPS

Don goggles when hammering or using a circular saw. Add gloves, long sleeves, and a dust mask when installing fiberglass insulation.

⚠ CAUTION

Precautions for Lead and Asbestos

Lead and asbestos, known health hazards, pervade houses built or remodeled before 1978. Before cutting into walls or ceilings, check painted surfaces for lead with a test kit from a hardware store, or call your local health department or environmental protection office. To test joint compound, ceiling and wall materials, and insulation for asbestos, mist the material with a solution of 1 teaspoon of low-sudsing detergent per quart of water; then remove small samples for testing by a National Institute of Standards and Technology-certified lab.

Hire a professional who is licensed in hazardous-substance removal for large jobs indoors, or if you suffer from cardiac, respiratory, or heat-tolerance problems that may be triggered by protective clothing and a

respirator. To remove lead or asbestos yourself, follow these precautions:

❗ *Keep children, pregnant women, and animals out of the work area.*

❗ *Indoors, seal off the work area with 6-mil polyethylene sheeting and duct tape. Cover rugs and furniture that can't be removed with sheeting and tape. Turn off air-conditioning and forced-air heating systems.*

❗ *When you finish indoor work, mop the area twice, then run a vacuum cleaner equipped with a high efficiency particulate air (HEPA) filter.*

❗ *Outdoors, cover the ground in the area with 6-mil polyethylene sheeting. Never work in windy conditions.*

❗ *If you must use a power sander on lead paint, get a model equipped with a HEPA filter. Never sand asbestos-laden materials or cut them with power machinery. Mist them with water and detergent, and remove with a hand tool.*

❗ *Always wear protective clothing (available from a safety-equipment supply house or paint store) and a dual-cartridge respirator. Remove the clothing—including shoes—before leaving the work area. Wash the clothing separately, and shower and wash your hair immediately.*

❗ *Dispose of the materials you removed as recommended by your local health department or environmental protection office.*

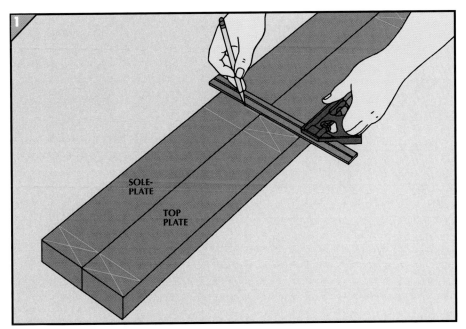

1. Marking the top and soleplates.

◆ Measure the ceiling the new wall will divide and, with a circular saw, cut two 2-by-4s to length to serve as the top and soleplates.

◆ Starting at one end of the top plate, mark stud locations $1\frac{1}{2}$ inches wide. Except at a doorway (page 41), space the stud centers 16 inches apart, finishing with a stud location at the opposite end of the plate.

◆ With a combination square, transfer the markings from the top plate to the soleplate (left).

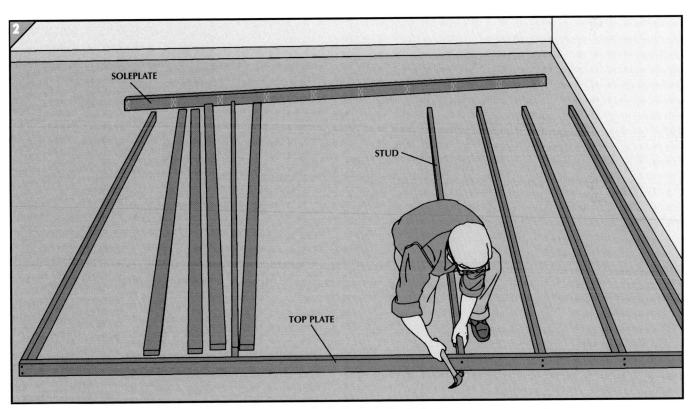

2. Assembling the frame.

◆ To determine the stud lengths, measure along a plumb bob dropped from the ceiling to the floor at each end and in the center of the new wall.

◆ Cut 2-by-4 studs $3\frac{1}{4}$ inches shorter than the smallest of the three measurements to allow for the combined thicknesses of the top and soleplates and for ceiling clearance when raising the wall.

◆ Orient any bowed studs so they all curve in the same direction.

◆ Set the top plate on edge and fasten it to each stud with two $3\frac{1}{2}$-inch common nails driven through the plate (above). A framing hammer speeds the work.

◆ Nail the soleplate to the other ends of the studs in the same way.

3. Locating the existing framing.

Use an electronic stud finder to pin-point joists behind the ceiling where you plan to install your partition *(right)*. If the wall will cross the room perpendicular to the joists, pencil a mark at the center of each one. For a wall running directly under a joist, draw a line indicating the center of the joist.

Use the same technique to find and mark studs where the new wall will meet existing ones. If the intersection falls between studs, cut slots in the walls for nailer blocks installed about one-third and two-thirds of the way up the walls *(inset)*. Patch the slots with wallboard.

⚠️ **CAUTION** *Turn off electrical power at the service panel to all circuits in the area before cutting into the wall; check outlets on both sides of the wall to confirm that the power is off* (pages 74-75).

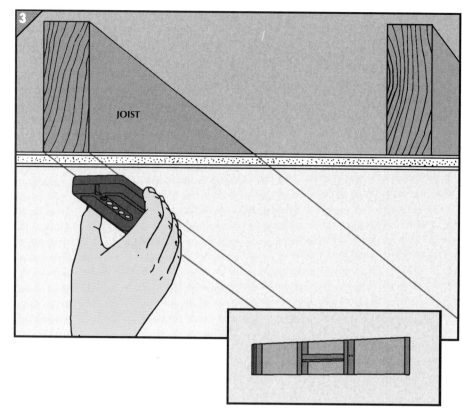

JOIST

4. Removing baseboard.

For a tight fit between a new wall and an old one, remove the baseboard and shoe molding, a narrow strip often fastened at the bottom of the baseboard.

◆ Beginning at a corner or at a baseboard joint, gently loosen the baseboard and shoe molding where the new and old walls will intersect. Use a pry bar backed with a thin scrap of wood to avoid damaging the wall, and insert a wood wedge behind the baseboard to hold it away from the wall after you loosen it *(left)*.

◆ Repeat the process, inserting wedges as you go, until the strip is completely detached.

5. Securing the frame.

◆ With a helper, tilt the wall upright.
◆ While your helper holds the frame in place, push pairs of tapered cedar shims into each side of the gap between the top plate and the ceiling where you will nail the plate to joists.
◆ Drive $3\frac{1}{2}$-inch nails through the top plate and shims into the joists *(right)*; then score protruding shims with a utility knife and snap them off.
◆ Secure the soleplate to floor joists where possible; otherwise, nail it to the flooring. In either case, use $3\frac{1}{2}$-inch nails spaced 16 inches apart. For concrete floors, drive $2\frac{1}{2}$-inch cut nails.
◆ Fasten the end studs of the new wall to studs or nailer blocks in the existing ones.

FRAMING AN OPENING

A rough frame for a prehung door.

As you assemble a new partition wall *(page 39)*, frame a doorway between two king studs and adjoining jack studs, both resting on the soleplate. The jack studs support a crosspiece called a header. Short, cripple studs fit between the header and the top plate.
◆ On the soleplate mark the width of the prehung door unit, adding $\frac{1}{2}$ inch to allow for shims.
◆ Saw partway through the underside of the plate at the marks.
◆ Cut a king stud for each side of the frame and nail it to the soleplate and top plate, $1\frac{1}{2}$ inches in from the marks, with $3\frac{1}{2}$-inch common nails.
◆ For each side of the frame, cut a jack stud $1\frac{1}{4}$ inches shorter than the top of the door unit's top jamb. Nail each jack stud to the soleplate with $3\frac{1}{2}$-inch nails and to the king stud with $2\frac{1}{2}$-inch nails at 1-foot intervals.
◆ Cut a header to fit snugly between the king studs. Nail it in place with $3\frac{1}{2}$-inch nails driven through the king studs.
◆ Cut cripple studs to fit between the header and the top plate. Position these at the same intervals as the wall studs and secure them with $3\frac{1}{2}$-inch nails driven through the top plate and the header.
◆ Raise the wall into position, and complete the kerfs cut in the soleplate to remove the unwanted section.
◆ Install the prehung door unit *(pages 61-63)*.

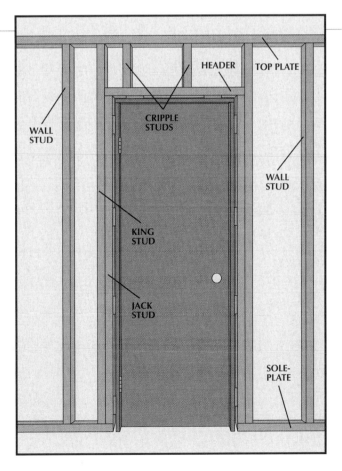

Staggering the studs.

◆ Locate and mark the ceiling joists *(page 40, Step 3)*.

◆ From 2-by-6s, cut top and soleplates equal to the length of the wall.

◆ Fasten the soleplate to the floor with $3\frac{1}{2}$-inch common nails.

◆ Mark each end of the soleplate for a 2-by-6 stud, and every 12 inches in between for staggered 2-by-4 studs.

◆ With a combination square, transfer the marks to the top plate *(inset)*, then fasten the top plate to the ceiling with $3\frac{1}{2}$-inch nails.

◆ Cut studs to fit between the plates, aligning them with the marks and toenailing them in place with $3\frac{1}{2}$-inch nails.

◆ Staple batts of fiberglass insulation, $3\frac{1}{2}$ inches thick and 24 inches wide, between the wall studs *(right)*.

For additional soundproofing, install the wallboard on resilient channels *(page 60)*.

Doubling a wall.

◆ Mark the floor and ceiling for two 2-by-4 soleplates and two top plates, 1 inch apart.

◆ Cut the plates, set them side by side, and mark them for 2-by-4 studs, 16 inches on center.

◆ Fasten the top plates to the ceiling and the soleplates to the floor with $3\frac{1}{2}$-inch common nails.

◆ Toenail the studs between the plates.

◆ With $\frac{1}{2}$-inch staples, fasten 6-inch-thick batts of fiberglass insulation between the studs.

For additional soundproofing, install the wallboard on resilient channels *(page 60)*.

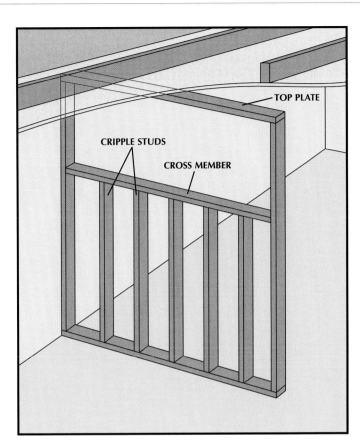

Constructing the new wall.
◆ Cut and assemble the top and sole-plates and the two end studs on the floor as you would for a standard partition *(page 39).*
◆ Cut a cross member to fit between the end studs, and nail it to the studs at the desired height with $3\frac{1}{2}$-inch nails.
◆ Cut cripple studs to fit between the cross member and the soleplate, spaced 16 inches apart, and nail them in place.
◆ Raise the wall into position *(left)* and fasten it to the floor, ceiling, and existing wall as described for a standard partition wall *(page 41, Step 5).*

ADDING A CLOSET

Framing a closet.
◆ Build and install the closet's front wall and door opening in the same way as for a partition wall *(pages 39-41).* For easy access to the closet, you may want to frame a large opening for bifold doors *(pages 63-65)* or a set of double doors.
◆ Cut two 3-inch-long nailer blocks from 1-by-3 lumber and, with $3\frac{1}{2}$-inch common nails, fasten them to the last stud at the end of the wall that will adjoin the shorter wall.
◆ Cut a reinforcing stud and nail it to the nailer blocks. Then toenail it to the top plate and soleplate.
◆ Construct a narrow wall to fit between the new wall and the existing wall in the room.
◆ Fasten this wall in place, nailing the end stud to the nailing blocks and end stud of the reinforced corner.

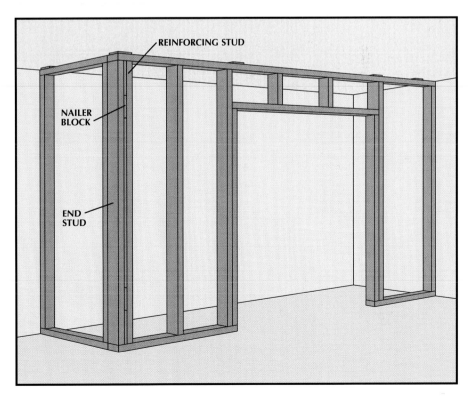

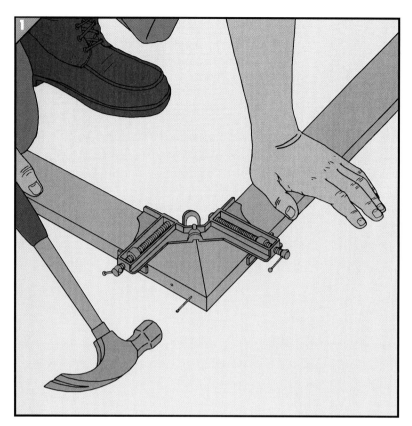

1. Constructing the frame.

To frame the screen, construct a rectangle $\frac{1}{4}$ inch shorter than the height of the room so the top edge of the screen won't catch against the ceiling when you are raising the divider into place. For light panel materials such as plastic, use 1-by-3 lumber for the frame; for heavier materials, use 2-by-3s or 2-by-4s.

◆ Miter four lengths of lumber for the frame so the inner edges are $\frac{1}{8}$ inch longer than the dimensions of the panel.

◆ Working from corner to corner, apply wood glue to the mitered ends, then secure the frame pieces in a corner clamp.

◆ Drive 2-inch finishing nails into the joints from each direction *(left)*.

2. Tacking lattice to the frame.

If the difference between frame and panel material thicknesses is 1 inch or more, secure the panel on both sides with quarter-round molding as described in Step 3. Otherwise, proceed as follows:

◆ Scribe a guideline around the back of the frame, $\frac{7}{8}$ inch from the inner edge.

◆ Miter four $1\frac{3}{4}$-inch lattice strips so their outer edges are the same length as the scribed lines.

◆ Apply wood glue to the back of the frame between the inner edge and the scribed line.

◆ Lay the lattice strips along the line and fasten them to the frame with $\frac{3}{4}$-inch brads driven at 6-inch intervals *(right)*.

◆ Turn the frame over and insert the panel, resting it on the lattice strips.

LATTICE STRIPS

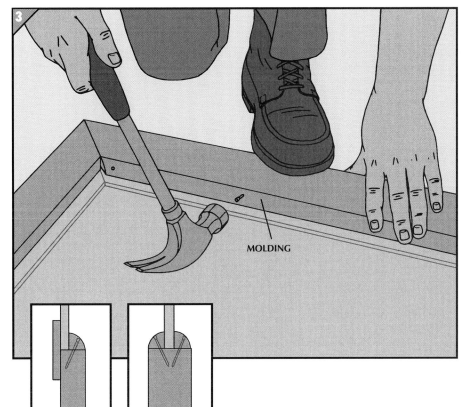

MOLDING

3. Securing the panel.

◆ Miter four lengths of $\frac{1}{2}$-inch trim such as quarter-round molding to fit the inside edges of the frame.
◆ To secure the panel, fasten the trim to the frame with glue and brads driven at an angle *(left and left inset)*.

For panels thicker than $\frac{1}{4}$ inch, secure the panel with quarter-round molding nailed to the frame on both sides *(right inset)*.

4. Securing a rectangular divider.

A three-sided, mitered channel anchors the divider to the ceiling and can also be used at the floor. To fit the divider snugly against the wall, notch either the baseboard and its shoe molding or a corner of the divider frame.
◆ For the ceiling, cut two pieces of molding that are equal in length to the width of the divider plus the thickness of its frame. With the molding in a miter box upside down, miter one end of each piece. Miter a third piece on both ends so the inside edge equals the thickness of the divider frame.
◆ Glue and nail one of the long pieces of molding to the ceiling at the panel location.
◆ Raise the divider against the molding *(right)* and nail through the molding into the divider frame.
◆ Place the second long piece of molding against the other side of the divider and then fasten it to the ceiling.
◆ Fit the short piece of molding between the ends of the longer ones *(inset)*.

At the floor, adapt the foregoing procedure or anchor the frame with nails or screws driven at an angle into the floor.

Often, there is no choice but to set up a home office in a room that also serves some other function. You do not necessarily need a separate room as long as your work space can be isolated. If you plan to use part of a room, the trick is to find some way to define the area that is to serve as your work space and claim it as your own. When it isn't possible to construct a permanent physical barrier such as a partition wall, work on creating a psychological barrier with less substantial materials or temporary setups.

A folding screen is one of the simplest ways to keep your work space separate from the rest of the room. Most commercial screens consist of at least three hinged panels and come in a wide variety of styles,

BELOW: This fabric-panel divider is ideal for defining a small office. The hinged wrought-iron frame allows the divider to be folded up and stored.

including wood panels, fabric-covered panels, and panels with inserts of fabric or lace. Screens can be made of bamboo or rattan, or can be custom-built to match your window treatment or some other decorative element of the room. Hinged screens are freestanding and add versatility to the area, as they can be folded up out of the way when not in use. A grouping of tall plants might also be used to define your work space.

Sliding doors or Japanese style shoji screens are another, more permanent way to close off the section of the room that you use for your office. Or, pairs of bookcases can be placed back to back to screen your work area and divide it from the rest of the room—and this also helps you gain valuable storage space.

The downside of screening, as compared to actual partition walls, is that while screening adds privacy, it does little to reduce noise. Noise levels are more easily controlled by reducing sound rather than by trying to absorb it. The best way to limit noise in a home office that shares a space with a living area may be to negotiate a schedule for sharing the room with the rest of the family.

When deciding on how to divide up the room to create your office nook, traffic lines are important: Situate your work space in an area that is out of the way of people walking through the room. Less obvious, but just as important, are sight lines. Is your work space the first thing people see when they walk into the room? Will the clutter on your desk remind you of unfinished work when you try to relax at the end of the day? And finally, since you will be unable to lock a door to keep others out, how do you signal "hands off" to the rest of the family so that you can ensure your work-in-progress remains undisturbed? If you can solve these problems to your satisfaction, then the divided-room office can work for you.

LEFT: Mounted on sliding tracks, these shoji screens provide access to a home office with ease and elegance. When the screens are shut to divide the office from the living areas of a home, the screen's translucent inserts enable light to filter through without compromising privacy.

Where you are fortunate enough to be able to devote more than one existing room to a home office, you may want to remove an intervening wall to create a sense of space.

Bearing or Nonbearing Walls: Before tearing out a wall, you must determine whether the wall bears weight from above, thus serving as a vital structural element of the house *(below)*. It is relatively easy to remove a nonbearing wall *(opposite)*—or part of one *(page 50)*. Removing a bearing wall is a project best left to professionals.

Dealing with Utilities: In making the decision to remove a wall, keep in mind that any plumbing, wiring, or ductwork will have to be rerouted. The number of receptacles and switches suggests how much wiring a wall contains. A bathroom above may be hooked to plumbing that descends

through the wall. From the basement try to detect any heating pipes or ducts rising within the wall.

Finishing the Job: After removing the wall, there will be breaks in the ceiling, walls, and floor. Wallboard on ceilings and walls can be patched, and gaps in the floor can be built up with any wood as thick as the flooring, and the whole room carpeted or tiled. However, professional help may be needed for hardwood floors that will remain exposed.

⚠ **CAUTION** *Before starting work, check for lead and asbestos in the wall (page 38).*

⚠ **CAUTION** *Turn power off at the service panel to all wiring in the wall before beginning work; then test outlets on both sides of the wall (pages 74-75) to confirm power is off.*

TOOLS
Pry bar
Circuit tester
Circular saw
Screwdriver
Handsaw
Wood chisel
Mallet
Hammer
Wallboard tools

MATERIALS
Drop cloths
Duct tape
2 x 4s
Framing lumber
Common nails
($3\frac{1}{2}$")
Wallboard materials

SAFETY TIPS
Protect yourself from the dust, flying splinters, and other debris created by demolition by putting on goggles, a dust mask, leather work gloves, long sleeves and pants, and sturdy shoes.

Bearing and nonbearing walls.
In a typical frame house, the roof is supported by long outer walls parallel to the ridge *(right)*. The weight of the remaining structure rests on joists, which transfer the load to the side walls. These walls pass the weight to the foundation and on to the footings. (End walls usually do not carry weight.) Since a standard joist cannot span the usual distance from one side wall to another, house framers provide two joists and rest their inside ends on an interior bearing wall. The interior bearing wall carries the weight down to a solid support, either to a bearing wall that rests on its own footings or, as shown here, to a girder with ends that rest on the foundation. A bearing wall can usually be identified by joists crossing its top plate, perpendicular to it, or by a girder or another wall running under and parallel to the wall. You can detect joists by looking in the attic and basement or by cutting a small hole in the ceiling. Nonbearing walls usually run parallel to the joists and perpendicular to the long walls of the house. If there is any doubt as to whether a wall bears weight, contact a qualified contractor or home inspector, or a structural engineer.

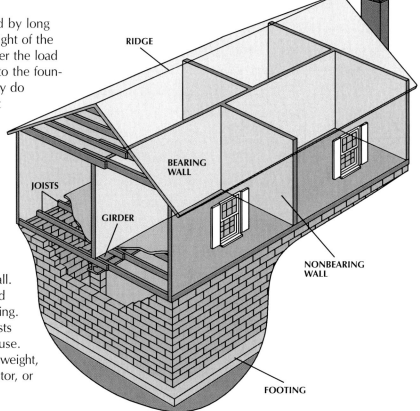

RIDGE

BEARING WALL

JOISTS

GIRDER

NONBEARING WALL

FOOTING

1. Stripping the wall.

◆ Turn off the power to the circuits in the area.
◆ Tear off the wall trim *(page 40)*.
◆ Tape down drop cloths in each room, close any interior doors, and open the windows.
◆ Cut strips of wall from between the studs with a circular saw set to the thickness of the wall surface; use a metal-cutting blade if the wall is made of plaster on metal lath. Alternatively, you can break a hole in the wall material with a hammer and pull it away with a crowbar.
◆ Saw the studs in two near the middle, and work the halves free from their nailing *(right)*.
◆ When you reach an outlet, remove its cover plate and strip off the wall surface around it. Trace the cable to the nearest electrical box, disconnect it, and pull it out of the wall. If you cannot discover a cable's origin or if unrelated cables pass through the wall, consult a professional.
◆ Work the bottom of the end stud loose from the adjoining wall with a pry bar, using a wide wood scrap to protect the wall surface. When the stud is safely away from the wall, wrench it free.

DROP CLOTH

DROP CLOTH

2. The top plate and soleplates.

◆ The top plate is often nailed upward to blocks between adjacent joists. Pry it down, beginning at the nailhead nearest one end, using a wood scrap to protect the ceiling.
◆ Near the center of the soleplate, make two saw cuts about 2 inches apart.
◆ Chisel out the wood between the cuts down to the subfloor.
◆ Insert a crowbar and pry up one end of the plate *(left)*. With a scrap of 2-by-4 as a fulcrum, pry up the other end.

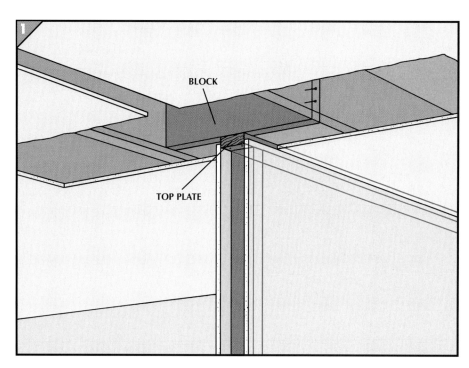

1. Securing the top plate.
◆ Designate a stud where you will stop demolition of the wall to preserve the remainder of it.
◆ Apply the methods on page 49 to demolish the unwanted part of the wall, but cut the wall surface and plates so they extend $1\frac{1}{2}$ inches beyond the designated stud; doing so creates a pocket for the stud to be added in Step 2.
◆ Cut a hole about 1 foot wide in the ceiling, centered on the upper end of the stud and running to the second joist on either side.
◆ Nail a block of joist-size lumber between the joists on each side of the top plate, with the face of the block flush with the end of the plate.
◆ Nail through the plate into the edge of the block (left).

2. Reinforcing the stud.
◆ Cut a reinforcing stud to fit snugly between the top plate and soleplate, and nail it to the end stud in the section of the partition that you have left standing (right).
◆ Surface the outer face of the reinforcing stud with wallboard and finish with corner bead (pages 51-52 and 54).

The simplest way to sheath the walls of your new office is to hang sheets of wallboard—also called drywall. It consists of a gypsum core sandwiched between layers of heavy paper; a standard sheet is 4 feet wide, 8 feet long, and $\frac{1}{2}$ inch thick. Wallboard with the long edges tapered makes finishing the joints easier.

Preparation: To calculate the number of sheets you need, determine the square footage of each wall, ignoring all openings except the largest, such as picture windows. Convert this figure into sheets by dividing it by the square footage of a panel. Be sure to complete any wiring before installing the wallboard *(Chapter 3).*

Installation: Vertical seams between wallboard sheets must align with the centers of wall studs. In most cases, this is easier to accomplish when the wallboard is laid horizontally *(page 52)*; however, for a narrow wall, you can avoid creating a seam if you lay the sheet vertically. Wallboard sheets can be installed with ring-shank wallboard nails or special wallboard screws driven slightly below the surface of the panels. To create a soundproof wall, install the wallboard on resilient channels *(pages 58-60)*.

Finishing the Job: Fill the holes in the wallboard left by the nail or screw heads with joint compound. Cover seams between sheets with paper or fiberglass joint tape before applying the compound *(page 53)*. Strengthen outside corners with angled metal strips called corner bead *(page 54)*. Finally, prime and paint the walls.

TOOLS
Tape measure
Carpenter's square
Utility knife
Hammer
Caulking gun
Wallboard hammer
Wallboard saw
Chalk line
Taping knives
  (6", 10")
Wallboard sponge

MATERIALS
Wallboard
Scrap 2 x 4s
Common nails ($2\frac{1}{2}$")
Ring-shank wall-
  board nails ($1\frac{1}{2}$")
Wallboard adhesive
Joint tape
  (fiberglass and
  precreased paper)
Joint compound
Metal corner bead

SAFETY TIPS
Goggles protect your eyes when you are nailing or working above eye level.

CUTTING THE SHEETS

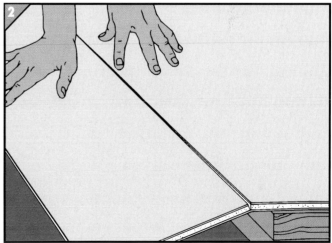

1. Scoring wallboard.
◆ Mark a sheet of wallboard for cutting.
◆ Position a carpenter's square at the mark at one edge of the sheet and draw a line. Then move the square to the opposite edge and complete the line. (A wallboard T-square allows you to draw this line in a single stroke.)
◆ Place a square along the line and score the surface of the wallboard with a utility knife *(above)*.

2. Snapping the core.
◆ Stack two 2-by-4 scraps under the wallboard just behind the scored line.
◆ With the palm of your hand, hit the short end of the sheet, snapping the core.
◆ Finish by slicing through the backing with a utility knife, then trim any ragged paper from the cut edge.

Putting up the panels.

◆ Mark the stud positions on the ceiling and floor.

◆ Drive $2\frac{1}{2}$-inch common nails partway into the wall studs 4 feet below the ceiling.

◆ With a caulking gun, apply a $\frac{3}{8}$-inch-thick zigzag bead of wallboard adhesive to each stud behind the sheet, starting and stopping 6 inches from the end of the sheet.

◆ With a helper, lift the wallboard, and rest it on the nails. Align the vertical edge with the center of a stud.

◆ Nail or screw the panel to each stud about 1 foot from the ceiling. Drive the fasteners straight and flush with the surface. Then drive them slightly below the surface without breaking the paper: A wallboard hammer works well for nails; for screws, use a screw gun designed for wallboard, or a variable speed electric drill with a dimpler attachment.

◆ Add fasteners every 2 feet on each stud, ending 1 inch from the top and bottom. Double the fasteners where the centerline of the sheet crosses each stud.

◆ Because ceilings and floors are rarely parallel, measure from the bottom of the sheet to the floor in at least four places, subtract $\frac{1}{2}$ inch and mark these distances on the second sheet. If the

distances are fairly uniform, snap a chalk line between the marks, then score and break the sheet at the line *(page 51)*. If not, connect marks with separate lines and cut the sheet with a wallboard saw.

◆ Trim the second sheet to a length one stud shorter than the sheet above to create staggered joints.

◆ With a helper, raise the sheet with scrap-wood foot levers *(inset)*.

TRICKS OF THE TRADE

Marking for Outlet Boxes

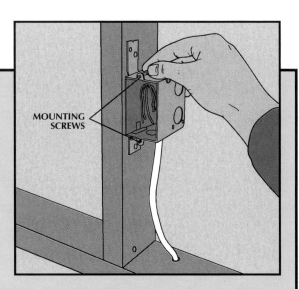

Fold the wires into the outlet box. Remove the mounting screws and insert them from back to front through their holes so that they protrude about $\frac{1}{2}$ inch *(right)*. Place the wallboard sheet in position on the studs and press it against the screw tips. Remove the sheet and place a spare outlet box on the wallboard, aligning the mounting holes with the marks made by the screws, then trace around the box. Cut just outside the lines with a wallboard saw, angling the saw so the hole is slightly wider at the back of the sheet.

DOORS AND WINDOWS

Marking and cutting the opening.

For a window, measure from the ceiling to the top of the jamb at both corners. Then measure from the last installed sheet to the nearest side-jamb edge. If the sheet will surround the window, also measure to the farthest side-jamb edge. For a door, measure the distances from the ceiling to the top jamb and from the last installed sheet to the side-jamb edge or edges.

◆ Mark these distances on the face of the sheet and connect the marks.

◆ If the sheet will enclose three sides of the window or door, cut along the two parallel lines with a wallboard saw.

◆ Score the remaining line and snap the core *(page 51)*. If the sheet will surround a window, cut around all the lines with the saw.

◆ Mark and cut the lower sheet the same way *(right)*.

TAPING SEAMS

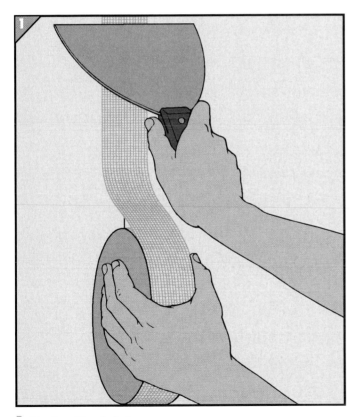

1. Taping the joint.

◆ Press the end of a roll of self-adhesive fiberglass-mesh joint tape against the top of the joint.

◆ Unwind the tape with one hand and, with a taping knife, press the tape to the joint *(above)*. Watch for wrinkles; if they appear, lift the tape, pull it tight, and press it again.

◆ Cut the tape off the roll when you reach the end of the joint.

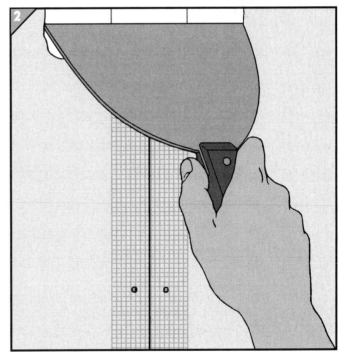

2. Applying joint compound.

◆ With the knife, spread compound over the joint tape and the adjacent wallboard in a layer approximately $\frac{1}{16}$ inch thick. On joints where nontapered ends of drywall abut, apply compound slightly thicker. While working, wipe the knife frequently against the lip of the pan so that the compound doesn't harden on the knife and score grooves in the wet compound.

◆ When the tape is covered, run the knife down the joint in one motion to smooth out the surface.

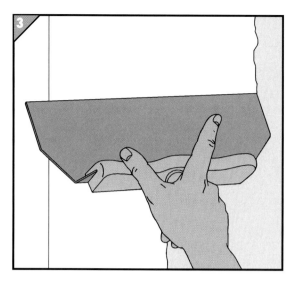

3. Feathering the joint.
◆ Run a clean 10-inch knife down each side of the joint, pressing hardest on the outer side of the knife so the mixture gradually spreads outward to a feathered edge *(left)*. Let the compound dry for a day.

◆ Hide fastener heads elsewhere by drawing joint compound across each one with a 6-inch knife held nearly parallel to the wallboard. Raise the knife blade and scrape off excess compound with a stroke at right angles to the first.

◆ Apply a second coat of compound thinned with 1 pint of water per 5 gallons. With a 10-inch knife, feather the compound to about 10 inches on either side of the joint. For non-tapered ends, apply more compound, feathering it to 20 inches on each side.

◆ When the last coat of joint compound is completely dry, rub it gently with a damp wallboard sponge. Do not wet the wallboard paper enough to tear, and rinse the sponge frequently. Repeat the procedure on the compound you applied to fastener heads.

DEALING WITH CORNERS

Taping inside corners.
◆ With a 6-inch taping knife, slather joint compound crosswise into the crack at an inside corner between two walls or a wall and the ceiling.

◆ After applying the compound, run the knife along each side of the joint to smooth the surface.

◆ Bend a length of paper tape in half down its crease line, and press the fold lightly into the corner joint with your fingers *(right)*.

◆ Draw the knife along each side of the corner, simultaneously embedding the tape and coating it lightly with compound.

◆ When applying the second and third coats use thinned compound *(Step 3, above)*. Do one side of the corner, allow the compound to dry one day, then do the other side.

◆ Smooth the compound with a wallboard sponge after it has dried *(Step 3, above)*.

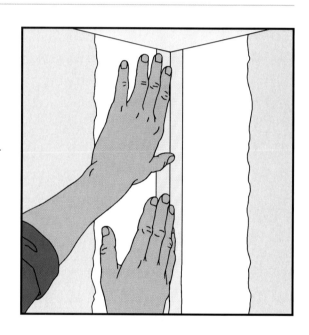

Strengthening outside corners.
◆ Nail a strip of metal corner bead so it fits flat on both sides of the corner *(left)*.

◆ Load the left two-thirds of a 6-inch taping knife with joint compound.

◆ With the right half of the blade overhanging the corner, run the knife from ceiling to floor down the left side of the bead, smoothing the compound over the perforations.

◆ Cover the right side of the bead in the same way.

◆ Clean the blade, then smooth and feather the joint by running the knife down each side of the bead.

◆ Let the compound dry for 1 day, then apply a second coat of thinned compound *(Step 3, above)*, feathering the edge about $1\frac{1}{2}$ inches beyond the dry compound.

◆ Wait 1 day, then apply a third coat using a 10-inch knife to feather the compound 2 inches farther on each side.

◆ Smooth the compound after it has dried *(Step 3, above)*. If the rounded tip of the metal bead still shows, it can be painted later with the rest of the wall.

Wallboard ceilings can be tricky to install, but they are the least expensive option, and most adaptable to different decorative treatments.

Planning: Sketch the layout of the sheets of wallboard carefully before the work begins *(below)*. Since electrical connections must remain accessible when the ceiling is in place, relocate existing junction boxes that would be covered by the ceiling. In addition, complete any new wiring before installing the wallboard *(Chapter 3)*.

Installation: Wallboard sheets for a ceiling are fastened the same way as those on walls—with adhesive and nails or screws *(pages 51-52)*. Cut the sheets by scoring them with a utility knife *(page 51)*; cut openings with a wallboard saw.

Other Ceiling Options: Acoustic tiles and panels are more expensive than wallboard, but are easier to install *(page 57)*. Suspended panels leave wiring accessible and can be used to conceal ducts and pipes; however, they lower the height of the finished ceiling.

TOOLS

Tape measure	Wallboard hammer
Circular saw	Taping knives
Hammer	(6" and 10")
Caulking gun	Wallboard sponge

MATERIALS

2 x 4s	Wallboard adhesive
Common nails (3")	Joint tape (fiberglass and
Ring-shank wallboard	precreased paper)
nails (1½")	Joint compound
Wallboard	Metal corner bead

SAFETY TIPS

When working overhead or when nailing, protect your eyes with goggles.

WALLBOARD FOR THE CEILING

1. Planning a wallboard ceiling.
Measure the ceiling dimensions at the top plates of the walls, and plan to install sheets perpendicular to the joists. When you diagram the ceiling, keep in mind several principles: The ends of the wallboard must be made to land at the centers of joists—by trimming the board if necessary; these joints must be staggered to prevent a continuous seam on a single joist; and any filler strips of wallboard should be installed in the center of the ceiling.

Where room dimensions create a narrow gap between the edge of a sheet and the wall, as in the L shown at right, trim back the sheet to widen the gap to at least 1 foot, and cut a piece to fill the gap. To support the edges of the wallboard if the last joist lies more than 4 inches out from the wall, install L-shaped 2-by-4 nailer blocks between the last joist and the band joist with 3-inch common nails *(inset)*. Measure and cut the sheets to fit around ceiling fixtures and other obstructions.

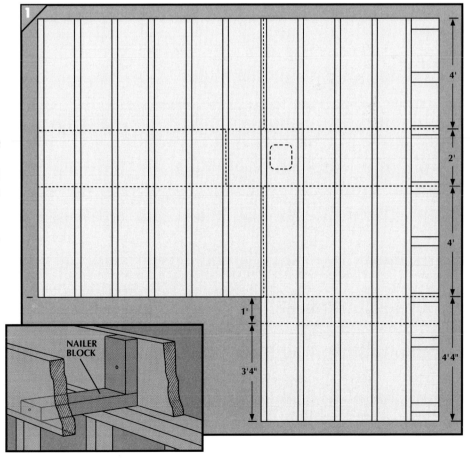

NAILER BLOCK

2. Marking guidelines for nails.

Make a vertical mark on the top plates below the center of each joist end *(left)*, and beneath the nailer blocks if you have any. The marks will establish the sight lines your wallboard nails must follow after the wallboard hides the joist itself.

3. Applying adhesive.

With a caulking gun, lay $\frac{3}{8}$-inch zigzag beads of wallboard adhesive along joists that will touch wallboard *(right)*.

T-BRACE

4. Putting up the wallboard.

◆ Make a 2-by-4 T-brace the height of the ceiling and have a helper hold up the sheet while you fasten it.
◆ Place the first sheet in a corner and center its end on the joist where it will join another sheet.
◆ Secure the board with pairs of $1\frac{1}{2}$-inch ring-shank wallboard nails or screws driven into each joist at the center of the sheet *(page 52)*.
◆ Fasten the tapered sides of the panel to each joist, 1 inch from the panel edges *(left)*.
◆ Secure the panel ends with fasteners 16 inches apart and $\frac{1}{2}$ inch from the edge.
◆ Conceal the nail or screw heads with joint compound and tape the seams *(pages 53-54)*.

A grid of tiles.
Easy to install, acoustic tiles help absorb sound from within the office. They are available in kits that provide metal strips and clips for support; alternatively, tiles can be stapled to a grid of wood furring strips nailed across joists *(left)*. Tiles can also be stapled directly to an existing ceiling if it is level and free of cracks. Pipes or ducts can be hidden by building a wood frame around the obstacle, then fastening tiles to the frame.

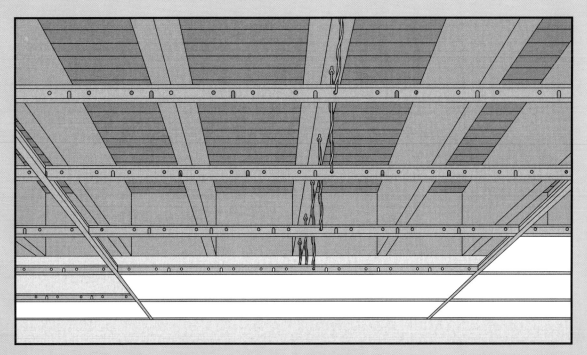

Suspended panels.
When a number of overhead pipes or ducts must be concealed—as in an unfinished basement— a ceiling made of suspended panels is the logical choice. Like acoustic tiles, panels are simple to install and serve to absorb sound in the office.

Lightweight metal runners are hung from the joists with wire; the panels are then set into the runners *(above)*. To hide ducts and pipes, runners can be hung lower to create a box around the obstruction. Fluorescent lighting panels can be substituted for regular panels.

Noise arises from two sources—sound reverberating within the room, and sound penetrating from elsewhere in the house. Sound from within can be absorbed by installing a ceiling of acoustical tiles or panels *(page 57)*, as well as by careful choice and placement of furniture and drapes *(page 108)*. Exclude external noise by sealing gaps in existing walls or by soundproofing the walls themselves.

Sealing Gaps: Holes and cracks in a wall leak a surprising amount of noise: Plugging a $\frac{1}{8}$-inch-wide gap around an electrical outlet box can improve the soundproofing effectiveness of a wall by as much as 10 percent. Other ways to suppress noise include damping vibrations in heating ducts *(opposite)* and sealing gaps around doors—but forced-air heating systems often require gaps under interior doors for adequate air circulation.

Soundproofing Techniques: The thin, flat surface of stud-and-wallboard construction is a poor sound barrier. The flexible wallboard picks up sound vibrations and transmits them through the studs, setting in motion the wallboard on the other side. Soundproofing properties can be built into new walls by staggering the studs or by constructing two independent walls with a gap in between *(page 42)*, then filling the wall with fiberglass insulation. Two layers of wallboard can then be mounted on $\frac{1}{2}$-inch resilient metal channels, leaving a gap between the wallboard and framing; exposed ceiling joists can be treated in a similar way *(opposite and page 60)*.

The soundproofing properties of existing walls and ceilings can be improved by fastening 2-inch Z-shaped metal channels to the existing wall and then adding 1 inch of insulation and a second layer of wallboard.

Whenever walls are built out for soundproofing, electrical outlet boxes will have to be extended—or deeper ones installed—so that the boxes will be flush with the finished wall surface.

TOOLS

Utility knife	Chalk line
Hammer	Carpenter's square
Screwdriver	Electric drill
Staple gun	Caulking gun
Tape measure	Wallboard tools

MATERIALS

Weather stripping	Wallboard
Door sweep	Cedar shims
Duct-lining kit	Wallboard screws
Fiberglass insulation	(1", $1\frac{1}{4}$", $1\frac{1}{2}$", $1\frac{5}{8}$")
Resilient furring	Wallboard materials
channels	Acoustic sealant

SAFETY TIPS

Goggles protect your eyes when you are driving nails or operating power tools. Wear goggles, a dust mask, gloves, and a long-sleeved shirt to handle fiberglass insulation. Gloves are a must when working with resilient furring channels.

BLOCKING HOLES

Sealing around doors.
◆ Cut lengths of weather stripping to fit around the perimeter of the door.
◆ Hold each piece flat against the door stop so the gasket is partly compressed against the closed door. Secure the strip to the stop with the nails provided *(right)*.

To seal the gap under the door, install a sweep on the bottom of the door so the gasket is slightly compressed when the door is closed against the threshold *(inset)*. You may need to trim the door to get the right fit.

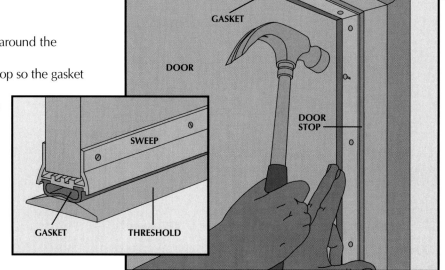

Installing duct liners.
◆ Unscrew the grille over the duct opening, then reach in and measure as far up the duct as you can.
◆ Cut acoustic duct liner to fit the measured areas and coat exposed surfaces with the adhesive sold by the liner manufacturer. Apply adhesive to the unbacked side of each piece of liner and press it into position inside the duct *(left)*.
◆ Let the adhesive dry, check that the pieces are secure, then replace the grille.

SOUNDPROOFING NEW WALLS

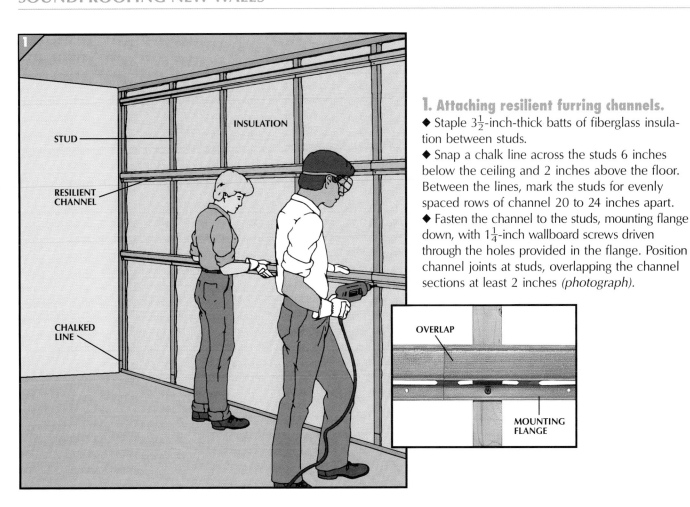

1. Attaching resilient furring channels.
◆ Staple $3\frac{1}{2}$-inch-thick batts of fiberglass insulation between studs.
◆ Snap a chalk line across the studs 6 inches below the ceiling and 2 inches above the floor. Between the lines, mark the studs for evenly spaced rows of channel 20 to 24 inches apart.
◆ Fasten the channel to the studs, mounting flange down, with $1\frac{1}{4}$-inch wallboard screws driven through the holes provided in the flange. Position channel joints at studs, overlapping the channel sections at least 2 inches *(photograph)*.

2. Attaching the wallboard.

Install two layers of $\frac{1}{2}$-inch wallboard panels, the first layer vertically, and the second horizontally.

◆ Trim the panels for the first layer $\frac{1}{4}$ inch shorter than the ceiling height *(page 51)*.

◆ Shim the first panel to support it $\frac{1}{8}$ inch above the floor, then fasten it to the channels with 1-inch, fine-thread wallboard screws at 24-inch intervals.

◆ Remove the shims and use them to install the rest of the first layer, leaving a $\frac{1}{8}$-inch gap between panels *(right)*.

◆ Caulk the gaps between panels and at the floor and ceiling with acoustic sealant *(inset)*.

◆ Install the second layer of wallboard, duplicating the $\frac{1}{8}$-inch gaps of the first layer, but using $1\frac{5}{8}$-inch wallboard screws spaced 16 inches apart.

◆ Caulk the gaps with acoustic sealant.

◆ Complete the joints between panels and at the corners and ceiling with tape and joint compound *(pages 53-54)*.

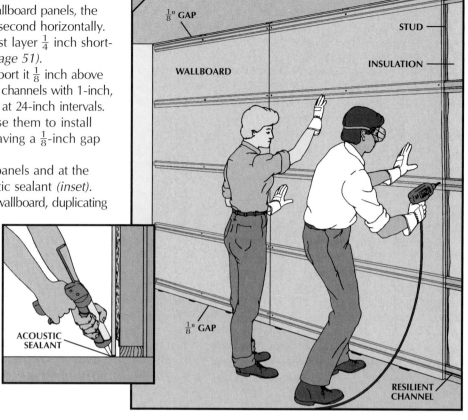

ACOUSTIC SEALANT

$\frac{1}{8}$" GAP

WALLBOARD

STUD

INSULATION

$\frac{1}{8}$" GAP

RESILIENT CHANNEL

A SOUNDPROOF COVERING FOR EXPOSED JOISTS

Soundproofing a ceiling.

◆ Install 6-inch-thick batts of fiberglass insulation between the exposed joists and against the subfloor above, stapling the batts to the sides of the joists at 2- to 3-inch intervals.

◆ Fasten resilient furring channels across the exposed joists, overlapping the channels by 2 inches, and fastening them with a $1\frac{1}{2}$-inch wallboard screw at each joist *(left)*.

◆ Fasten wallboard panels across the resilient channels with 1-inch wallboard screws, leaving a $\frac{1}{8}$-inch gap around the perimeter of the ceiling. Center joints between panels on channel flanges and fasten the panels to the channels with 1-inch fine-threaded wallboard screws at 24-inch intervals.

◆ Caulk all the gaps with an acoustic sealant and tape the seams *(pages 53-54)*.

The traditional way to provide access to your new office is to install a prehung door. However, if your office space has a very wide entry, you'll need to consider other options such as accordion, sliding, or bifold doors. Bifold doors are an attractive solution. They open and close easily, and can be left ajar to let in light, or closed to hide the work area. They are also a good choice for a large closet converted to an office.

Prehung Doors: The simplest type to install is a split-jamb model. These units consist of two pre-assembled sections that are slipped between the jack studs of the rough opening *(page 41)* from opposite sides to sandwich the wall. However, for a more soundproof barrier, you can install a solid-core door,

available prehung but without integral casing.

When you order a door from a lumberyard, you must specify the width of the jamb (the thickness of the wall) and the width of the finished door. You must also specify whether you want the door to open clockwise (a right-handed door) or counterclockwise.

Bifold Doors: These consist of panels hinged together lengthwise in pairs; the louvered style of doors let through some air even when they are closed. One or more pairs can be mounted at one side of the opening and pulled all the way across; more commonly, a pair of panels is installed at each side of the opening and brought together at the middle *(pages 63-65)*.

TOOLS

Carpenter's level	Nail set
Flush-cutting saw	Putty knife
Hammer	Hacksaw
Utility knife	Electric drill
	Screwdriver
	Plumb bob

MATERIALS

Split-jamb door	Wood putty or spackling compound
Shims	
Finishing nails ($1\frac{1}{2}$", 2", $3\frac{1}{2}$")	Bifold door and hardware kit

SAFETY TIPS

Always wear goggles to protect your eyes when hammering.

GROOVE

TONGUE

SPLIT JAMBS

CASING

An interior split-jamb door.
This door unit has two jamb sections that fit together with a tongue-and-groove joint *(right).* The casing, or visible trim, on both sections is factory-installed.

1. Installing the door.

◆ Slide the jamb section containing the door into the rough opening, resting the door on two pairs of shims. Insert pairs of shims behind the side jambs at the heights of the hinges.

◆ Adjust the shims behind the hinge-side jamb until the jamb is plumb *(right)*.

◆ If the gap between the lock-side corner of the head jamb and the door is more than $\frac{1}{8}$ inch, trim the bottom of the lock-side jamb by about $\frac{1}{16}$ inch; leave the door in place and use a flush-cutting saw *(photograph)*.

◆ Nail the hinge-side casing to the wall with $1\frac{1}{2}$-inch finishing nails into the jamb and 2-inch nails into the framing.

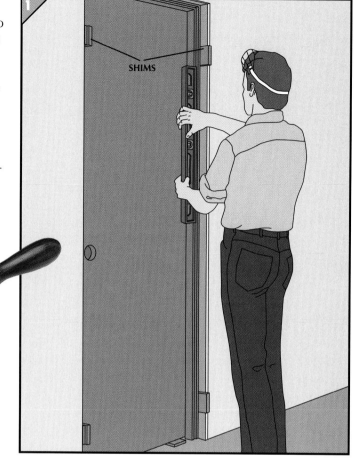

2. Adjusting the casing.

◆ With a $\frac{1}{8}$-inch gauge such as a piece of corrugated cardboard, adjust the top casing until there is a $\frac{1}{8}$-inch gap between the head jamb and the door, then nail the casing to the header with 2-inch finishing nails *(left)*.

◆ Adjust the gap between the door and the lock-side jamb in the same way, and nail the lock-side casing.

◆ From the other side of the door, insert pairs of shims above the head jamb, behind the middle of the hinge-side jamb, and behind the lock-side jamb.

◆ Drive two $3\frac{1}{2}$-inch finishing nails through each pair.

◆ Score the shims with a utility knife, then break them off flush with the edge of the jambs.

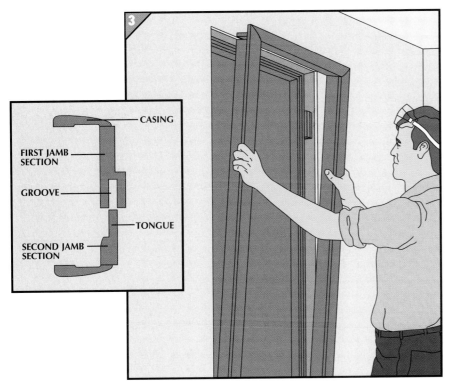

CASING

FIRST JAMB
SECTION

GROOVE

TONGUE

SECOND JAMB
SECTION

3. Finishing the jamb installation.

◆ Fit the tongue of the second jamb section into the groove of the first one *(inset)*, then push the second section inward until the attached casing rests against the wallboard *(left)*.

◆ Fasten the casing as in Step 1 *(opposite)*.

◆ Drive $3\frac{1}{2}$-inch finishing nails through the second jamb section and the shims into the rough framing.

◆ Set all the nails and, with a putty knife, fill the holes with wood putty—if you intend to stain the casing—or spackling compound.

PUTTING IN BIFOLD DOORS

TRACK

1. Mounting the track.

◆ Measure the width of the top of the opening and the length of the track, which should be $\frac{1}{8}$ inch shorter. If necessary, cut the track to size with a hacksaw.

◆ Center the track at the top of the opening and mark the screw holes; set the track aside.

◆ Drill pilot holes to match the screws provided with the kit.

◆ Attach the track *(right)*.

2. Installing the bottom bracket.

◆ From the center of the top pivot bracket (which comes attached to the track), drop a plumb line to the floor *(left)* and lightly mark the floor at the indicated point.
◆ Set the bottom pivot bracket *(photograph)* in place against the side wall of the opening, with the floor mark centered between the sides of the notched slot.
◆ Drill pilot holes for the screws provided; screw the bottom bracket to the wall and the floor.

For a two-door set, follow the same procedure on the opposite side of the opening.

3. Preparing the door.

◆ With a hammer, gently seat the bottom pivot in the hole at the bottom of the door panel nearest the wall.
◆ Follow the same procedure to insert the top pivot into the hole at the top of that door panel, and the roller guide into the hole at the top of the other panel. Both the top pivot and the roller guide are spring-loaded to simplify installation.
◆ Fold the door and slip the top pivot into the top pivot bracket *(right and top inset)*. Push the door upward to compress the top pivot and insert the bottom pivot into its bracket *(bottom inset)*.
◆ Unfold the door, hold down the spring-mounted roller guide, and slip it into the track.

For a two-door set, install the other door in the same way.

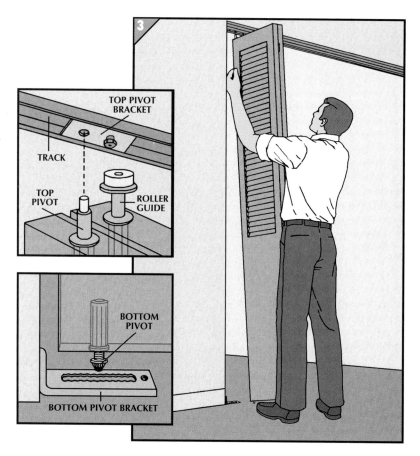

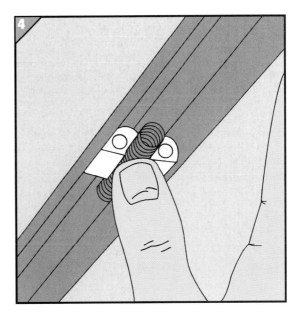

4. Securing the snugger.

Insert the snugger into the track *(right)*. For a single door, place the snugger between the roller guide and the top pivot; in the case of a two-door set, put the snugger between the doors.

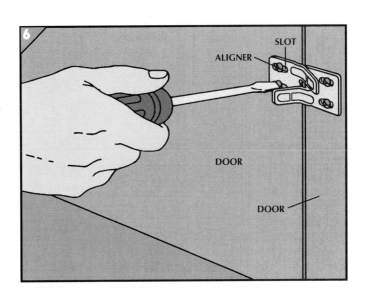

BOTTOM PIVOT

BOTTOM PIVOT BRACKET

ADJUSTING WHEEL

5. Adjusting the doors.

To raise or lower a door slightly, note which notch the bottom pivot occupies in its bracket. Then lift out the pivot and turn the adjusting wheel—counterclockwise to lower the door, clockwise to elevate it *(left)*. Reseat the pivot in the correct notch.

You can move the bottom of a door sideways by lifting the bottom pivot and moving it to another notch.

To shift the top of a door, remove the door, loosen the screw holding the top pivot bracket, and move the bracket. Retighten the screw and replace the door.

After positioning the doors so that they align well, attach the handles.

6. Mounting the aligners.

Bifold doors mounted on each side of an opening and meeting in the middle when closed are usually held flush and in line with metal aligners. To install the aligners, mount one on the back of each closed door *(right)*. You can fine-tune the position of each aligner by loosening the screws and sliding the aligner along the adjustment slots.

SLOT

ALIGNER

DOOR

DOOR

CHOOSING FLOOR COVERINGS

When selecting a floor covering for your home office, there are two main considerations to bear in mind: aesthetics and practicality. Certainly, appearance is important, but don't neglect to ask the following questions about a flooring material. How will it wear? Is it easy to maintain? Will it contribute to noise, or absorb it? Consider, too, how a floor covering affects indoor air quality (IAQ). Some flooring materials release chemicals into the air or may harbor biological contaminants that, in sensitive individuals, can cause symptoms such as dizziness and nausea, headaches and eye problems, nose and throat irritation, a dry cough, difficulty concentrating, and fatigue.

Commercial carpeting, available in a wide range of colors and patterns, has become an affordable luxury for home offices. Carpet is a good choice as it helps absorb sound and cushions feet; the low-looped pile of the commercial type allows office chairs to slide easily. There are two main textures: level-loop carpeting, which has tufted loops all of the same height, and multi-level loop, which has loops of different heights. Most commercial carpeting is made from nylon or polypropylene. Both types of fibers wear well, are resilient, and easy to clean.

Because electrostatic discharge can cause severe damage to sensitive electronic equipment, static electricity is a vital concern in the home office. Most commercial-grade carpeting is now factory-treated to prevent it from generating static shock above 3.5 kilovolts at a relative humidity of 20 percent at 70°F. Another proven way to control static electricity is by using a humidifier: Moisture in the air will be absorbed by carpet fibers and help dissipate electrical charges. You can also spray the carpet surface with a commercial anti-static agent, or mist it with a solution made by mixing equal parts fabric softener and water.

There has been some concern about carpeting's effect on IAQ; make sure any you buy has the green label indicating that it has passed the Carpet and Rug Institute's IAQ tests. After installation, increase the ventilation to the room for a few days; periodic deep-extraction cleaning will help to control biological contaminants such as pollen, mold, and bacteria.

Vinyl flooring, sold in sheets or as tiles, comes in a wide variety of colors and patterns. Durable and easy to clean, it absorbs sound, and provides a little cushioning. However, vinyl gives off some emissions that can affect IAQ.

Rubber flooring is also available in many colors and can be purchased in sheets or as tiles. It has good insulation value and helps absorb sound. It is durable and easy to maintain. Although it can give off odors, the emissions are not dangerous.

Cork sheets or tiles come in a range of attractive natural colors. Cork offers good insulation value and also helps absorb sound. In addition, it is very durable and has good IAQ characteristics.

Hardwood planks have good IAQ properties, are very durable, but require periodic refinishing. Wood parquet flooring is less durable than hardwood.

TIPS FOR BUYING WALL-TO-WALL CARPETING

Questions to ask the salesperson:
- Will a salesperson come to my home to measure the office accurately?
- What is the charge for removing old carpeting and taking it away, shaving doors, etc.?
- Has the new carpet been treated to avoid problems with static electricity?
- Are padding and installation included?
- Where will the carpet be seamed? (If necessary, purchase extra carpeting to ensure that the seam is in an inconspicuous location.)

- Is there a guarantee or warranty on the purchase and/or installation?

Make sure your written contract includes the following:
- The manufacturer's name, the carpet color, and its style number (you should ask for a sample of the carpet and padding);
- The exact amount of carpeting purchased and the cost per yard;
- A diagram showing where seams will be placed;
- The total cost of the job.

WIRING FOR THE HOME OFFICE

WHEN YOUR HOUSE WAS BUILT, LIKELY NO ONE COULD HAVE anticipated the electrical needs of a home office. Your chosen space will require outlets for plugging in computers and printers, fax machines and photocopiers, perhaps even a coffee machine and a microwave. You'll also need more extensive and more versatile lighting, and you may have to modify or upgrade your present telephone system.

The first step is to evaluate the electrical system in your home office: how many circuits are in place and how much, if any, extra capacity they can spare. Chances are you'll need to expand the system by extending one or more existing circuits or wiring a new one from the service panel. Either way, this chapter explains what you need to know.

Once the wiring, outlets, and switches you need are in place, it's time to choose and install lighting fixtures that will blend with your decor and make your office a comfortable and productive place to work in.

RIGHT: With enough outlets to run a computer system and other equipment, this home office has sufficient capacity left over to power a bank of recessed lights in the ceiling and task lights mounted under the cabinets.

Today's fully equipped office, with its wide array of electronic equipment, and lighting, heating, and ventilation needs, can place heavy demands on a home's electrical system. Adding new outlet boxes to your office may be adequate to serve your needs *(pages 83-88)*; however, you may need to install new circuits to avoid overloading the existing ones *(pages 76-82)*. The amount of current each piece of equipment draws is generally indicated in amps on the device—if indicated in watts, divide the watts by the circuit's voltage to obtain the amperage. Consult the chart *(right)* for typical ratings so you can anticipate the electrical needs of new equipment.

Electronic Safeguards: Protect any sensitive electronic apparatus from power fluctuations by plugging it into a circuit that serves no equipment with a motor that cycles on and off, such as refrigerators. To avoid voltage surges, keep microwave ovens and coffeemakers on a circuit separate from electronic equipment. In addition, items that need to be shielded from power spikes can be hooked up to a surge protector, some of which also shield telephone lines, modems, and fax machines. You may want to provide some equipment with an uninterruptible power source, or UPS *(opposite, bottom)*. The chart at right suggests the type of backup device each piece requires.

Lighting: As you plan new electrical circuits for your home office, try to anticipate your lighting needs *(page 73)*. Light fixtures can generally be wired to the same circuit as computer equipment.

Other Equipment: Include any proposed heating, cooling, and ventilation apparatus in your wiring plan. Air conditioners and electric baseboard heaters that are permanently wired to the house circuitry require their own separate circuits *(page 72)*.

POWER REQUIREMENTS FOR OFFICE EQUIPMENT

Equipment	Amperage	Surge Protection	UPS
Answering machine	0.1	no	no
CD-ROM drive, external	0.2	yes	yes
Computer with 300-watt supply	2.7	yes	yes
Disk drive, external	0.2	yes	yes
Disk drive, removable	0.2	yes	yes
Fax machine	1.5	yes	no
Lamp	0.5	no	no
Modem, external	0.1	yes	yes
Monitor, 14" to 15"	1.5	yes	yes
Monitor, 17"	1.9	yes	yes
Monitor 20"	2.4	yes	yes
Photocopier, desktop	8.0	no	no
Plotter	2.0	yes	no
Printer, medium laser	7.6	yes	no
Printer, personal laser	6.0	yes	no
Printer, ink jet	0.4	yes	no
Printer, dot matrix	1.0	no	no
Scanner	1.5	yes	no
Speakers, self-powered	0.1	yes	no

Calculating the load on a circuit.

The chart above shows the amperage drawn by typical office equipment. Add up the amps drawn by all the pieces that might be placed on the same circuit. To avoid overloading a 15-amp circuit, the total cannot exceed 12 amps; for a 20-amp circuit, the maximum is 16 amps. The chart also indicates whether surge protection or an uninterruptible power source is recommended for the equipment.

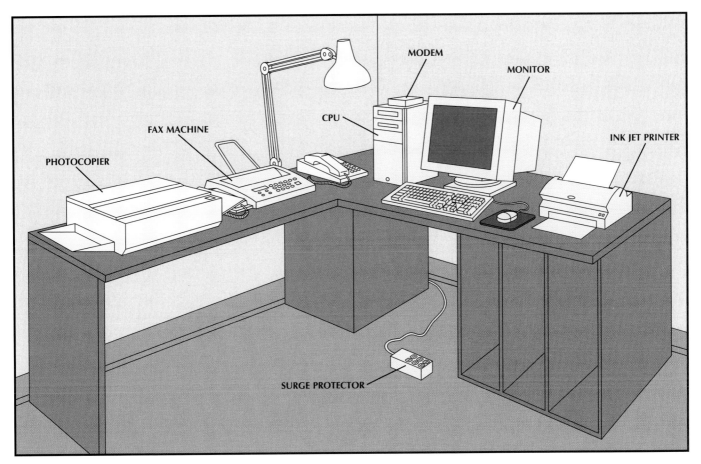

PHOTOCOPIER

FAX MACHINE

MODEM

CPU

MONITOR

INK JET PRINTER

SURGE PROTECTOR

Planning the circuits.

All the office equipment highlighted here requires surge protection. For convenience, some can be connected to the same circuit by way of a multi-receptacle surge protector. However, laser printers, photocopiers, and other big power users require a circuit of their own.

UNINTERRUPTIBLE POWER SOURCES

If you live in an area subject to frequent power outages, consider plugging your computer equipment and peripherals into an uninterruptible power source (UPS). In the event of an outage—or the power drop that is common in older buildings—the device provides power long enough for you to save your work and shut down the computer. Depending on the model, a UPS may provide backup power up to 30 minutes. To determine which equipment benefits from a UPS, consult the chart opposite.

Buy a model with a sufficient number of receptacles for your current and anticipated future needs, and check that the unit's power cord is long enough. Some UPS units offer protection for an entire computer network, but this is seldom necessary for a home office.

Most units incorporate surge protection, so you can also plug any equipment needing surge protection into a UPS.

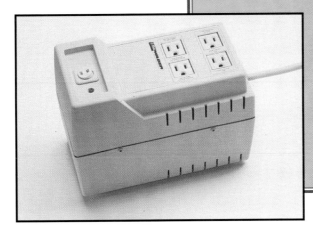

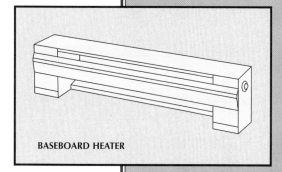

BASEBOARD HEATER

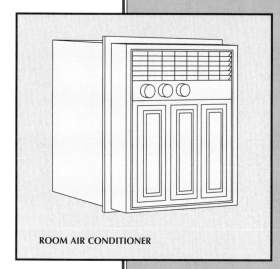

ROOM AIR CONDITIONER

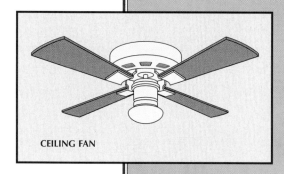

CEILING FAN

If your office is in a room of your home, its temperature will likely be comfortable. For a newly finished room in a basement or attic, you may be able to tap into the existing heating and cooling system. When this is not possible, you will need to provide independent heat and air-conditioning, which must be taken into account in your wiring plan.

A simple heat source to install is a baseboard heater. Some small units can be plugged into a wall receptacle, provided the receptacle is on an independent circuit. To obtain more heating capacity, buy a direct-wired model; 120-volt heaters are available, but 240-volt units are more common. To install the unit on a wall, remove the baseboard and fasten the heater to the wall. You'll need to run cable for a circuit to the wall and connect the cable to the heater's wires. If you don't feel comfortable doing this work yourself, consult an electrician; and always have an electrician hook up the cable to the service panel.

To cool an office, a room air conditioner is a good choice. Check the power requirement for your model and run a dedicated circuit for the air conditioner; depending on the model, a 240-volt circuit may be required. Also check the type of receptacle required—some air conditioners require a special one—and locate the outlet box as close as possible to the window. In some areas, you may be permitted to wire an air conditioner and a heater to the same circuit—check your local codes.

A ceiling fan will help keep the air moving in a room. Frugal in its electrical needs—a unit can be on the same circuit as the lighting fixtures in a room—and will increase the efficiency of your heating and cooling system. Some models also incorporate a light fixture. A fan can be hooked up to an existing ceiling outlet box, or you may want to choose a new location. Fans are heavy, so use a metal box approved for this use and attach it securely to the ceiling joists.

Working without adequate light or with the wrong kind of light can cause eyestrain, burning eyes, headaches, and drowsiness. Interior lighting is of two main types—ambient and task—and the ideal lighting plan should provide for both. When buying light fixtures, consider the type of bulb they take *(pages 91-93)*.

Ambient Lighting: With or without windows, an office requires a certain level of gentle, diffuse light. Light from a window, skylight, or glass door gives the most comfortable light to work by. Additional light can be provided by suspended incandescent lights, fluorescent lights attached to a ceiling outlet box, or recessed lights, if they spread illumination widely enough *(pages 96-100)*. Wall or ceiling fixtures that point up to bounce light off the ceiling provide indirect lighting with little shadow. Track lights are best suited to lighting individual objects such as artwork; they do not generally diffuse light evenly enough for working environments.

Task Lighting: Light that is directed to the working area can be provided by desktop lamps *(pages 93-95)* or by lamps or light fixtures attached to a wall or shelf above a desk and pointed downward. Small, specially designed halogen or fluorescent fixtures mounted under a shelf over a work surface also provide good task lighting. Ceiling fixtures are not a good source of task lighting because they cast shadows as you bend over your work.

Although most task lights are designed to be movable, it is best to plan their locations so you can place outlets nearby, avoiding a mess of wires.

A well-lit office.

In this office, a large window admits ample natural light; the computer's screen is placed at a right angle to the window to reduce glare. Depending on the direction the window faces, blinds may be required *(pages 168-169)*. A wall fixture pointed at the ceiling supplements the natural light from the window, and task lights direct light onto the drafting table and desk.

Working with wiring is not dangerous, provided that you follow all the safety rules and take the time to do the job correctly. Before beginning any wiring job, make sure you are well versed with the basics of how a home electrical system works, as well as familiar with all the safety tips given below. If you are at all uncertain of the techniques, hire a professional.

Working to Code: Local electrical codes, which have the force of law, govern the type and size of all electrical equipment as well as installation methods. You must be familiar with your local code before starting any wiring job. Also ask the building authorities whether you need a permit and what kinds of inspections will be required during and after the work. Some jurisdictions allow only licensed electricians to work on home wiring.

Volts, Amps, and Watts: Voltage is the measure of the "force" in a circuit. Normally, house circuits carry 120 volts, but some large appliances may require 240 volts. Amps measure the amount of current actually flowing in a circuit. Most house circuits carry 15 or 20 amps; determine your wiring needs according to the equipment you plan to install *(page 70)*.

Grounding: A typical circuit has two conductors. Wires encased in black insulation carry current from the service panel to the outlet boxes; white wires return it to the service panel and from there to the earth, or ground. Fire or electric shock may occur if current leaks from a black (hot) wire to a metal fixture.

A person touching the fixture can conduct the current to ground, with possibly fatal consequences. For this reason, electrical cable must include a third wire, usually bare copper, to provide a safe path to ground. Every receptacle, switch, light fixture, and metal outlet box in the house must be grounded by a wire connected to this copper wire. If you find an ungrounded outlet box, consult an electrician.

Choosing Cable: The three wires bundled together in standard cable vary in size according to the amount of amperage they are designed to carry—too small a wire can overheat, possibly melt its insulation and cause a fire. Select No. 12 cable for a 20-amp circuit, or No. 14 for a 15-amp circuit.

Cutting the Power: Never work on an outlet box or cut into a wall without being certain that the circuit is off. First, flip the breaker or pull the fuse for the circuit at the service panel. Insert the probes of a voltage tester into the vertical slots of a receptacle served by the circuit; if the tester glows the power is still on. Where there is any doubt, turn off all the circuits at the service panel. Before working directly on a fixture, switch, or receptacle, check again with a voltage tester after removing the cover plate *(opposite)*.

Joining Wires: All electrical connections must be made in an outlet box. First remove about 10 inches of the outer insulation from the cable with a cable ripper, being careful not to damage the insulation of the individual wires. Then remove about $\frac{1}{2}$ inch of insulation from each wire with a wire stripper. Join wires with plastic wire caps, available in a variety of sizes; ensuring that the cap completely hides the bare wire.

Checking the Work: With the job done and the power still off, check for short circuits with a continuity tester. Unscrew any light bulbs on the circuit, then touch the tester's alligator clip to the black wire in the circuit's last box. Touch the other probe to the white wire, then to the bare copper wire, and finally to the box itself.

A glowing tester bulb in any of these cases indicates a short circuit: Check any new connections for damaged insulation or bare wires contacting each other and make the necessary corrections. Mount cover plates over receptacles and switches. Once you've replaced the cover plate, turn the power on and check a receptacle for power with a voltage tester.

Electrical Safety Tips

✔ Never work on a live circuit. Until you have determined the circuit is off *(above)*, assume it is live—work carefully to avoid touching any screw terminals or bare wire.

✔ When turning off power as described above, stand on a dry surface and use only one hand. Do not touch a sparking, blackened, or rusted panel. Never work on the wiring inside the panel.

✔ Label or lock the panel so that no one can turn the power back on by mistake while you are working on the electrical system.

✔ Never work on wiring in wet conditions or with wet hands, feet, or hair.

✔ Do not touch a metal pipe or any other potential conductor when you are working on wiring.

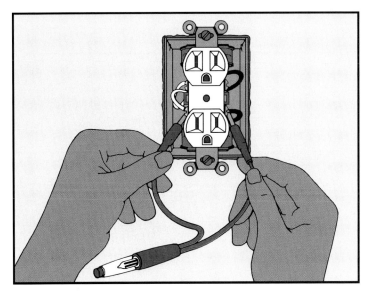

Testing a receptacle for power.

Before working, turn off power to the circuit at the service panel and make the following checks with a voltage tester. If the tester's neon bulb glows at any stage of the process, the circuit still has power; stop and try a different fuse or circuit breaker at the service panel.

◆ Before removing the cover plate, check that power is off by inserting the probes of a voltage tester into the receptacle's vertical slots.

◆ Remove the cover plate. Working carefully to keep your hands away from any bare wires or metal parts, touch the probes to the terminal screws where the black and white wires attach to the receptacle *(left)*. On a dual receptacle, test both pairs of terminals.

◆ Test from each black wire to the ground wire to check for defects or improper wiring in the neutral circuit.

Testing a switch for power.

◆ To verify that electricity to a switch has been shut off, unscrew the cover plate, then the switch. Pull the switch from the box by the mounting strap.

◆ Working carefully to keep your hands away from any bare wires or metal parts, touch one probe of a voltage tester to the outlet box if it is metal—or to the ground wire if the box is plastic—and touch the other probe to each of the brass terminals on the switch. The tester's bulb will not glow if electricity to the switch has been turned off.

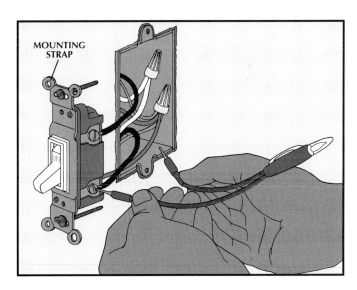

MOUNTING STRAP

Checking a light fixture.

◆ Turn off power to the fixture at the service panel. Flip the wall switch to OFF.

◆ Unscrew the fixture and pull it away from the box to expose the wires.

◆ Hold the fixture in one hand and remove the wire caps with the other. Work carefully to avoid touching any bare wires or metal parts. Keep black and white wires away from each other and from the box if it is metal.

◆ Gently loosen each fixture wire from the corresponding house wire. Set the fixture aside.

◆ In the following checks, a voltage tester will not glow if the power is off: Touch one probe of the tester to the black wire in the box and the other to ground—the box if it is metal *(left)*, or the ground wire in a plastic box. Check also for voltage between the black wire and the white wire and between the white wire and ground.

To equip your new office with sufficient receptacles, as well as outlet boxes for light fixtures, you may be able to simply extend an existing circuit. However if the equipment you plan to power will overload the circuit, or if you want separate circuits for computer equipment *(pages 70-71)*, you will need to add new circuits. The steps for extending or adding a circuit are essentially the same except that in one case you tap into a circuit at an existing outlet box, and in the other you run the cable directly from the service panel.

Locating the New Boxes: Turn off the power to all circuits in the room. Select a location for the first new box and, if the room is already finished, make an opening for it in the wall or ceiling *(pages 78-79)*.

Routing the Cable: If you're tapping into an existing circuit, find a box as close to the new box site as possible to provide power for the extension. Only certain types of boxes can be rewired for an extension *(below)*. If your cable must be routed behind the ceiling, try to tap into a box that allows you to run the cable along the joists, rather than across them. Draw a map of the room showing the existing box or service panel, the new box, and the positions of studs and joists. This will help you plan a route for running the new cable. You can then estimate how much cable you will need. Provide 8 extra inches of cable for each box, and add another 20 percent to allow for unexpected deviations in the cable's route.

To run the cable, cut access holes in walls and ceilings, drill a path for the cable through studs or joists, and fish the cable through *(pages 80-82)*; or run the cable along the surface *(pages 83-84)*.

Hooking Up: With the new cable in place, clamp it to the new box and install the box *(pages 85-88)*. Connect the cable to the switch or receptacle *(pages 88-89)*, or install the light fixture *(pages 96-100)*. Then, for an extension, hook up the cable to the existing box following the diagrams opposite. For new circuits, have an electrician hook up the cable to the service panel.

Wrapping Up: Once the job is complete, carefully check your work *(page 74)*. Then, shut off the electricity again and patch the holes that you have made in the walls or the ceilings. Finally, turn the power back on. Your new circuit is ready for use.

HOW A BOX IS WIRED

Close inspection of an existing outlet box will reveal whether it is a good candidate for extension. After shutting off the power at the service panel, remove the cover plate from the box to determine the type of box and the number of connections it already contains. Middle-of-the-run switch and outlet boxes identified by the two cables clamped to them—one incoming and one outgoing—can easily be extended. So can end-of-the-run receptacles, identified by their single incoming cable. However, end-of-the-run switches, which are also attached to only one cable, cannot serve as circuit extenders. Nor can any outlet box controlled by a wall switch, since the switch would then control the entire extension.

Most boxes are wired with 14-gauge cable. If the box contains only one or two such cables, a second or third can be added. In a kitchen area, receptacle boxes may contain thicker 12-gauge cable. If a box contains only one 12-gauge cable, a second can be added. If you are unsure of the type of cable, or for a box containing more than one switch or receptacle, consult your local building department.

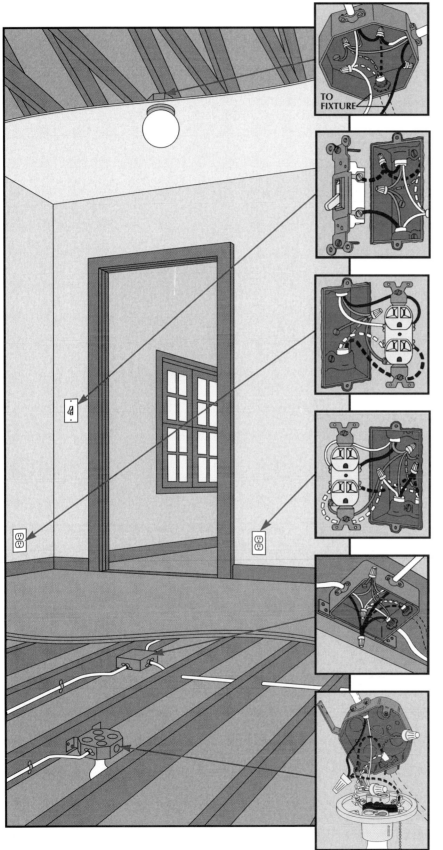

Middle-of-the-run ceiling box.
Attach the black, white, and ground wires of the new cable *(dashed lines)* to the corresponding wires in the cable bringing power from the service panel.

Middle-of-the-run switch.
Disconnect the incoming black wire from the switch terminal and join it to the black wire from the new cable and a black jumper *(dashed lines)*. Connect the jumper to the switch terminal. Attach the new white and ground wires *(dashed lines)* to the corresponding wires already in the box.

End-of-the-run receptacle.
Attach the black and white wires of the new cable *(dashed lines)* to the unused terminals on the receptacle. Connect the new ground wire *(dashed line)* to the existing ground wire and to the jumper.

Middle-of-the-run receptacle.
Remove a black wire from a receptacle terminal and join it with both the black wire of the new cable and a black jumper *(dashed lines)*. Attach the jumper to the terminal. Repeat for the white wires. Attach the new ground wire *(dashed line)* to the other ground wires and the green jumper.

Junction box.
After identifying the cable from the circuit you wish to extend, attach the black, white, and ground wires of the cable to the new cable's corresponding wires *(dashed lines)*.

End-of-the-run pull-chain fixture.
Disconnect the black and white wires. Join each to its corresponding wire in the new cable and to a jumper *(dashed lines)*. Attach the black jumper to the brass-colored screw on the fixture, and the white jumper to the silver-colored screw. Connect both ground wires to a jumper *(dashed line)*, then fasten the jumper to a ground screw in the box.

Before installing a new outlet box, cable must be run from an existing box or the service panel, around or through the structural framework of studs and joists, to the new outlet's position. The path should involve the least amount of labor and wall and ceiling damage.

An Advantageous Route: In unfinished basements or attics, you can fasten new electrical boxes directly to exposed studs or joists *(box, page 86)*. In a finished room, however, you must install surface wiring *(page 83)* or cut openings in the wall or ceiling *(below and opposite)*. Whenever possible, run the cable through an unfinished basement or attic, where studs and joists are exposed or readily accessible *(pages 80-81)*. You can either staple the cable along studs and joists, or drill holes and thread the cable through them.

When tapping a wall box in a finished room just above the basement or below the attic, you can reach the box by drilling through the boards, called plates, at the top or bottom of the wall. Fish tapes —hooked wires—are then used to pull the cable along this part of its course.

Opening Hidden Paths: To run cable in a finished room that cannot be reached from either basement or attic, you must make access holes in walls or ceilings to get at studs, joists, and plates along the intended route *(page 82)*.

Wherever the room's wooden framework blocks the intended route of the electrical cable, you will have to bore a path for it. Fish tapes are then used to guide the cable through the hidden spaces and bored holes.

Code Requirements: Cable running along an exposed joist or stud must be stapled at intervals no greater than $4\frac{1}{2}$ feet. Holes for threading cable must be drilled at least $1\frac{1}{2}$ inches from the edge of a stud or joist. Exposed cable must be stapled within 12 inches of a metal box or plastic box with an internal clamp, and 8 inches from a plastic box with no internal clamp.

⚠ **CAUTION** *Before beginning any of these tasks, turn off power to the work area and check that all circuits on both sides of the wall are also turned off (pages 74-75).*

TOOLS

Voltage tester
Electric drill
Spade bits ($\frac{3}{8}$", $\frac{3}{4}$")
Wallboard saw
Electronic stud finder
Screwdriver
Hammer
Fish tapes
Cable ripper
Wire stripper
Utility knife

MATERIALS

Outlet box
Hanger wire
Cable
Cable staples
Electrician's tape
Lightweight chain

SAFETY TIPS

Wear goggles when operating a power tool.

CUTTING A WALL-BOX OPENING

1. Outlining the box on the wall.

◆ Place the box face down on a sheet of thick paper and outline the box on the paper. Leave out the ears at the top and the bottom of a metal box *(right)*, or at each corner of a plastic box. Mark an X within the shape, then cut out the shape. This will serve as a template.
◆ With the marked side against the wall, hold the template where you want the box, then transfer its shape to the wall.

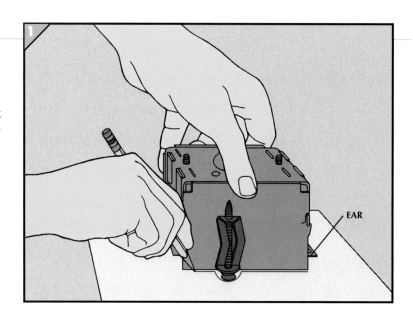

EAR

2. Cutting the opening.

◆ Turn off power to the work area and check that all circuits are off *(pages 74-75)*.

◆ Drill a small hole in the center of the outline. Bend hanger wire to a 90-degree angle, insert one end through the hole, and rotate the wire to check for obstructions. If you find any, relocate the box.

◆ With a $\frac{3}{8}$-inch spade bit, drill eight holes, positioned around the box outline *(right)*. Omit the side holes for metal boxes without clamps and for plastic boxes.

◆ Cut around the outline with a wallboard saw *(photograph)*, being careful not to cut into any wires. Use short strokes in order to avoid jabbing the saw blade into the other side of the wall.

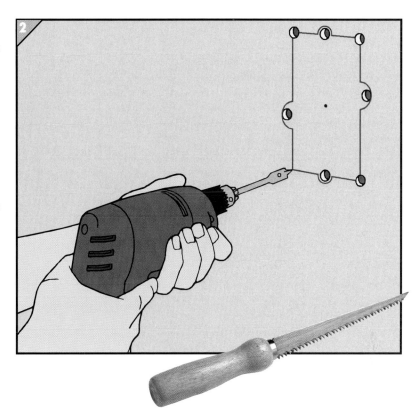

MAKING A HOLE FOR A CEILING BOX

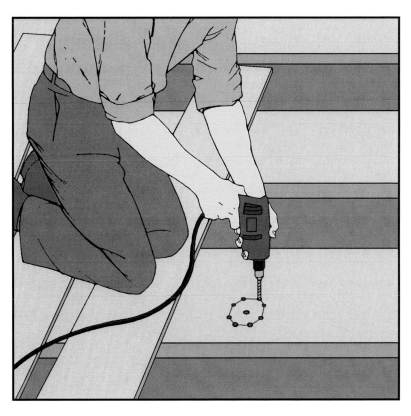

Cutting the opening.

◆ Turn off power to the work area and check that all circuits are off *(pages 74-75)*.

◆ From the room below, use an electronic stud finder to choose a location for the new box that is at least 4 inches from a joist. Mark the spot on the ceiling and drill a $\frac{1}{8}$-inch locator hole through the ceiling.

◆ In the attic, check that no wires will obstruct the new box, then center the box over the locator hole and trace the box outline on the exposed surface of the ceiling below.

◆ Drill $\frac{3}{8}$-inch holes at the outline's eight corners, positioning the bit just outside each corner *(left)*.

◆ From below, cut along the outline marked by the drilled holes with a wallboard saw.

1. Accessing an existing box.

◆ Turn off power to the work area and check that all circuits on both sides of the wall are turned off *(pages 74-75).*

◆ Bore a $\frac{1}{8}$-inch location hole through the floor directly below the front of the box you plan to tap.

◆ Poke a thin wire or other marker through the hole, then go to the basement and find the marker.

◆ In line with the location hole, bore up through the soleplate of the wall with a $\frac{3}{4}$-inch spade bit, drilling at a slight angle if necessary *(right).*

◆ Below the opening for the new box *(pages 78-79),* drill a hole through the plate.

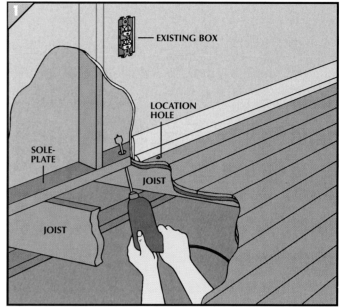

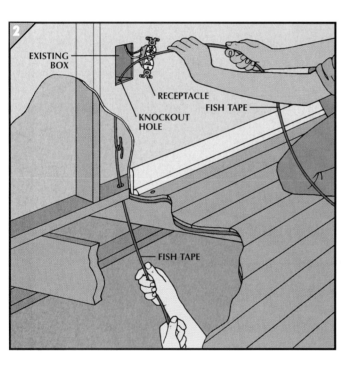

2. Fishing tape from box to basement.

◆ Detach the receptacle from the existing box and pull it out of the way; you need not disconnect the wires.

◆ With a screwdriver, remove a knockout from a hole in the bottom of the box *(page 85, Step 1).*

◆ Push the end of a fish tape through this hole and down behind the wall.

◆ Have a helper in the basement push a fish tape up through the hole in the soleplate. Maneuver them behind the wall to hook their ends together *(left).*

3. Feeding cable to the existing box.

◆ From the basement, pull the fish tapes that have been joined through the soleplate until the end of the upper one is exposed; unhook the tapes.

◆ With a cable ripper, strip 3 inches of sheathing from one end of the cable, then remove the insulation from the exposed wires using a wire stripper. Run the bare wires through the hook of the upper tape, then fold the wires back over themselves to secure them to the hook. Fasten the looped wires together with electrician's tape.

◆ As your helper feeds cable up through the hole in the soleplate, pull the fish tape back through the knockout hole in the existing box until the end of the cable emerges.

◆ Detach the cable from the fish tape and trim the uninsu-lated wires from the cable.

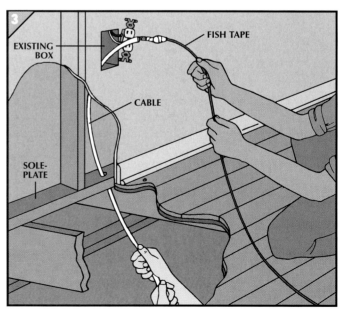

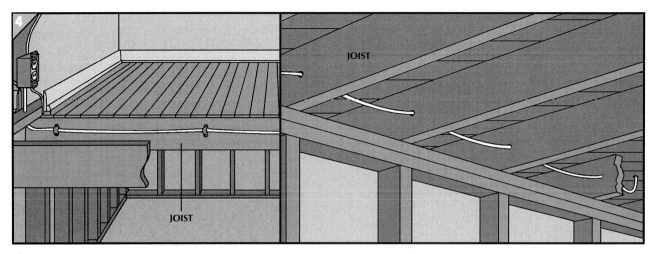

4. Running the cable.

◆ To run the cable along a joist, fasten it with cable staples *(above, left)*, taking care not to damage the cable sheathing as you nail the staples.

If you must cross joists, drill a $\frac{3}{4}$-inch hole through the middle of each joist, aligning the holes, and thread the cable through them *(above, right)*.

◆ When you reach the hole you have drilled in the opposite sole-plate, fish the cable up to the new box opening by the method shown in Steps 2 and 3.

ROUTING CABLE THROUGH AN ATTIC

Fishing cable to the attic.

You can run cable along or across exposed attic joists by the same methods used in the basement, but a light chain used in place of one fish tape simplifies the procedure.

◆ Remove a knockout from a hole in the top of the existing box *(page 85, Step 1)*.

◆ Bore a location hole in the ceiling directly above the front of the box *(opposite, Step 1)*. Then go to the attic and drill a hole through the wall's top plates in line with the location hole.

◆ Return to the room and have a helper in the attic drop a light chain down through the hole in the top plates to a point that is below the level of the box.

◆ Push a fish tape through the knockout hole, catch the chain *(right)*, and pull it into the box. Secure the chain to the hook at the end of the fish tape with electrician's tape.

◆ Have your partner pull the chain up until the fish tape reaches the attic. Remove the chain and attach the cable to the tape hook.

◆ From the room, pull the fish tape down until the end of the cable emerges in the existing box.

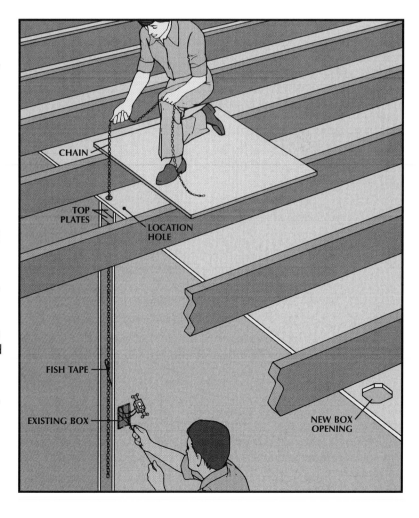

1. Exposing the studs.

◆ Make an opening for the new box *(pages 78-79)*.
◆ With a stud finder, locate the stud nearest the existing box. Use a utility knife or wallboard saw to cut a hole 3 inches high and wide enough to extend

2 inches beyond the edges of the stud *(above)*.
◆ Locate the remaining studs and cut holes over them by the same method.
◆ Drill a $\frac{3}{4}$-inch hole at the center of each stud, angling the holes slightly as necessary.

2. Threading cable through the studs.

◆ After removing a knockout tab in the bottom of the existing box, have a helper push a fish tape through the hole and down into the wall.
◆ Thread a second tape through the hole in the nearest stud, hook your helper's tape *(above)*, and pull it through the stud.

◆ Release your tape, attach cable to the free end of the first tape, then have your helper pull tape and cable back through the stud and into the existing box.
◆ Using the same two-tape method, fish the other end of the cable through each stud and into the opening for the new box.

Cutting into finished walls to install new receptacles can be a daunting task. If you have a minimal amount of rewiring to do, this can be avoided in a number of ways: by installing surface-mounted conduit, multi-outlet strips, power bars, or a receptacle adapter. All these methods can help avoid an unsightly and potentially dangerous mess of extension cords, although the wires will be visible. Whatever method you choose, be sure that the equipment you plan to plug in won't overload the existing circuit *(page 70)*.

Surface-Mounted Conduit: A system of channels and outlet boxes, surface-mounted conduit is installed along baseboards, door-frames, and the ceiling *(below)*; the rigid

channels that protect the wires all but vanish when painted to match the room. Follow the manufacturer's instructions for installation.

Multiplying Outlets: If you require new outlets primarily along one wall, you can add them without running new cable. One way is to install a multi-outlet strip, which is direct-wired to the circuit *(page 84)*. An easy, but less permanent-looking alternative is to simply purchase a power bar or receptacle adapter *(box, page 84)*.

⚠ *Before installing surface raceways or a multi-outlet strip, turn off* **CAUTION** *power to the affected circuits and check that it is off on both sides of the wall* (pages 74-75).

TOOLS

Screwdriver
Cable ripper
Wire stripper

MATERIALS

Raceway channel
and fittings
Multi-outlet strip
Electrical cable
Wire caps

SURFACE RACEWAYS

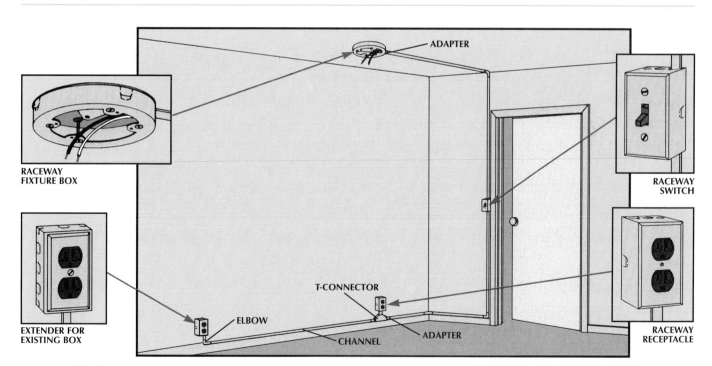

A network of raceway fittings.
Raceway elements are available in both metal and plastic. Fittings like boxes and elbows come in two pieces: a backplate that screws to the wall and a cover, which snaps over the plate. The backplate of each fitting has tongues

that slip into the ends of the single-piece channel; the width of channel to use depends on the number and gauge of the wires in the circuit. Metal raceway systems accommodate cable, but individual wires labeled type TW on the insulation are easier to install. Only

hot and neutral wires are needed; the channel itself, along with wires inside each outlet box, takes care of grounding. Plastic systems, however, require running a ground wire alongside the black and white ones and connecting it to each fixture in the circuit.

Mounting the strip.

◆ Mark the desired location of the multi-outlet strip, indicating the position of the small junction box.

◆ Run cable to the junction-box location.

◆ Separate the base from the strip and screw it to the wall *(right)*.

◆ Cut the sheathing from the end of the cable with a cable ripper and strip the ends of the wires using a wire stripper.

◆ With wire caps, connect the bare cable wire to the green wire of the outlet strip; the white cable wire to the white outlet wire; and the black cable wire to the black outlet wire.

◆ At the other end of the strip, connect the green wire to the grounding clip that clamps into the outlet-strip base. Cover exposed wire ends with wire caps.

◆ Snap the outlet strip onto the base.

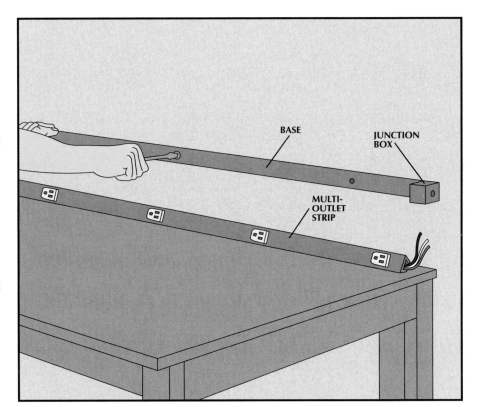

BASE

JUNCTION BOX

MULTI-OUTLET STRIP

POWER BARS AND RECEPTACLE ADAPTERS

The simplest way to accommodate new equipment is to use a power bar or a receptacle adapter. Power bars sit on the floor or can be fastened to a desk or wall, serving as extensions and additional receptacles. Receptacle adapters simply increase the number of slots at a receptacle. The model shown has slots on the side so it occupies less space between the back of a desk and the wall. Many power bars and receptacle adapters include a built-in circuit breaker; for sensitive computer equipment, choose one with a surge-suppression feature.

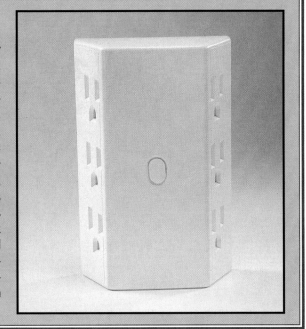

The central element in any electrical installation is an outlet box mounted in a wall or ceiling. The box supports switches, receptacles, and light fixtures, and protects connections to the house wiring.

Installing the Boxes: Outlet boxes that house receptacles, switches, and wall lights are generally rectangular. They can be made either of metal or plastic. In finished walls, they are clamped to the wallboard, while in an unfinished room, they can be attached directly to the studs *(below and page 86).*

Boxes for ceiling lights are octagonal or circular. To support most ceiling fixtures, the box must be metal and be firmly fastened to two joists. One type is fastened to joists from an unfinished attic *(page 87),* while another type can be installed from below when the area above is inaccessible *(box, page 88).* To support a ceiling fan, use only boxes approved for that purpose. Before installing an outlet box, clamp the wire securely to the box; the method differs depending on the type of box.

Connecting the Wires: Once the box is in place, the receptacle or switch can be hooked up. When you buy a new receptacle, make sure it is rated for the correct voltage and amperage, and ensure that it can be grounded. The way the receptacle is hooked up to the cable depends on whether it is located in the middle or at the end of the circuit *(page 88).*

The function of a switch is to interrupt a hot wire in a circuit. As with receptacles, the wiring method for a switch depends on its location in the circuit *(page 89).* One common arrangement is a middle-of-the-run switch—where the current encounters the switch before the fixture. A switch loop is used where power runs to a light before it reaches the switch.

Once the receptacle or switch is hooked up, connect the other end of the cable to the old outlet box *(page 77)* or, for a new circuit, have an electrician connect it to the service panel. Finally, check your work *(page 74).*

TOOLS			MATERIALS		
	Wire stripper	Hammer		Two-part	Machine
Screwdriver	Wallboard	Nail set	Wall box	connectors	screws
Pliers	saw	Wrench	Ceiling box	Bar hanger	Jumper wires
Cable ripper	Electric drill	Tin snips	Cable	Receptacles	Wire caps

INSTALLING A METAL WALL BOX

1. Clamping the cable.
◆ Insert the tip of a screwdriver into the slot of a U-shaped knockout, and pry the knockout away from the box *(inset).*
◆ Work the knockout back and forth until it breaks free; if necessary, twist it out with pliers.
◆ With a cable ripper, cut 3 inches of sheathing from the end of the cable, then strip the ends of the wires with wire strippers. Pull the cable into the box through the knockout hole and under the internal clamp, leaving 6 inches of cable extending past the front of the box.
◆ Holding the cable so the clamp rests on the sheathed portion, screw the clamp tightly against the cable *(right).*

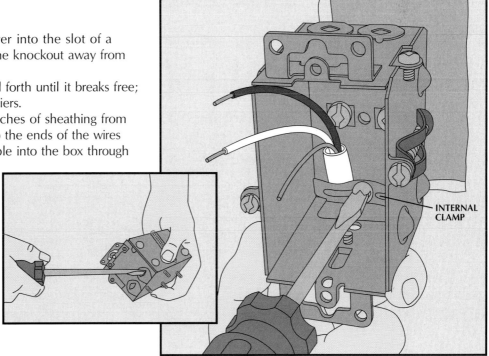

INTERNAL CLAMP

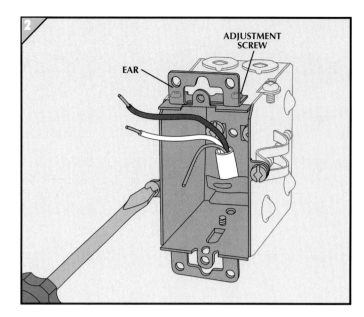

2. Setting the box in the wall.

◆ Check for fit by pushing the box into the wall opening. Remove the box, enlarge the hole as necessary with a wallboard saw, and move the ears by turning the adjustment screw to bring the box flush with the wall.

◆ Return the box to the opening. Tighten the clamp screws on the sides, expanding the clamps and drawing the box against the wall *(right)*.

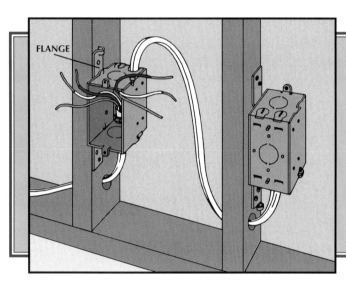

BOXES FOR AN UNFINISHED ROOM

In an unfinished room, rough in the wiring before putting up the wallboard. Nail flanged outlet boxes to the studs so the edge of the flange is flush with the edge of the stud. Drill $\frac{3}{4}$-inch holes through the studs near the soleplate and run the cable, clamping it securely to each box. Avoid placing outlet boxes that serve adjacent rooms within the same stud space; doing so will conduct sound between the rooms. Staple the cable to the studs.

A PLASTIC BOX

Attaching the box.

◆ With a wallboard saw or a drill, enlarge the holes in the upper right and lower left corners of the opening to accommodate the clamps.

◆ Press firmly on the clamp from the rear of the box with your finger or a screwdriver to break the thin plastic locking it closed.

◆ Cut the sheathing from the cable with a cable ripper, then strip the ends of the wires with a wire stripper.

◆ From outside the box, push the wires under the flap, then pull the cable into the box. Press the clamp against the cable sheathing to ensure a good grip.

◆ Insert the box into the opening.

◆ Tighten the screws on the top right and bottom left corners of the box *(right)*. Doing so extends the clamps and draws them toward the inside of the wall, pulling the box tight.

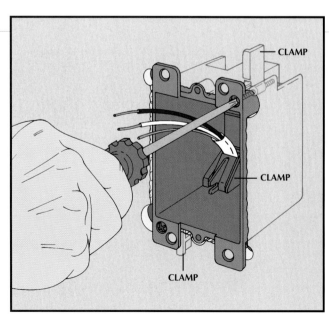

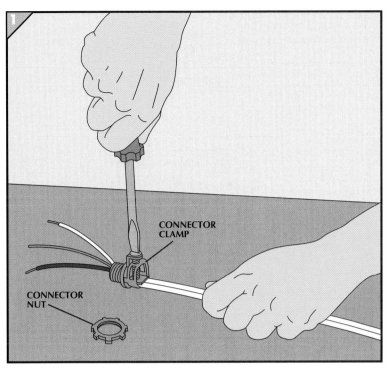

1. Clamping the cable.

◆ Remove a round knockout from the side of the box with a hammer and nail set.
◆ Cut the sheathing from the end of the cable with a cable ripper, then use wire strippers to strip the ends of the wires.
◆ Slip the clamp portion of a two-part connector onto the cable, with the threaded portion facing the stripped wires and flush with the end of the sheathing. Tighten the clamp screw on the cable *(left)*.

Some ceiling boxes have an internal clamp; in this case, clamp the cable as for a wall box *(page 85, Step 1)*.

CONNECTOR CLAMP

CONNECTOR NUT

2. Installing the box.

◆ Insert the stripped wires and the threaded end of the connector into the box through the knockout hole. Slip the nut over the wires and screw it onto the connector so it is finger tight.
◆ Fasten the box to the hanger with the hardware provided.
◆ Cut the tab from each end of an extendable bar hanger with tin snips.
◆ Holding the box in the ceiling hole with its front flush against the inside surface of the ceiling, extend the arms of the hanger to the joists on either side. Mark the positions of the hanger screw holes on the joists, drill pilot holes, and screw the hanger to the joists *(right)*.
◆ From below, position a nail set against one of the protrusions on the rim of the connector nut; tap the nail set, tightening the nut *(inset)*.

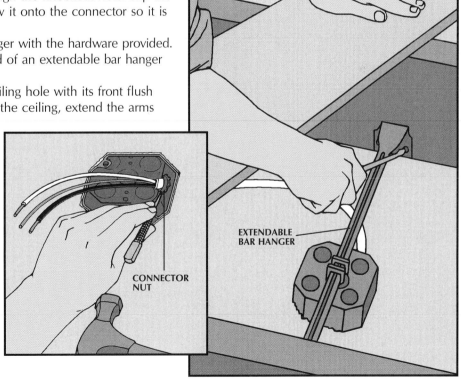

CONNECTOR NUT

EXTENDABLE BAR HANGER

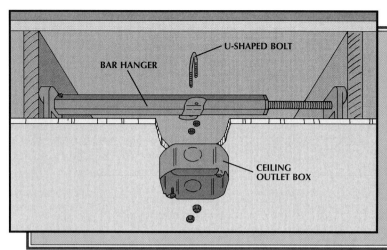

BAR HANGER

U-SHAPED BOLT

CEILING
OUTLET BOX

A screw-type bar hanger is designed to be installed from below when the joists are not accessible from an unfinished attic above. The bar hanger is inserted into the hole in the ceiling and turned by hand to extend the ends to reach the joists. An adjustable wrench is used to turn the bar, forcing the teeth on each end into the joists. Once the bar is in place, the ceiling outlet box is attached to it with the U-shaped bolt and nuts provided.

WIRING A RECEPTACLE

Middle-of-the-run

Two cables enter a box in the middle of a circuit run, each containing black, white, and bare copper wires.
◆ Connect each black wire to a brass-colored terminal in any order.
◆ Attach the white wires to the silver-colored terminals.
◆ In a metal box, attach a short jumper to the back of the box with a machine screw and attach another jumper to the green grounding terminal on the receptacle.
◆ Fasten these jumpers and the two bare copper wires from the cables with a wire cap (right). For a plastic box, there will be no jumper needed to the box.

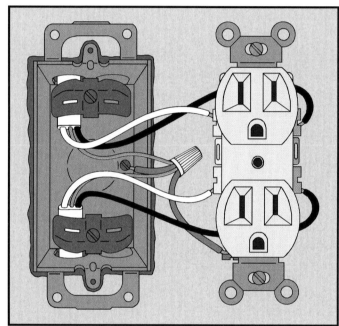

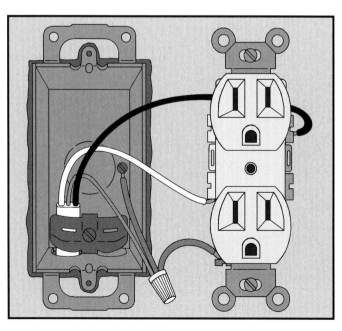

End-of-the-run.

Only one cable enters an end-of-the-run box.
◆ With plastic-sheathed cable, connect the one black wire to either brass-colored terminal and the white wire to either silver terminal.
◆ With a metal box, attach ground jumpers to the box and receptacle, and connect them to the bare copper wire with a wire cap. With a plastic box, there is no jumper to the box.

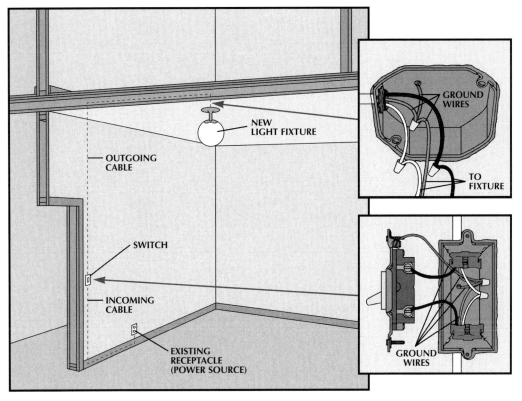

GROUND WIRES

NEW LIGHT FIXTURE

OUTGOING CABLE

TO FIXTURE

SWITCH

INCOMING CABLE

EXISTING RECEPTACLE (POWER SOURCE)

GROUND WIRES

A middle-of-the-run switch.

◆ At the switch *(bottom inset)*, attach the black wires of the incoming and outgoing cables to the switch, join the white wires with a wire cap, and screw a ground wire to the box—if it is metal.

◆ Connect the black and white fixture wires to their counterparts in the cable *(top inset)*. Do likewise with the ground wires, adding a jumper to the box if it is metal.

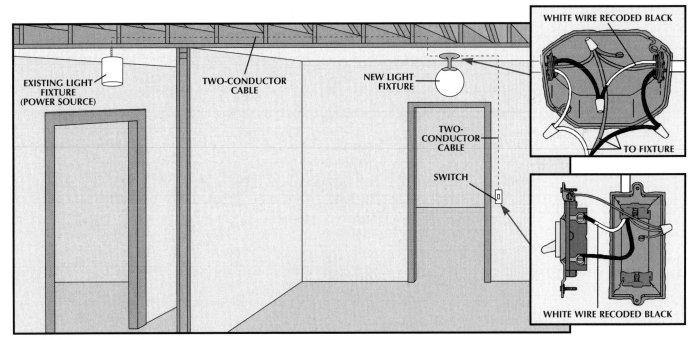

WHITE WIRE RECODED BLACK

EXISTING LIGHT FIXTURE (POWER SOURCE)

TWO-CONDUCTOR CABLE

NEW LIGHT FIXTURE

TWO-CONDUCTOR CABLE

SWITCH

TO FIXTURE

WHITE WIRE RECODED BLACK

A switch loop.

◆ At the new fixture *(top inset)*, join the incoming white wire to the white fixture wire. Blacken the end of the white wire of the outgoing, switch-loop cable to show that the wire is hot and connect it to the black wire of the incoming cable. Attach the black fixture wire to the black wire in the switch loop. Join the ground wires and connect them to the box, if it is metal, with a jumper.

◆ At the switch *(bottom inset)*, recode the white wire black, and connect both conductors to the switch. Connect the ground wire with jumpers to the switch and to the box—if it is metal.

CHOOSING LIGHT FIXTURES

Adequate lighting and proper illumination are both essential for a comfortable working environment. Aside from the eye strain and headaches that can result from insufficient light—or the incorrect type of light—you can suffer from other physical problems. Surprisingly enough, some instances of neck and back pain can be attributed to poor or improper lighting—such as when individuals strain and contort their necks to see their work or computer screens. There is another—even more compelling—argument for proper lighting. Many people working in environments without adequate or proper light have been found to suffer from depression.

ABOVE: *In this bright, comfortable home office, natural light from the two windows is augmented by track lights mounted on the ceiling. The lights are directed away from the work area to avoid both direct and reflected glare.*

Fortunately, obtaining the proper balance between glare-free ambient lighting and adjustable task lighting can alleviate all of these problems.

How much light is enough? To a large extent, the answer depends on one's age. A 20-year-old needs less light than a 40-year-old. Most people, as they grow older, become "far-sighted." This condition, called presbyopia, occurs as the lenses of the eyes gradually become harder and cannot change shape in response to the action of the ciliary muscles. This makes focusing on near objects difficult. Sufficient light combined with corrective eye wear can help to correct this problem.

A BUNDLE OF BULBS

Incandescent light bulbs are the most common type of light in both household and commercial applications. These bulbs are usually pear-shaped *(left, top)*, although tube-shaped models are available *(left, bottom)*. The glass can be either frosted or clear. Manufacturers now make long-life and reduced wattage bulbs.

Fluorescent lamps provide good ambient light. The tube type *(right, top)* is the most common, can measure from 5" to 96" long, and requires special fixtures and a ballast. Compact fluorescents *(right, bottom)* work in much the same way as tubes, but often come with an integrated ballast and a screw base so they can be used in an incandescent fixture.

With a longer life than standard incandescents, quartz-halogen lamps produce a whiter, brighter light. The standard type features a quartz glass envelope *(left, top)*. Other types are available in which quartz-halogen lamps are enclosed inside a protective glass bulb *(left, bottom)*.

Indoor light comes from three types of bulbs or lamps: incandescent, halogen, or fluorescent. Incandescent light bulbs haven't changed much since their invention by Thomas Edison in 1878. A coiled tungsten filament enclosed inside a glass bulb glows—or incandesces—as the electric current passes through it. The bulb is filled with an inert gas to stop the filament from burning too quickly. The tungsten slowly evaporates as it burns and builds up on the inside of the glass. Incandescent bulbs have a shorter life expectancy than other types and are considered the least efficient at converting electrical energy into light. Long-life and reduced wattage incandescent bulbs, designed to compensate for these shortcomings, are available.

Halogen bulbs—also called quartz-halogen or tungsten-halogen—are a variety of incandescent lamp. The tungsten filament is enclosed inside a quartz glass envelope filled with halogen gas. The halogen causes the evaporated tungsten particles to be redeposited on the filament, which contributes to longer bulb life. The bulbs burn at a higher temperature than other incandescents do, and produce a brighter, whiter light. Although they are also somewhat more energy-efficient, the quartz glass envelope must not be touched, as oils from the skin can react with the quartz glass and cause it to fail prematurely. Some manufacturers are now producing bulbs in which the halogen lamp is enclosed inside a larger glass bulb to prevent this problem.

Fluorescent tubes last longer and are more energy-efficient than other types of bulbs. You can now buy fluorescents that

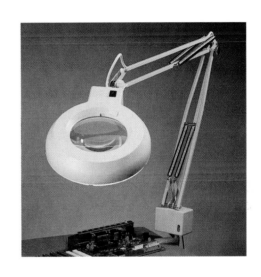

produce warm-colored light, and improved ballasts have done away with the annoying flickering and buzzing that plagued older models. The color of the light—color temperature—is determined by the phosphor blend coating the inside of the tube. Compact fluorescents work in the same way as fluorescent tubes, but they are smaller, and often come with a ballast integrated into a screw base so that they can be used to replace incandescent lamps.

TASK LIGHTING

Task lighting, as the name suggests, is specifically designed to direct light to the surface on which you are working. Properly used, this type of light makes working more comfortable and helps the eyes remain healthier—improper use of task lights can actually make things more difficult to see. For task lighting to be effective, there are a few simple guidelines you should follow.

Use a desk lamp that is strong enough to provide light for your most difficult visual tasks without creating too great a contrast in which too much light actually obscures vision by reducing contrast. Veiling typically occurs when bright light shines directly on thermal fax paper or glossy magazine paper.

The best place to mount task lights is to the side of the work—on the left side for right-handed people and the right side for left-handed people. Adjust the lamp head so the bulb does not shine into your eyes or onto a computer screen.

Some people feel that incandescent or halogen task lights give a more neutral or natural light than fluorescents, which can be an important consideration if you work with color. The light from these lamps is usually easy to direct, but because it emanates from a small area, it can cause sharp shadows. Another point to keep in mind is that this type of lamp gives off a lot of heat.

Fluorescent lamps provide a more diffuse light and the shadows they create are

between the light on your work surface and the level of light in the rest of the room.

Purchase task lights that are easily adjustable and that hold their position once adjustments are made. The lamp head should stay cool so that you can reposition it as necessary. Adjusting a task light to maximum advantage can be a bit tricky. Avoid aiming light directly onto a computer monitor—the light should be focused primarily on your work surface, with a little aimed toward the keyboard. It's also important to avoid the problem of reflected glare, which can cause "veiling," a condition not as sharp. They don't generate as much heat as incandescent lights, so the fixtures tend to stay cooler. Some lamps—architect's lamps, for example—use a combination of incandescent and fluorescent bulbs for a good color balance.

One final point: task lights do not merely illuminate your work area better. Proper task lighting consumes less energy than would be needed to maintain adequate light levels with ambient lighting—and this translates into lower energy bills.

TAKING CARE OF YOUR EYES

Follow these tips to keep your eyes healthy:

■ Take a break at least every half hour and stare off into the distance for 15 to 20 seconds to give your eye muscles a chance to relax.

■ Remember to blink.

■ If dry eyes are a problem, ask your pharmacist to recommend an eye lubricant.

■ Have your eyes examined regularly and remember to tell your doctor that you use a computer.

■ Use an anti-glare filter made of optically coated glass on your computer monitor.

■ If you wear glasses, have your optician apply an antireflective coating.

■ Good nutrition is important and Vitamin A is especially good for your eyes—eat some dark leafy greens every day.

■ Go for a walk on your lunch break and look at the scenery.

■ Get sufficient sleep.

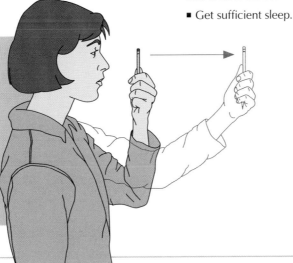

Practice focusing: Hold a pencil in front of your face and focus on it for a few seconds. Follow the pencil with your eyes as you move it in and out slowly (right). Repeat several times, then when your hand is outstretched, focus on a distant object.

Relax your eyes: If you can't lie down and close your eyes, here's the next best thing: While sitting at your desk, cover your eyes with your hands and sit quietly for a few minutes (above). Relax and enjoy the dark.

The most suitable ceiling fixtures for a home office are standard suspended fixtures, recessed fixtures, and fluorescent lights. Suspended fixtures and fluorescents are hooked up to a ceiling box—to support any fixture heavier than 5 pounds, ensure that the box is metal and is securely fastened to the joists *(pages 87-88)*. Most fixtures come with mounting hardware, and the recessed types—both halogen and standard incandescent—include their own junction boxes.

Suspended Fixtures: Incandescent light fixtures that hang from a ceiling box can sometimes be attached directly to the mounting tabs in the box. In other cases, you will have to adapt the box with a crossbar *(below)*.

Recessed Lights: Incandescent fixtures designed to sit flush with the ceiling hang from a mounting plate inserted into an opening in the ceiling *(opposite and page 98)*. When installing several such units on a single circuit, make sure that all but one are rated for "through-wiring" with two cables; the last fixture needs only a single cable. Halogen fixtures are unusual in that, as well as having a built-in junction box, they incorporate a transformer to convert the house current to the lower voltage required by halogen bulbs *(pages 99-100)*.

A recessed fixture installed in an insulated ceiling is a potential fire hazard: Keep insulation at least 3 inches away from the fixture or buy a fixture rated IC (for insulation contact).

Fluorescent Lights: Available in a wide variety of shapes, the most common fluorescent fixture is the rectangular single-tube model *(page 100)*.

⚠️ **CAUTION** *Before installing a light fixture, turn off power to the work area and check that all circuits on both sides of the wall or ceiling are also turned off* (pages 74-75).

TOOLS

Fish tape	Electronic
Cable ripper	stud finder
Wire stripper	Electric drill
Screwdriver	Spade bits
Hacksaw	($\frac{5}{8}$", $\frac{3}{4}$")
Tin snips	Wallboard
Hammer	saw

MATERIALS

Light fixture	Two-part
kit	connector
Cable	Wallboard
Jumper wire	patching
Machine	materials
screw	Toggle bolts,
Wire caps	washers
Crossbar	Hickey
Lock nut	Nipple

SAFETY TIPS

Wear goggles when sawing or drilling.

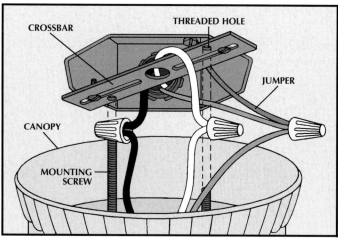

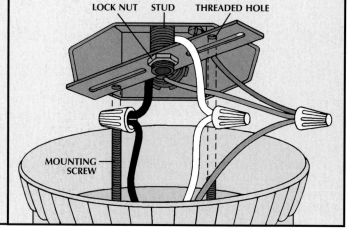

A suspended fixture.

◆ Fish a cable to the ceiling box, clamp it, remove the insulation from the end of the cable, and strip the wires.
◆ With wire caps, connect black wires to black, and white wires to white. In a metal box, fasten a short grounding jumper to the box with a machine screw, then connect the jumper and the bare copper wires with a wire cap. (For a plastic box no jumper is needed.)

◆ Where canopy holes do not align with the mounting tabs in the ceiling box, adapt the box with a slotted crossbar. Screw the crossbar to the tabs *(above, left)* or, for a box with a stud in the center, slip the crossbar onto the stud and secure it with a lock nut *(above, right)*.
◆ Fasten the canopy to the threaded holes in the crossbar with screws trimmed, if necessary, so they do not press against the back of the box.

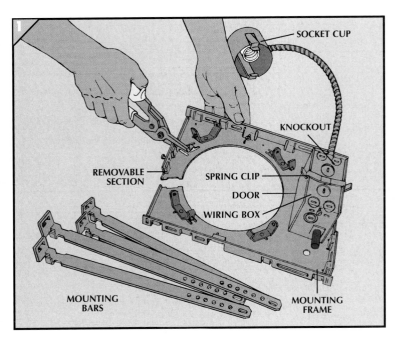

1. Preparing the mounting frame.

◆ If a template is not provided with the fixture, create one by removing the frame's mounting bars and placing the frame on a piece of cardboard. Outline the frame and circular opening with a pencil, then cut along the lines to create a template.

◆ With tin snips, cut out the removable section of the frame opposite the wiring box *(left)*.

◆ Lift the spring clip on top of the wiring box and remove one of its two detachable doors.

2. Cutting a ceiling opening.

◆ With an electronic stud finder, locate the ceiling joists. Using the template, mark fixture locations on the ceiling between joists.

◆ Drill a small hole in the center of each circular mark. Bend hanger wire to a 90-degree angle, insert one end through the hole, and rotate the wire to check for obstructions. If you find any, relocate the fixtures. Otherwise, cut openings as shown on page 79.

◆ At each joist running between fixtures, cut an access opening in the ceiling as shown for studs on page 82. Drill a $\frac{3}{4}$-inch hole through the center of each joist.

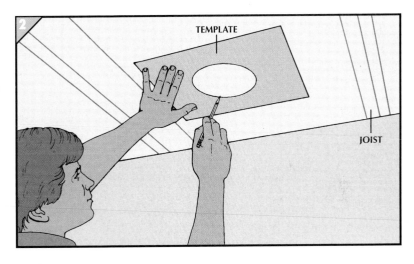

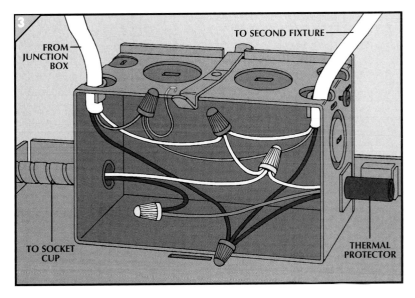

3. Wiring connections.

◆ Fish a cable from a junction box to the first fixture opening, followed by another cable from the second fixture opening to the first—and so on downstream. Remove insulation from the ends of the cables and strip the wires.

◆ At the first ceiling opening, rest a fixture-mounting frame atop a stepladder, and clamp the cable ends to opposite sides of the box.

◆ Red wire caps *(left)* indicate the connections to be made between the cable and fixture wires. Connect black to black, white to white, and the ground wires.

◆ Reattach the box door.

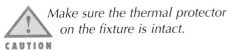

Make sure the thermal protector on the fixture is intact.

CAUTION

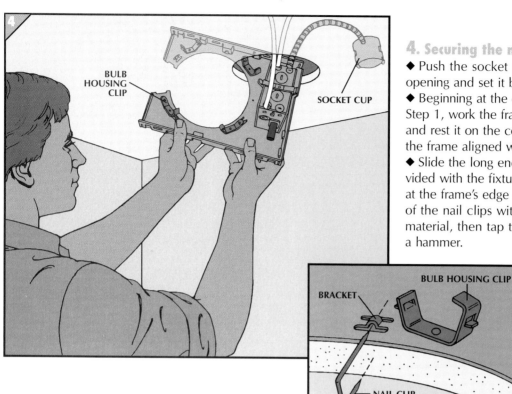

4. Securing the mounting frame.

◆ Push the socket cup through the ceiling opening and set it beside the lip of the hole.

◆ Beginning at the opening cut in the frame in Step 1, work the frame through the hole *(left)*, and rest it on the ceiling with the opening in the frame aligned with the ceiling hole.

◆ Slide the long ends of the four nail clips provided with the fixture partway into the brackets at the frame's edge *(inset)*. Align the short ends of the nail clips with the center of the ceiling material, then tap them into the ceiling with a hammer.

5. Installing the bulb housing.

◆ Bring the socket cup back through the opening. Rotate the bulb housing clips inward.

◆ Insert the socket cup into the top of the bulb housing so that tabs in the cup snap into slots in the housing.

◆ Push the assembly into the frame *(right)* until the bulb housing flange rests against the ceiling, completing the installation.

◆ At the second fixture opening, connect cables from the first and third fixture openings to the second fixture in its wiring box, and complete the installation as described above.

◆ When all fixtures are in place, patch the access holes at each joist.

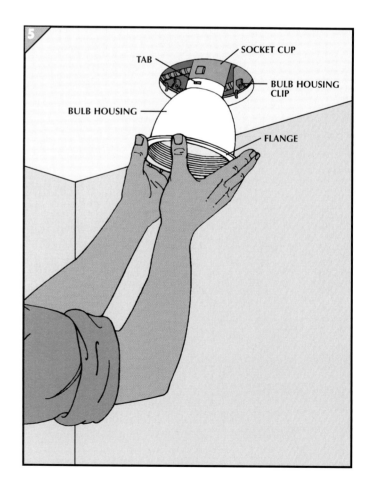

1. Making the wiring connections.

◆ Using the template provided, cut a hole in the ceiling *(page 97, Step 2)*. Route cable to the opening.

◆ Remove the insulation from the end of the cable and strip the wires.

◆ Set the fixture on a ladder near the opening. Remove the cover from the junction box. Then, remove a knockout and clamp the cable to the box with a two-part connector *(page 87, Step 1)*.

◆ Red wire caps indicate the cable and fixture wires to be connected: the black wire to the black, the green wire to the the copper ground wire, and the white wire to the white *(right)*.

◆ Push the wires into the box and replace the cover.

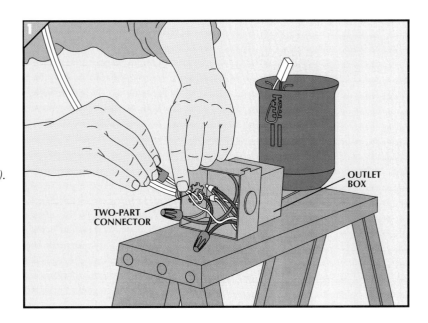

OUTLET BOX

TWO-PART CONNECTOR

2. Installing the fixture.

◆ Lift the fixture into the opening with the outlet box first *(left)*, then center the housing over the opening.

◆ Reaching inside the housing, push up on the metal prongs to press the springs down against the wallboard, then clip the prongs into the slots in the housing *(inset)*. If the spring is overly tight, remove it and reattach it to a higher pair of tabs. If it is too loose, attach it to a lower pair of tabs.

HOUSING

SLOT

PRONG

TAB

SPRING

HOUSING

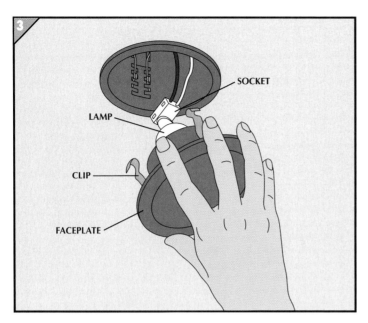

3. Attaching the lamp.

◆ Remove the cardboard covering the glass lens of the faceplate and slip the lamp into place.

◆ Insert the prongs on the end of the lamp into the socket hanging from the wires inside the housing.

◆ Push the faceplate up into the housing until it is flush with the ceiling.

A FLUORESCENT FIXTURE

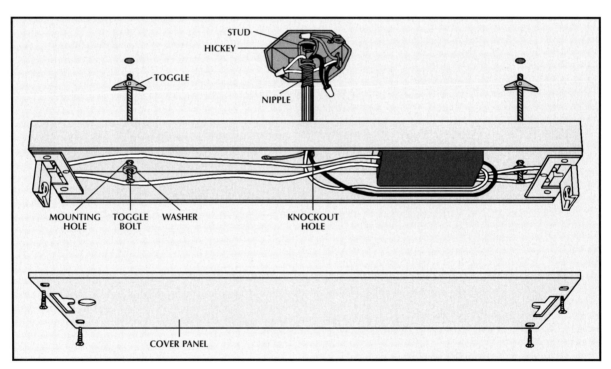

Mounting a one-tube ceiling fixture.

◆ Position the fixture with the knockout hole for the wires centered on the ceiling box, and mark the ceiling through the fixture-mounting holes. Lower the fixture and, with a $\frac{5}{8}$-inch spade bit, drill holes at the marks.

◆ Slip a toggle bolt and washer through the fixture-mounting holes and screw a toggle onto the end of each of the bolts.

◆ Thread a hickey to the stud and a nipple to the hickey; if there is no stud, attach a crossbar *(page 96)* to the box tabs and a nipple to the crossbar.

◆ Have a helper support the fixture or hang it from the box with a wire hanger, then lead the fixture wires through the nipple and connect them to those that are in the box, black to black and white to white. Connect the ground wires from the fixture and the house circuit to each other and to the grounding jumper in the box if it is metal.

◆ Raise the fixture. While folding the wires into the box, push the toggles through the ceiling holes and guide the fixture onto the nipple. Tighten the toggle bolts.

◆ Finally, install the cover panel and the tube.

Home offices require one or more jacks for fax and modem connections. You will most likely also want to install independent phone lines for the office.

A typical home telephone system is linked to the network by a special jack or by a box called a network interface. The device serves as a point of demarcation between the phone company's jurisdiction and the homeowner's. This link and everything beyond it is installed and maintained by the phone company, but anywhere on your home's side of the boundary, you are free to modify and expand the system. Within the house, jacks are wired either to each other or to a central connecting block, usually located in a basement, attic, or utility room.

Adding New Jacks: Phone jacks can either be mounted on a baseboard or set into the wall like an electrical receptacle *(page 102)*. To merely extend a line, it's easiest to wire new jacks to a nearby jack on an existing phone line; locate them at least 6 inches from the nearest electrical outlet.

Adding New Lines: Every independent phone line serving a home requires a pair of wires—two pairs are usually provided by the phone company so that two separate phone lines can be accommodated. To add more lines, the phone company will need to bring in additional wires.

To hook up only a second line, you can reconfigure an existing jack *(box, page 102)*, purchase a two-line telephone, or install a special two-line jack. Another alternative is to route cable called telephone station from each jack serving the new line directly to the point of demarcation, and have the phone company make the connection there.

This approach allows for greater flexibility later on, since any of these jacks can be switched to a new line simply by changing the connections at the point of demarcation. If you are installing new jacks with home-run wiring, consider using three-pair twisted wire *(below)* to permit future upgrades to the system.

Running Cable: Telephone station wire can be run inside walls and through unfinished attics and basements much as electrical cable can *(pages 80-82)*, as long as it is kept 6 inches from electrical wiring. However, since it carries such low voltage, it can also be run along baseboards *(page 103)* and around door and window frames, or you can hide it behind shoe molding or under the edge of wall-to-wall carpet. To bring station wire from one floor to another, you can route it through closets or take advantage of the open space around a plumbing stack vent *(page 104)*.

⚠️ **CAUTION** *Although the message-carrying current in a phone line is harmless, the phone is rung by bursts of current strong enough to deliver a shock. To prevent phones from ringing while you are working with wires, remove all phone handsets from the hooks.*

TOOLS
Screwdriver
Wire strippers
Diagonal cutters
Staple gun for wires
Electric drill
Fish tapes
Fishing weight

MATERIALS
Telephone jacks
Telephone
  station wire
Wire clips
Telephone-wire
  staples
Heavy string

SAFETY TIPS
When drilling, protect your eyes with goggles.

OPTIONS IN TELEPHONE WIRE

Older homes usually have telephone wires that carry quad wire—two pairs of untwisted wires, with each pair designed to serve a separate telephone number. When both lines are in use with this type of wire, you can experience "crosstalk" between the two lines. While crosstalk may be merely annoying when you are speaking on a phone, on a modem or fax line it can disrupt the transmission of data. If you are installing new runs of telephone wire, consider buying three-pair twisted wire. Twisted wire prevents crosstalk; the three-pair type can accommodate a third line.

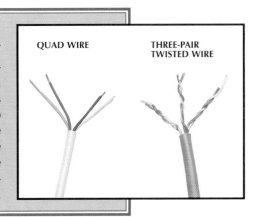

QUAD WIRE   THREE-PAIR TWISTED WIRE

Putting in a surface-mounted jack.

◆ Loosen the four terminal screws on the jack about three turns each.

◆ Remove 3 inches of sheathing from a length of telephone station wire to reveal the colored conductors.

◆ Insert each colored wire into the slot of its corresponding color-coded terminal *(right)*.

◆ Attach the jack to the baseboard with the screws provided.

◆ Insert the spade tips on the jack-cover wires into their corresponding color-coded terminals and tighten the screws.

◆ Break out a wire-channel tab from the jack cover, route the station wire through it, and then screw the cover to the jack.

◆ Route the station wire to an active jack, securing it with wire clips, and connect the conductors to the appropriate color-coded terminals there.

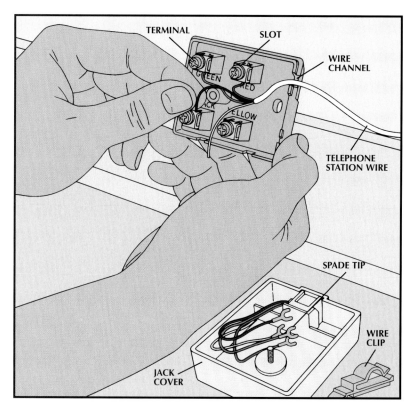

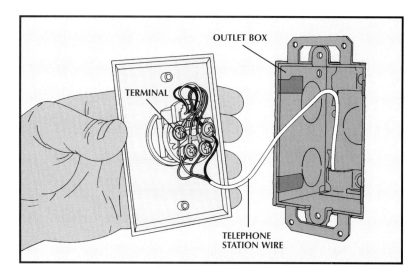

Installing a flush-mounted jack.

◆ Install a standard electrical outlet box *(pages 85-86)* and route a length of telephone station wire from an active jack into the box.

◆ Remove 3 inches of sheathing from the station wire and $\frac{1}{2}$ inch of insulation from each colored conductor.

◆ One at a time, loosen the four terminal screws about three turns.

◆ Wrap the bare end of each conductor around a terminal, matching the color of the wire already installed there *(left)*. Tighten the screws.

◆ Trim stray wire ends with diagonal cutters, and attach the jack to the outlet box with the screws provided.

WHICH PHONE RINGS WHERE

Jacks installed by the telephone company are always wired to serve two lines. To reconfigure a surface-mounted jack to serve only the second line, open the jack and remove the red and green spade tips from the terminals. Wrap the tips with electrical tape and fold them out of the way. Leave all the colored conductors from the telephone station wire connected to the terminals; they supply jacks farther down the lines.

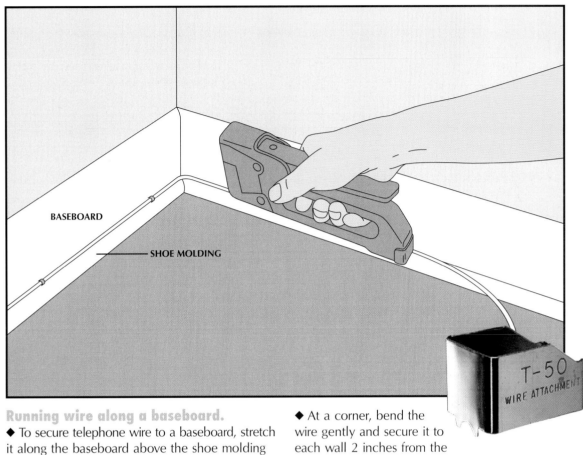

BASEBOARD

SHOE MOLDING

T-50
WIRE ATTACHMENT

Running wire along a baseboard.

◆ To secure telephone wire to a baseboard, stretch it along the baseboard above the shoe molding and staple it in place every 16 inches with a staple gun designed for telephone-wire staples. Some standard staple guns can be fitted with a special attachment for this purpose *(photograph)*.

◆ At a corner, bend the wire gently and secure it to each wall 2 inches from the bend *(above)*.

An alternative method is to staple the wire to the wallboard just above the baseboard.

TRICKS OF THE TRADE

Pushing Phone Wire Through a Wall

To route phone wire through a hollow wall, drill holes in both sides of the wall and push a drinking straw through *(right)*. If the straw will not exit the second hole, push a straightened coat hanger through first and then slide the straw over it. Pull out the hanger and pass the telephone wire through the straw. Then, remove the straw and patch the gaps around the wire with spackling compound.

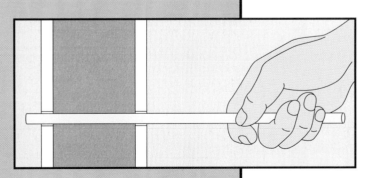

Wiring through closets.
Use the following procedure when closets are not stacked directly above one another:
◆ Fish wiring from the basement through a hole drilled in the floor of a closet above.
◆ Drill a hole through the closet ceiling into the space between the joists above *(right)*.
◆ Drill a hole down into the same joist space through the floor of a closet on the next floor.
◆ Tack one end of a heavy string to the floor of the upper closet. Wrap the other end into loops, and stuff the loops down into the joist space.
◆ Push a fish tape through the hole in the lower closet and snag the string *(inset)*. Pull the string into the lower closet, tie it to the wiring, and pull them into the upper closet.

If the closets do not share a joist space, remove a section of baseboard in an upper room and drill behind it on an angle into the joist space above the lower closet. Fish wiring through and run it along the baseboard to the nearest jack location.

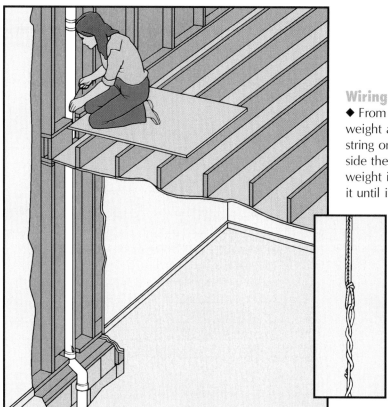

Wiring along a stack vent.
◆ From the attic, lower a small fishing weight attached to a long piece of string or chain into the space alongside the plumbing stack *(left)*. If the weight is blocked, jiggle and bounce it until it falls past the obstruction.
◆ When the string reaches the basement, attach cables to the string, staggering the points of attachment to avoid a bulky connection *(inset)*.
◆ Pull the string and cables back up beside the stack.

Once you've found a corner of the house for your office where you'll be undisturbed, you may still need to communicate with family members in other rooms or a visitor who comes to the front door. This is best done with an intercom, of which there are three main types: In one, units located throughout the house communicate by radio waves; in another, the units plug into electrical receptacles and communicate over the house wiring.

These two systems are easy to install and relatively inexpensive; however, for much clearer sound—free from interference—you may want to consider a hard-wired type, in which the units are connected by low-voltage wire run through the walls or along baseboards in the same way as telephone wire *(pages 103-104)*. In the simplest system, a master unit is installed in a closet or other hidden spot, and a number of stations are each wired directly to it. Some intercoms also allow "daisy chain" wiring, in which each station is wired to the previous one, rather than to the master unit.

Stations include indoor and outdoor units that can receive and initiate a communication with the push of a button. Other systems have a "hands-free" feature, which allows the person at the receiving end to respond to a communication without pushing a button.

Most models also include special units that allow you to talk to someone at the front door, although communication cannot be initiated from the door units. In some cases, a special door chime wired to the intercom will transmit the signal to all the stations. Some systems even allow you to unlock the door remotely.

In addition to the standard indoor stations, a desktop unit in the office can be kept within easy reach. For rooms where you want the station to be less conspicuous, a small control unit installed in an accessible spot can be wired to independent speakers hidden in a corner or in the ceiling. On many models, you can hook up a cassette deck or CD player to the master station, allowing music to be transmitted to all the stations.

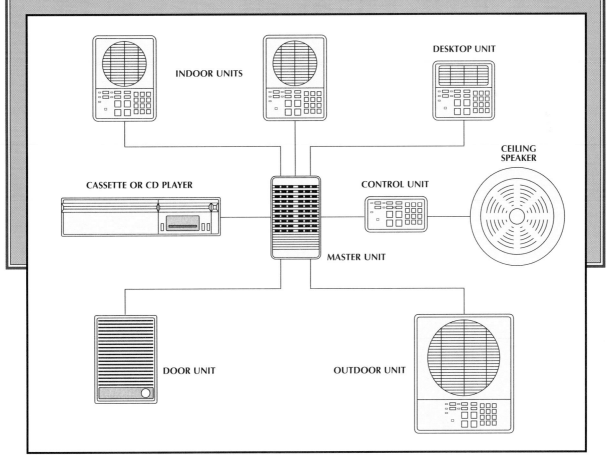

INDOOR UNITS

DESKTOP UNIT

CEILING SPEAKER

CASSETTE OR CD PLAYER

CONTROL UNIT

MASTER UNIT

DOOR UNIT

OUTDOOR UNIT

CHAPTER 4

CREATING A WORKING ENVIRONMENT

WHILE THE WONDERS OF MODERN TECHNOLOGY CERTAINLY simplify the task of operating a business, the cornerstones of any office still remain a spacious desk and a comfortable chair. Although these furnishings don't play an active role in your work, the care you take in selecting them will go a long way toward determining how pleasurable and productive your office hours are.

With the emergence of ergonomics, furniture makers have developed pieces that cradle people in healthy postures as they work, easing the aches and pains that can accompany long hours. Although much of this furniture has earned a niche in the business world, building your own can often be the only way to meet your needs. After providing a sampling of office furniture, this chapter shows you how to fashion a customized workstation. With a little care and attention, you can build an environment that reflects your tastes and personality—and helps make your work more pleasant and efficient.

RIGHT: Designed to fit into a corner, this desk provides ample room for a computer, task lights, file trays, and research material. Two of the desk supports double as file cabinets, and wall-mounted shelves in matching wood offer additional storage space.

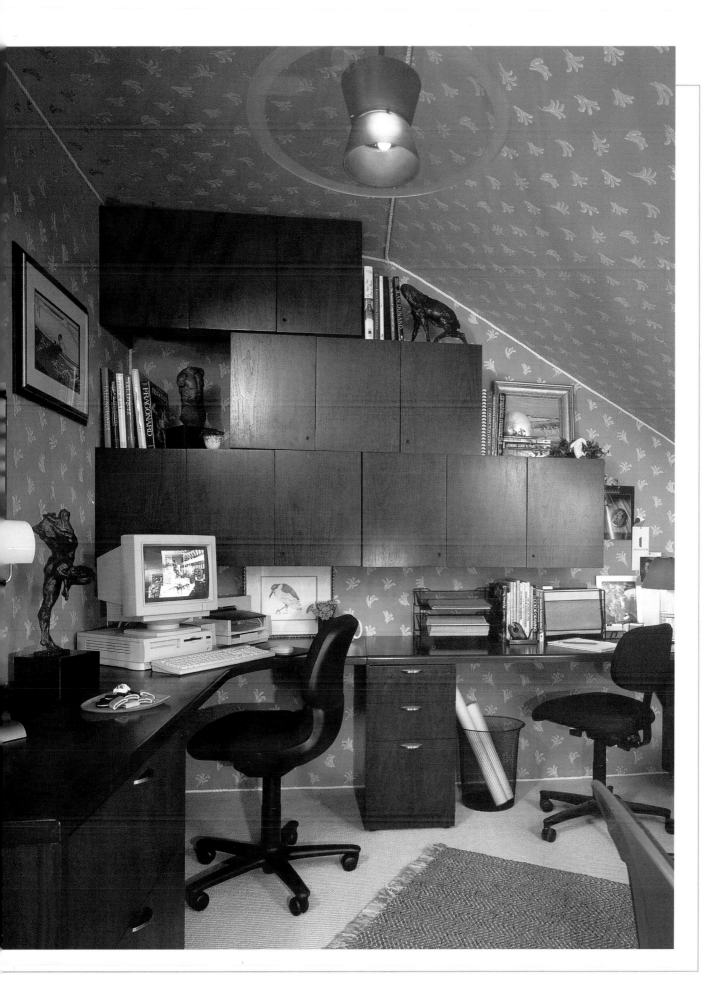

You are likely to spend more waking hours in your home office than in any other part of the house. Thus, it's important to properly plan and lay out the office and everything in it to avoid compromising your comfort and health. Designing a working environment for human comfort and safety—the science known as ergonomics—includes furnishings such as desks and chairs, and environmental factors like lighting and air quality.

Workstation Design: Much office work consists of sitting at a computer workstation. A poorly designed desk or an ill-fitting chair can contribute to back, shoulder, and neck pain; a keyboard that is incorrectly positioned can lead to repetitive stress injuries to the wrists. When building your own desk, design it so the keyboard, monitor, and documents are set at the correct height *(opposite)*. If you are buying a workstation *(pages 110-114)* and can't find one with the right dimensions

for your size, you can compensate with adjustable supports for the monitor and keyboard. Adjust the chair to keep your arms, legs, and back at the angles shown in the diagram.

Protecting Your Eyes: To avoid eyestrain, place the monitor at the correct distance from your eyes *(opposite)*. Provide the room with adequate light *(pages 73 and 90-95)*; frequent breaks and exercises can ease the strain on your eyes *(page 95)*.

Keeping Things Within Reach: To avoid having to stretch frequently across your desk—and perhaps strain back or shoulder muscles—set up your workstation so that the items you regularly need to use are within easy reach *(below)*. If a single work surface is not adequate, consider adding an L-shaped extension to your desk that you can reach by simply swiveling your chair.

Hearing Yourself Think: Low-level noise in your office may not be imme-

diately noticeable, but with time it can take a toll on your concentration and efficiency. Block noise from outside the office with soundproofed walls and ceilings *(pages 58-60)*, and with carpet on the floor in the room above. Control noise originating inside the office with acoustic tiles *(page 57)*. Also, try to furnish the room so "hard" surfaces such as bare walls stand opposite "soft" ones such as bookcases or drapes. Two hard surfaces across from each other often reflect too much noise.

Breathing Easy: Vapors emitted by certain types of carpets—as well as by the toner used in photocopiers and laser printers—have been linked to respiratory disorders. The air quality in your office, particularly after installation of new carpeting, can be improved by proper ventilation. A further step to take is to filter airborne particles out of the air by installing an air purifier. Also be sure to keep your office at a comfortable temperature and humidity.

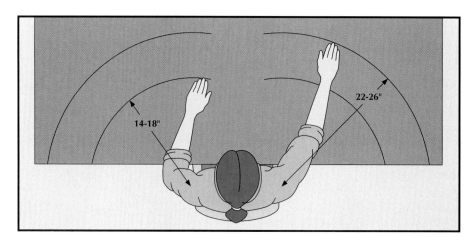

Everything within easy reach.
Position items on a desk so you can reach them without straining. The area within 14 to 18 inches of the shoulders can be reached by moving the hands only *(above)*—keep the computer mouse within this arc. Reaching the area in the 22- to 26-inch range requires extension of the arm without straining forward—ideal for documents and regularly used supplies. Reserve the area outside these arcs for seldom-used items.

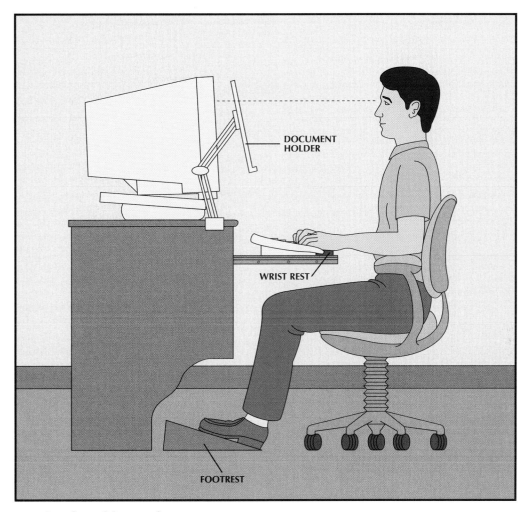

DOCUMENT
HOLDER

WRIST REST

FOOTREST

Comfortable seating.

When designing or adjusting your workstation *(page 122)*, observe the following guidelines: Set the chair height so the soles of your feet are flat on the floor or a footrest, and your thighs are parallel to the floor or slope down slightly. Place the monitor 18 to 30 inches from your eyes, with the top line of the display at eye level. If you type from documents, set up a document holder close to the monitor. The keyboard must be positioned so that when your elbows are at your sides your forearms are parallel to the

floor or angled slightly downward, with your wrists in line with your forearms. Position the mouse so you can reach it with your arm close to your body and with your hand and forearm in a straight line.

A padded wrist rest can help keep your wrists from bending and cushion them from a sharp desk edge, both common causes of repetitive stress injuries. Purchase a wrist rest long enough to span the length of both the keyboard and mouse area—or get a second, smaller wrist rest for the mouse alone.

COMMERCIAL POSSIBILITIES

In recent years, many manufacturers have turned their attention to the growing market for home office furniture. As a result, there is a wide choice of ready-made and ready-to-assemble furniture. How do you choose what is right for you? Architect Ludwig Mies van der Rohe once made a three-word statement that contains good advice for most decorating situations: "Form follows function." Simply start by defining what you need. What jobs will you be performing in this space? What equipment do you use? Will you have to accommodate other people, either employees or clients? Is the room yours alone, or will you be sharing it with other family members? When you know what you need, then you can add in what you want.

Many home workers neither need nor want the cold sterile look that defines

ABOVE: This contemporary workstation features a rounded bookcase return, an adjustable swivel monitor stand, a sliding keyboard/mouse shelf, and a file drawer. All of these items can be set up on either the left or the right side of the desk.

BELOW: An entire home office is housed in this attractive wood cabinet. Two sets of doors open to reveal work surfaces, shelves, and plenty of room for a computer and a telephone.

many corporate workplaces, especially if the home office is sitting in the middle of the family room or other communal space. They want home office furniture that is functional and comfortable. For others, their work area, even one at home, must say "office" in no uncertain terms or they can't seem to function. Ultimately, there is no one "right" solution. By considering the many options available and your personal work style and space, you will eventually find the setup that is right for you.

Whatever your job, you will need a surface on which to work. How big should this surface be? In theory, it should be big enough to have everything you need to work within arm's reach and it should be wide enough to accommodate your largest

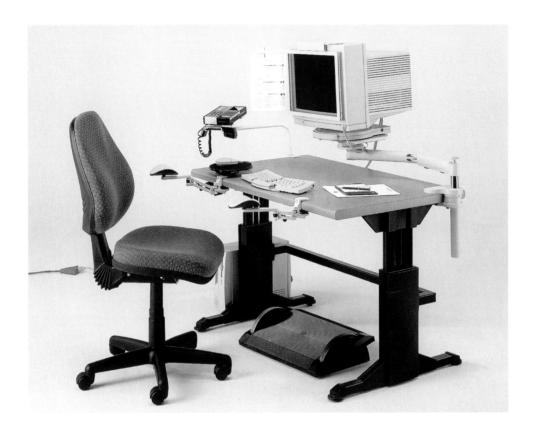

piece of equipment; if you use a computer, that is probably the monitor. What about the rest of your accessories? How much space will your phone, fax, printer, mouse, calculator, scanner, speakers, and other desktop equipment occupy? Think this through carefully before you buy. Imagine yourself sitting at the workstation and try to visualize your equipment layout. (You may want to use a graph and cutouts similar to those used in Chapter 1 to plan office layouts.) Where will all the wires go? It may be that a single, large, rectangular work surface is not the best solution.

Workstations built in L- or U-shaped configurations make your work space more efficient by bringing more of the work surface within your reach.

Remember, too, that when buying furniture, cheap doesn't always save you money. Look for quality, whatever your budget. The pieces you buy now should be able to adapt and grow with your changing needs. There are many lines of reasonably priced modular furniture that offer flexibility and adaptability. They include desks in a variety of dimensions, corner connectors, fixed or mobile filing cabinets, CPU stands,

printer carts, hutches, shelves, and other pieces. Units can always be purchased as needed or as permitted by your space and budget constraints.

Another important consideration is the finish on the furniture. Is it durable or does it scratch and stain easily? A high-gloss finish will not only show scratches, dust, and fingerprints, but also will create problems with reflected glare, which can cause eyestrain and headaches. White furniture,

SPACE-SAVING SOLUTIONS

whether the finish is matte or glossy, also reflects too much light. The best finishes are low-luster natural wood or matte surfaces, preferably gray or beige. Your computer keyboard should be positioned in line with your forearms *(page 109)*. If you can't adjust the height of your work surface, add an adjustable tray for your keyboard and mouse underneath it.

A mobile computer work center may be the solution if finding enough space is your problem. These workstations are equipped with shelves and trays to hold your entire computer system, including printer and

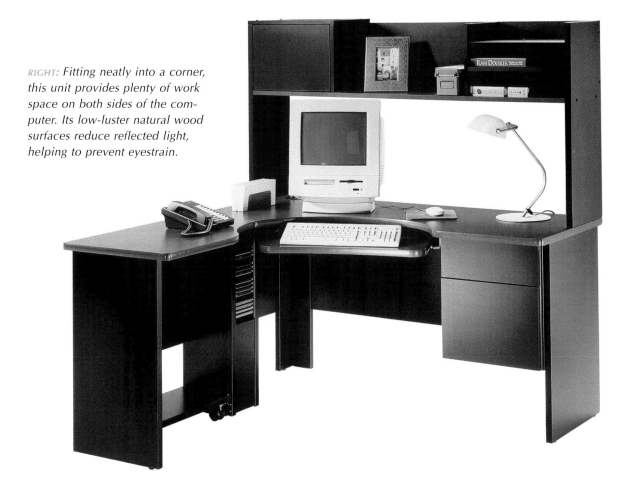

RIGHT: *Fitting neatly into a corner, this unit provides plenty of work space on both sides of the computer. Its low-luster natural wood surfaces reduce reflected light, helping to prevent eyestrain.*

paper. Most designs allow you to adjust the height of the work surface. These work centers have casters for easy mobility, allowing you to move them from room to room for quiet or privacy, or to roll the whole thing into a closet out of the way when you are finished working. If your work area is in plain sight of your living space, you might consider one of the units that are all-in-one offices hidden inside what looks like a fine wood armoire. These cabinets disguise your office when closed, but open up to reveal pullout keyboard trays, various drawers and shelves, and other storage elements—some even feature wire management systems and task lights. Keep in mind that these compact workstations are often quite expensive.

Choosing your office chair may be one of the most important decisions you make when setting up your office. Sitting is hard work. Our bodies were designed for activity—walking, running, jumping, motion of all kinds—not for long periods of sitting. Although sitting takes less energy than standing and relieves strain on hips, knees, and feet, it increases the strain on the back, the buttocks, and the thighs. The muscles in your back, legs, and trunk are constantly contracting to keep your body upright. Sitting without proper support strains the back muscles and puts pressure on the disks. The result? Back pain that leads to decreased productivity and, eventually, lost work time. With a well-designed, ergonomic chair you can avoid most of these problems.

While there is some controversy about the proper sitting posture—some experts favor a backward tilt; others a forward tilt; and still others maintain that the best posture

ADJUSTABLE ARMREST

CONTOURED BACKREST

LUMBAR SUPPORT

DEEP SEAT CUSHION

FIVE-PRONGED BASE WITH CASTERS

RIGHT: For a chair to be comfortable, the padding should support the user's weight evenly. Adjustable armrests help reduce shoulder, back, and neck strain.

is straight with the thighs at a 90-degree angle to the torso—there are certain basic guidelines that will help you select a good chair, whatever sitting position you prefer. Start with an overall chair size that is suited to the size of your body. The chair should be firm enough to support you, especially in the lumbar (lower back) area, yet flexible enough to allow movement. You should be able to adjust the height of the chair, the angle of the seat surface, the backrest, and the armrests. And you should be able to make all of these adjustments while seated. The upholstery fabric should keep you from sliding forward; the armrests should be padded; and the front of the seat should have a waterfall design—a rounded front edge—so that it doesn't cut off circulation in your legs. Finally, the chair should rest on a five-pronged base with casters that will roll easily on your floor surface.

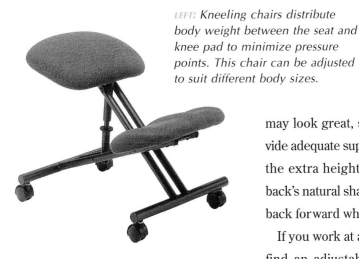

Experts say that your chair should fit your body as well as your shoes fit your feet. And the more time you spend sitting each day, the better the fit needs to be. How do you know if your chair fits? First, the backrest must match the curves of your spine in order to provide adequate lumbar support. Chair height should allow you to place both feet flat on the floor—if the chair must be higher to allow proper positioning of the arms and hands at the keyboard, then use a footrest. Your thighs should be well-supported at a 90- to 105-degree angle to your torso, and pretty much parallel to the floor. Your elbows should rest comfortably on the armrests.

Don't let appearances fool you when shopping for a chair. Although a high-backed, lushly upholstered executive chair may look great, some models fail to provide adequate support for the back. In fact, the extra height may even distort your back's natural shape by pushing the upper back forward while you sit.

If you work at a drafting table, you may find an adjustable work stool a better choice than a standard office chair. Because the stool seat is quite a bit higher, you will probably need a footrest to support your feet if it isn't already built into the stool.

Kneeling chairs are supposed to help you maintain the natural curve in the lumbar region and reduce the strain on the muscles in your neck and back. Furthermore, circulation to the legs is not restricted in the same way that it can be with a standard chair. However, some people have experienced knee and leg pain when using this type of chair.

ABOVE: *This chair comes with its own integrated footrest. This is useful for work at a drafting table or other high work surface that prevents the feet from touching the floor.*

RIGHT: *This versatile chair supports a variety of body positions. Its upholstery is different from traditional fabrics—as well as conforming to the user's shape, it allows air to pass through, preventing heat buildup.*

BACK SUPPORT

There are various accessories that can be used to make existing seating more comfortable. For lower back support, options range from a simple lumbar support cushion to a cushion system of interchangeable foam inserts or an inflatable lumbar cushion that can be adjusted and re-adjusted to suit individual needs. If you suffer from back problems, there are also special back supports that are molded to fit your spine's natural contours and provide the needed horizontal and lateral support. By eliminating pressure on the spine and promoting good posture these supports help relieve back discomfort. They can be used with or without a lumbar support cushion and can be used with most chairs.

Cushions can also be used to change seat height or shorten seat depth for short people. If, after making these adjustments, your feet do not rest flat on the floor, you should use a footrest.

Orthopedic back supports can be used with or without a lumbar cushion to make a conventional chair more comfortable.

A good chair is a major investment. Whatever type of chair you are thinking of buying, try it out before you take it home. Sit in it for awhile. Move around in it. Try different sitting positions—leaning forward at the keyboard, leaning back to talk or to read. Stretch in it. Put your feet up. Ask the salesperson what all the levers do and how to operate them. Then make sure you can work them from a seated position. If possible, buy your chair from a dealer who offers a trial period. That way you can test it under your own real working conditions.

If space permits, you will probably want to invest in one or two comfortable seats for clients. Although standards for these chairs do not need to be as rigorous as for the chair you use all day, meetings will be more pleasant for all concerned if the chairs meet the minimum requirements for comfort. A waterfall edge, back support, and armrests should keep your guests comfortable.

Chair mats: A chair mat may be necessary either to protect your floor covering or to allow the casters on your chair to roll freely on a carpeted surface. These mats come in different sizes and thicknesses. The ones designed to protect carpets have cleats to keep them in place and ensure that they don't slide around. A clear mat

will allow the carpet to show through. Tapered edges are a good idea as they allow your chair to roll on and off the mat more easily.

STORAGE

Your productivity will be greatly increased by having needed materials organized and readily available. Well-planned storage is an important component of a successful home office.

Underestimating storage needs is a common mistake. What seems to be perfectly adequate when you start out in your new home office will soon be outgrown when your business takes off, so make allowances for expansion when planning your storage system. To determine how much storage you will need, start by making a list of the equipment and supplies you need to store now. Think about what you will need to add in the next year or two. How long will you need to keep files? Do they have to be close at hand or can you store them in some other area? Once your storage requirements are clear, the

LEFT: A chair mat both protects the floor and allows a chair to roll more easily.

next step is to look for efficient, attractive ways to keep everything tidy.

Whatever your business, you will probably need some sort of shelving. The options here are almost limitless: free-standing bookcases, built-in shelving, industrial shelving, wall-mounted shelving, as well as modular units or custom-built shelving systems to accommodate special needs. Make sure the shelves are wide and deep enough to hold the items you need to store. Shelves should have enough support to bear the load you place on them. For safety's sake, secure high shelving units to the wall with a few long screws.

Don't limit yourself to traditional or commercially available storage options. Wicker baskets can provide attractive and

efficient storage for rolled up plans or blueprints. A cutlery tray or a tool caddy can keep small desktop items neat. A favorite mug or small vase is an attractive place to store pens and pencils. Small baskets can organize stationery and correspondence. Storage bins with wheels can help organize a "mobile" office.

A traditional filing cabinet is probably still the best way to keep your files in order. If you handle lots of paper, you will need the four-drawer version. If you have room for it, consider a lateral file cabinet. It will give you more surface space in your office. Commercial file cabinets tend to be sturdier and the drawers slide more easily than the cheaper models sold for home use. This is one time where buying second-hand is a good idea. If the color of the file cabinet doesn't fit your decorating scheme, enamel spray paint is a simple way to bring everything together.

If storage space in your office area is limited, classify items by how often you use them. Inactive files can be stored in a basement, garage, or other area. Keep sufficient office supplies for a one-week period nearby, and store the rest in another part of the house where there is available space.

ABOVE: Work is easier when it's organized. This simple wall-mounted shelf unit helps keep current files in order.

LEFT: A built-in shelving arrangement provides an elegant backdrop to this work area. The closed storage at the bottom holds supplies, files, and other items best kept out of sight.

The workstations and amenities shown here and on the following pages represent only a selection of the possibilities that you can fashion from the instructions that follow in this chapter. Individual elements, each built separately, can be adapted and combined to create various setups.

You can build working surfaces to a comfortable height *(pages 108-109)*, and include as many compartments, drawers, and shelves as necessary to house equipment and meet storage needs.

The Work Surface: A standard desk is 60 inches long by 30 inches deep and 29 inches high. Because sitting at a desk this large would place many items out of reach *(page 108)*, you can include a special cor-ner unit that joins two desks at right angles *(below and opposite)*. A desk should be large enough to accommodate a computer; other equipment such as printers and fax machines can also go on a desk, or on shelving above it or on a separate rolling unit.

Designing for Computer Gear: If you have a large computer monitor and your work surface won't be able to accommodate both the monitor and the keyboard, a pullout keyboard tray *(page 152)* will enable you to position the keyboard at the correct distance from the screen, and at a comfortable height. Plan the height of the keyboard tray so your forearms will be roughly parallel to the floor when you are typing; to ensure the tray will clear your knees, you may have to mount the tray or desktop a bit higher. When the monitor and central processing unit (CPU) are separate compo-nents, the monitor may fit on top of a CPU that comes in a horizontal housing; take care that the monitor isn't too high for comfort *(page 109)*. A vertical CPU can rest on the floor or in a special compartment built into a work-surface support.

Storage Space: In addition to the cabinets supporting the work surface, you can add storage space by placing a shelf unit on the desk. You can also build independent storage units such as a rolling cabinet, a cabinet with drawers for blueprints, or a wall unit with pigeonholes *(pages 124-125)*.

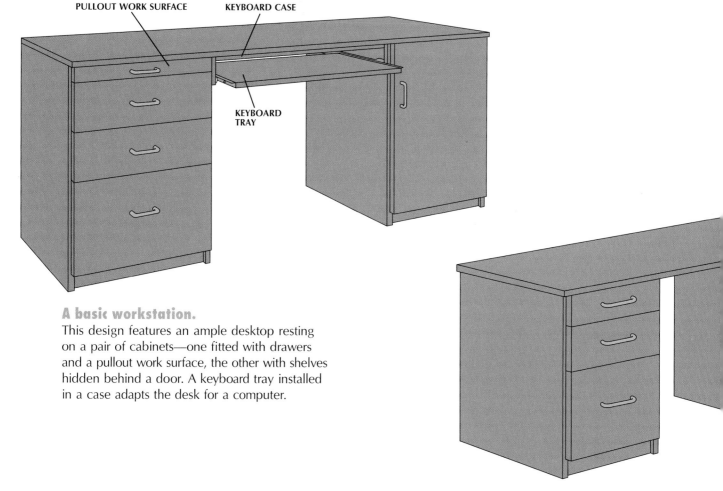

PULLOUT WORK SURFACE   **KEYBOARD CASE**

KEYBOARD TRAY

A basic workstation.
This design features an ample desktop resting on a pair of cabinets—one fitted with drawers and a pullout work surface, the other with shelves hidden behind a door. A keyboard tray installed in a case adapts the desk for a computer.

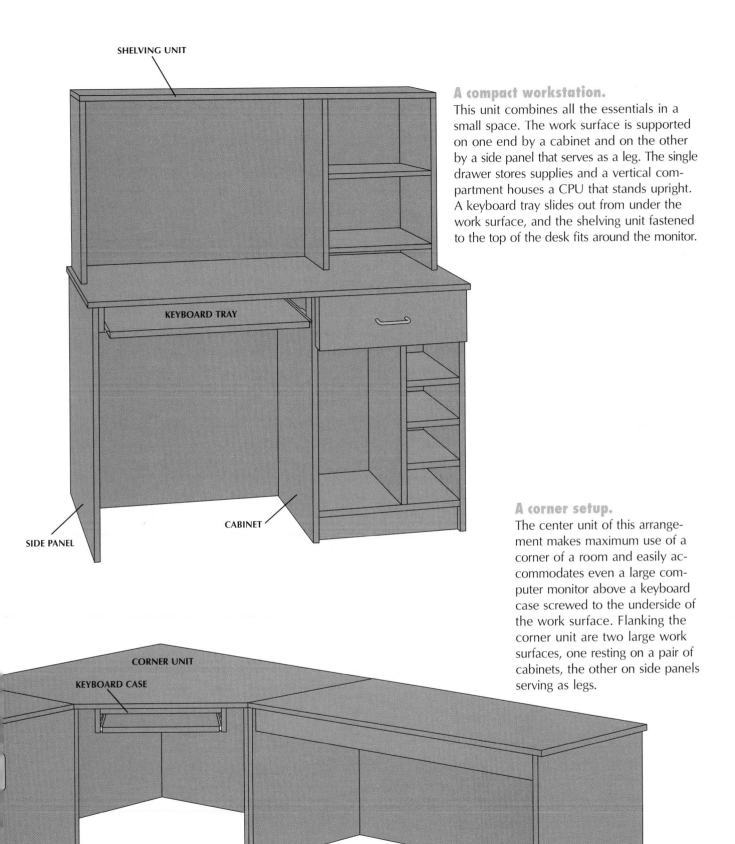

SHELVING UNIT

KEYBOARD TRAY

SIDE PANEL

CABINET

A compact workstation.
This unit combines all the essentials in a small space. The work surface is supported on one end by a cabinet and on the other by a side panel that serves as a leg. The single drawer stores supplies and a vertical compartment houses a CPU that stands upright. A keyboard tray slides out from under the work surface, and the shelving unit fastened to the top of the desk fits around the monitor.

A corner setup.
The center unit of this arrangement makes maximum use of a corner of a room and easily accommodates even a large computer monitor above a keyboard case screwed to the underside of the work surface. Flanking the corner unit are two large work surfaces, one resting on a pair of cabinets, the other on side panels serving as legs.

CORNER UNIT

KEYBOARD CASE

A rollout cabinet.

The desk shown at right is ideal for an office in a closet or other restricted space. Rather than resting on cabinets, the desk is free-standing, and a separate storage cabinet on casters is rolled underneath. The cabinet can be pulled out to serve as an extra work surface and tucked under the desk when not in use.

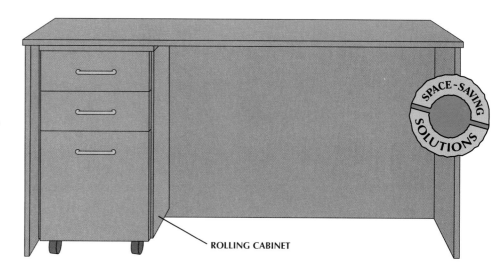

ROLLING CABINET

SPACE-SAVING SOLUTIONS

A mobile unit.

A wheeled workstation *(left)* can pack many features into a tiny space: a vertical compartment for a CPU; a desktop storage unit with space for a monitor; and a pullout keyboard tray that must extend far enough to provide knee and foot space. Mounting the printer shelf on drawer-glide hardware facilitates access to the top or back of the printer.

STORAGE UNIT

KEYBOARD TRAY

PRINTER SHELF

VERTICAL COMPARTMENT

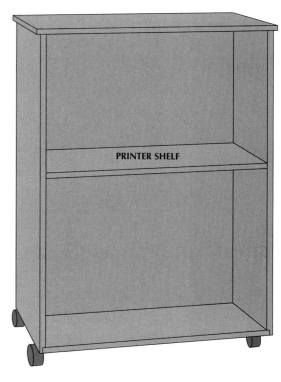

PRINTER SHELF

A rolling cabinet.

This unit is ideal for a printer and related supplies; the casters are handy for a printer that serves more than one computer. If your printer uses continuous-feed paper, thread the paper upward through a slot cut in the printer shelf.

Filing units.

These two wall-mounted units offer handy pigeon-holes for temporary filing. The unit with shallow shelves *(right)* is built much like a cabinet with adjustable shelves *(pages 134-139)*. For instructions on building the unit with vertical dividers *(below)*, turn to page 157.

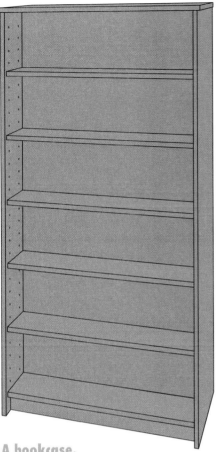

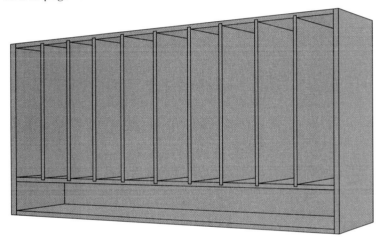

A bookcase.

This six-shelf unit is a variation of the cabinet with adjustable shelves shown on pages 134 to 139. The bookcase can be made any size as long as the shelf material can span the distance between the sides without bowing *(page 126)*.

EQUIPPING A SPACE FOR GRAPHIC ARTS OR SEWING

You can adapt the instructions in this chapter to build furniture specially suited to graphic design and sewing. For a graphic arts studio, it is best to buy a commercial drafting table, but you can build a cabinet *(right)* for storing photographs, artwork, or blueprints. Adapt the design on pages 134 to 137 and add shallow drawers *(pages 141-146)*.

To customize a desk *(page 122)* for a sewing machine, make the work surface at least 5 feet long and 18 to 24 inches deep. If you want the bed of the machine to sit flush with the table top, cut an opening in the surface and install brackets to hold a shelf sturdy enough to support the machine.

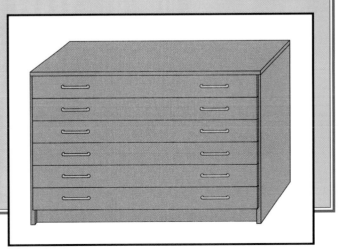

The highest quality furniture is made of solid wood. However, it is costlier than manufactured panels such as plywood or medium-density fiberboard (MDF). Moreover, solid wood is not generally available in widths over 12 inches, and many parts of a workstation are wider than this. To create a desktop of solid wood, for example, you would have to glue together several boards, edge to edge, to create a wide panel.

The Material of Choice: Available in 4- by 8-foot sheets, plywood and MDF are easier to work with than wood. Only MDF can be bought with a plasticlike coating, available in several colors, but both come in a variety of wood veneers. If you are planning to apply a stain or clear finish to your furniture, select an A-C grade for softwood veneer, A-2 for hardwood.

The material featured in this chapter is $\frac{3}{4}$-inch plywood. Although more expensive than MDF, it holds screws better and can span longer distances without sagging *(chart, below)*. For the back panels of the cabinets that support the desktop, you may want to substitute $\frac{1}{8}$-inch hardboard.

Cutting the Pieces: The easiest way to cut large panels is with a circular saw *(opposite)*. Smaller pieces can be cut on a table saw.

Before assembling your furniture, finish exposed edges with commercial edge banding—thin, self-adhesive strips of veneer applied with a household iron—or with solid wood *(page 128)*.

TOOLS

Chalk line	Clamps
Tape measure	Household iron
Circular saw	Hand roller
Plywood blade	Utility knife

MATERIALS

Manufactured panels	Edge banding
2 x 4s	Sandpaper (medium-grade)

SAFETY TIPS

Protect your eyes with goggles when using a circular saw.

MAXIMUM SPANS FOR MANUFACTURED PANELS

	½ inch	⅝ inch	¾ inch
Plywood	20 inches (24 inches for light loads)	28 inches (36 inches for light loads)	36 inches (48 inches for light loads)
MDF	16 inches (20 inches for light loads)	20 inches (36 inches for light loads)	24 inches (48 inches for light loads)

No-sag shelves and desktops.
The chart above suggests the maximum unsupported span for different thicknesses of plywood and MDF. Thin materials need supports spaced more closely than thick ones—as do heavy loads, which include items such as books and computer equipment. All the plywood and MDF in the chart can span greater distances if you strengthen it. To do so, double the material or fasten a 2-inch-wide strip of it to the underside of the shelf or desktop, stopping the strip short of desktop supports or shelf pegs.

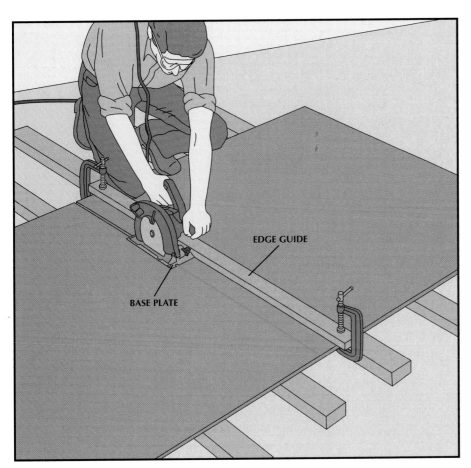

EDGE GUIDE

BASE PLATE

Using a circular saw.

To prevent plywood from splintering as you cut it, mount a plywood-cutting blade in your circular saw, apply a strip of masking tape across the panel before marking the cutting line with a chalk line, or score the cutting line with a utility knife.

◆ Support the panel on 2-by-4s spaced about a foot apart. Reposition the 2-by-4s as necessary to place one board 3 inches on each side of the cutting line.

◆ Measure the distance from the saw blade to the edge of the base plate and clamp a plywood or MDF strip as an edge guide this distance from the cutting line. Orient the guide with the factory-cut edge toward the cutting line. Hold the saw against the guide to confirm that the blade meets the cutting line.

◆ Kneeling on the panel over one of the 2-by-4s, cut the panel with the saw's base plate against the edge guide (left).

TRICKS OF THE TRADE

A Circular-Saw Guide

A two-piece edge guide can be positioned at the cutting line, saving you the trouble of having to measure between the saw blade and base plate to position a guide. To make a guide for sawing a full-length manufactured panel, cut two 8-foot-long strips from the factory-cut edges of a $\frac{3}{4}$-inch plywood panel. (Four-foot strips make a guide that's more convenient for shorter cuts.) Make one strip 4 inches wide and the other 12 inches wide. Fasten the strips together with $1\frac{1}{4}$-inch No. 8 wood screws driven in a staggered pattern so the factory-cut edge of the narrow strip sits across the wider piece. Clamp the jig to a work surface, then cut the wide strip, holding the

saw's base plate against the narrow strip (below). Varnish the jig to reduce warping. To use the jig, secure it with the sawed edge along the cutting line, extend the saw blade an inch, and run the saw base plate along the narrow strip.

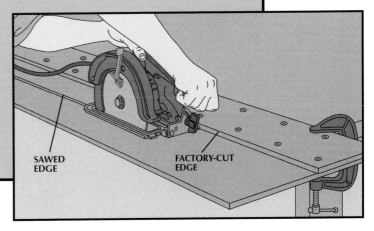

SAWED EDGE

FACTORY-CUT EDGE

Applying edge banding

◆ Support the panel vertically with clamps, and set a household iron to HIGH (without steam).

◆ Cut a strip of commercial banding slightly longer than the edge to be covered, and place the strip on the edge with the adhesive side down.

◆ Run the hot iron slowly along the edge, pressing the banding flat with one hand *(right)*; to prevent scorching the banding, avoid holding the iron in one spot for more than a few seconds.

◆ Applying even pressure, run a small block of wood or hand roller *(photograph)* back and forth along the edge.

◆ After the glue has set, turn the panel onto the banded edge, and run a utility knife along the adjacent face and edge to trim excess banding.

◆ Smooth the edges with medium-grade sandpaper.

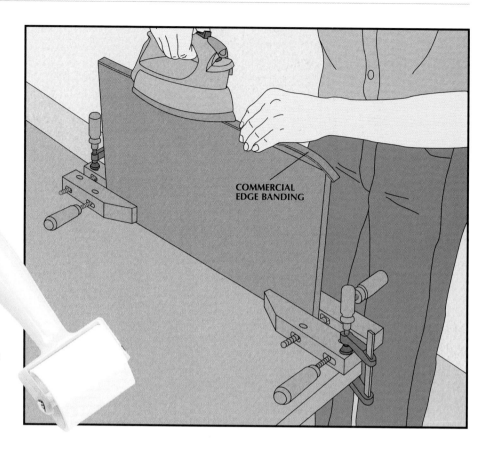

COMMERCIAL EDGE BANDING

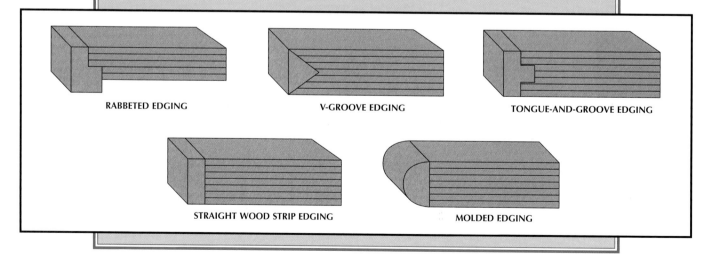

SOLID WOOD EDGING FOR PLYWOOD PANELS

Edging plywood or MDF panels with solid wood gives you a broad choice of woods and decorative effects. As an added benefit, rabbeted edging also helps to reinforce the edge of the panel. Order custom-made edging from a lumber dealer, then for rabbeted, V-groove, or tongue-and-groove edging, cut the panel edge with a router to accept the shape. Fasten the edging with wood glue, clamping it firmly until the glue dries.

RABBETED EDGING

V-GROOVE EDGING

TONGUE-AND-GROOVE EDGING

STRAIGHT WOOD STRIP EDGING

MOLDED EDGING

There are several ways to fasten the panels of your workstation together. You can use screws *(below and pages 134-164)*, but dowel joints and plate joints also work well for plywood and medium-density fiberboard (MDF) panels. Metal brackets are suitable if they can be concealed *(page 133)*.

Joining with Screws: In furniture construction screws are usually countersunk—driven so the heads are flush with the surface. For a more finished look, you can conceal the fasteners completely by counterboring the holes; this involves driving the screw heads below the surface and filling the holes with wood plugs, available in hardware stores precut in a variety of diameters. Select plugs in a contrasting

wood, or stain them to match. A combination bit *(below)* drills the pilot, countersunk, and counterbored holes, all in one operation.

Purchase flooring screws to connect the panels; they are less likely to split the material than standard wood screws. To join two boards face to face, use screws $\frac{1}{4}$ inch shorter than the combined thickness of the two pieces. For a right-angle joint, 2-inch screws offer a strong hold. The $\frac{5}{8}$-inch wood screws used to install hardware do not require pilot holes; make starting holes with an awl.

Biscuits for Strength: Plate joints are glued joints reinforced by oval wood wafers—called biscuits—inserted into semicircular slots cut into the mating pieces *(pages 132-133)*. You

will need a plate joiner to make the slots, but the technique is simple to master, and the resulting joints are invisible and exceptionally strong.

The biscuit size depends on the thickness of the stock—$\frac{3}{4}$-inch wood requires No. 10 biscuits, for example. The plate joiner is adjustable to cut slots of the appropriate size.

Dowel Joints: Glued into holes drilled in the mating pieces *(pages 130-131)*, dowels also yield a joint that is invisible and easy to make, but not as strong as screws or biscuits. Pointed metal dowel centers make it easy to mate the panels exactly *(page 131)*. Use grooved dowels 1 to $1\frac{1}{2}$ inches long with a diameter no more than half the thickness of the stock.

TOOLS

Bar clamps
Electric drill
Combination bit
Stop collar
Screwdriver
Wood chisel
Doweling jig
Dowel centers
C-clamps
Mallet
Plate joiner

MATERIALS

Flooring screws
Wood glue
Wood plugs
Sandpaper
  (medium grade)
Dowels
Wood biscuits

SAFETY TIPS

Protect your eyes with goggles when drilling.

FASTENING WITH SCREWS

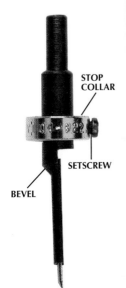

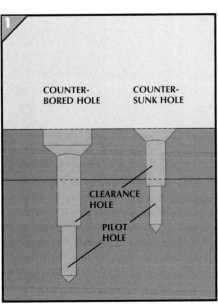

1. Hiding the screw heads.

Before drilling any screw holes, clamp the panels together as shown on pages 135 and 136.

◆ For a counterbored hole, position the stop collar on the shank $\frac{1}{4}$ inch above the beveled part of the shank *(photograph)*. For a countersunk hole, place the collar at the bevel. Tighten the setscrew to lock the collar in place, then install the bit in an electric drill and bore the holes.

◆ Disassemble the joint and spread a thin bead of wood glue on the mating surfaces.

◆ Reassemble the joint and drive a screw into each of the holes.

2. Hiding the screws.

◆ To conceal counterbored screws, buy wood plugs of the same diameter as the holes. Or, make your own plugs with a drill press equipped with a plug-cutting bit *(photograph)*.
◆ Squeeze a small amount of wood glue into the bottom of the hole. Push the plug into the hole and wipe up any excess glue with a damp cloth. Allow the glue to dry.
◆ With a wood chisel bevel side up, cut the plug flush with the surface *(right)*, then sand the surface smooth with medium-grade sandpaper.

PLUG CUTTER

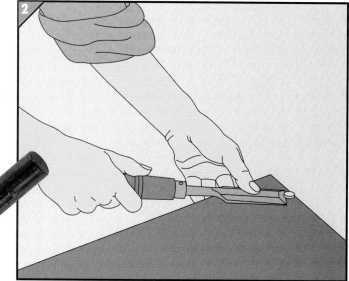

MAKING DOWEL JOINTS

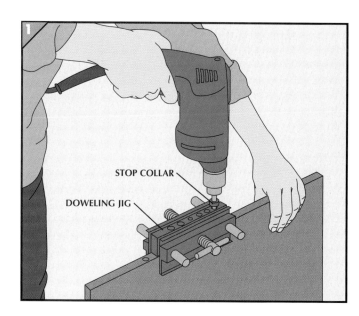

STOP COLLAR

DOWELING JIG

1. Drilling holes in one panel.

◆ Clamp one of the panels in a vise with the edge to be drilled facing up. Starting at one corner, mark the edge every 4 inches.
◆ Position a commercial doweling jig on the edge. Find the hole that matches the dowel diameter and center it on the first mark. Tighten the jig.
◆ Attach a stop collar or a piece of tape to the bit to mark the drilling depth equal to half the length of the dowel plus $\frac{1}{8}$ inch—plus the height of the doweling jig.
◆ Insert the bit through the jig and drill the hole.
◆ Bore the remaining holes *(left)*, repositioning the jig for each one.

TRICKS OF THE TRADE

A Handy Prop

You can hold a panel upright with simple wood props. Cut two short lengths of 2-by-6 stock, then make a slot halfway through each piece slightly wider than the thickness of the panels. To support a panel, fit a prop around each end of the piece.

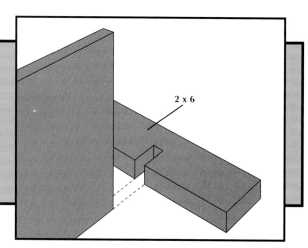

2 x 6

2. Marking the second panel.

Make a right-angle brace by fastening two boards together at a 90-degree angle. Clamp the brace to your worktable, then at a right angle to it, clamp a straightedge board to align the outside edges of the panels.

◆ Insert dowel centers into each of the holes drilled in the first piece *(inset)*.

◆ Hold the second panel upright against the brace, and set the drilled panel flat on the table.

◆ Tap the drilled panel with a rubber mallet, driving the dowel-center points into the vertical panel *(left)*.

◆ Drill holes in the second panel at the dowel-center marks as shown in Step 1.

◆ Repeat the process to drill holes for the remaining corners of the cabinet.

RIGHT-ANGLE BRACE

STRAIGHTEDGE BOARD

3. Joining the boards.

◆ Dab a little wood glue in the holes in one of the panels at each corner of the cabinet and insert the dowels loosely *(right)*.

◆ Drip glue in the holes of the other panels and spread a thin bead of glue on the mating surfaces.

◆ Orient the panels as in Step 2, lining up dowels with holes, and tap the corners together with a mallet.

◆ Clamp the cabinet as shown on page 135 until the glue has dried.

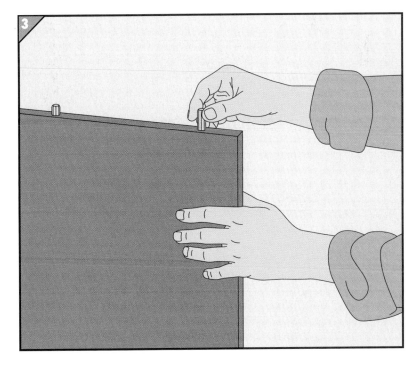

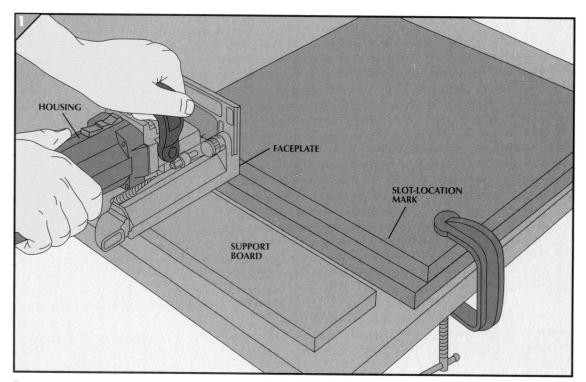

1. Cutting slots in the first panel.

◆ Lay one of the panels outside-face down on a work surface and set the other outside-face up on top of it. Mark reference letters to identify adjoining edges.

◆ Set the edge of the upper panel back by an amount equal to the thickness of the stock, then clamp the two pieces to the work surface.

◆ Place a support board the same thickness as the panels in front of the workpieces, then mark slot location lines on the top panel every 6 inches.

◆ Resting the plate joiner on the support board, align the guideline on its faceplate with a slot location mark on the stock. Holding the tool with both hands, push in the housing to cut the slot *(above)*. Repeat the process at the other marks.

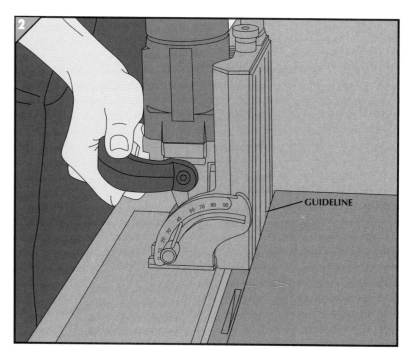

2. Slotting the second panel.

◆ Holding the plate joiner upright, align the guideline in the center of the tool's base plate with a slot mark and make a cut.

◆ Cut the rest of the grooves along the edge in the same way *(left)*.

◆ Mark slot-location points on the other three corners of the carcass, then cut slots at the marks.

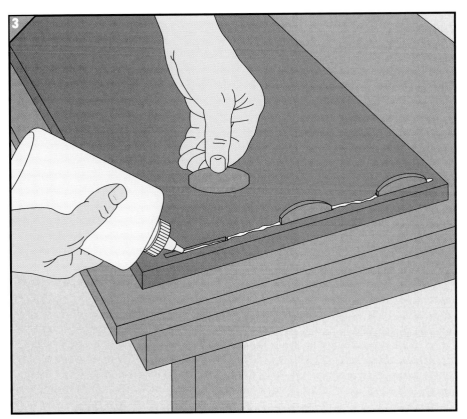

3. Inserting the biscuits.

◆ Set the panels with slots in their faces on a table, and squeeze a bead of wood glue into each slot and along the surface of the panels between the slots, inserting biscuits as you go *(left)*.

◆ Apply glue to the slotted edges of the other panels.

◆ Press the pieces together and clamp the cabinet as shown on page 135 until the glue has dried.

JOINING WITH METAL BRACKETS

Sturdy joints can be made with metal angle irons, although this method is best reserved for areas where the brackets will not be visible, such as an inside corner. For a very tight joint, attach the angle iron to one piece, setting it in slightly from the edge. Then fasten the angle iron to the second piece—the panels will be pulled tightly together as you drive the screws *(right)*.

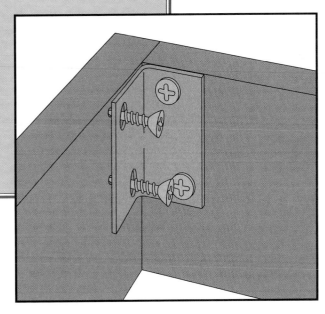

Intended primarily to serve as a support for one end of a desktop, the cabinet shown below can also stand alone as a storage unit or bookcase. In that role it can provide a surface for equipment such as a fax machine or printer. This versatile unit can accommodate any combination of shelves, vertical dividers, drawers, or doors *(pages 138-148)*.

Planning: This cabinet can be made virtually any size. If it will help support a desktop, decide on the size of the top first, then make the cabinets 3 inches shallower so the top overhangs 2 inches at the back and 1 inch in front. Design the cabinets $\frac{3}{4}$ inch shorter than the desired height of the desk to allow for the top's thickness. In addition, plan for a top long enough to provide space for legroom and a keyboard tray between the cabinets.

If you plan to install shelves, consider the maximum span of the shelf material *(page 126)* in establishing the cabinet width. Where you intend to add a vertical divider for a CPU *(page 140)*, make the cabinet deep enough to allow 3 inches of space behind the unit for air circulation. If doors are part of the design, keep in mind that doors wider than 20 inches tend to sag on their hinges.

Building the Cabinet: Cut all the panels to size from $\frac{3}{4}$-inch plywood *(page 127)*, and install edging on each piece *(page 128)*. You can make the back from $\frac{1}{8}$-inch hardboard *(page 137)*. Then assemble the cabinets using one of the joinery methods described on pages 129 to 133.

TOOLS

Tape measure	Screwdriver
Circular saw	Bar clamps
Electric drill	Combination square
Combination bit	Hammer

MATERIALS

Plywood ($\frac{3}{4}$")	Wood screws
Hardboard ($\frac{1}{8}$")	($\frac{5}{8}$" No. 6)
Finishing nails (1")	Angle irons
Flooring screws	(1" x 2")
(1", $1\frac{1}{4}$", 2" No. 8)	Wood glue

SAFETY TIPS

Protect your eyes with goggles when drilling and nailing.

Anatomy of a cabinet.

This simple cabinet is basically a box, or carcass, with two sides, a top, a bottom, and a back. Tack a hardboard back to the edges of the other panels. A plywood back can be recessed $\frac{1}{2}$ inch as shown here. The result is a more appealing cabinet, especially in settings where the back is exposed.

The bottom of the cabinet is anchored to cleats fastened inside the side panels. A kickplate set in $\frac{1}{2}$ inch from the front conceals the cleats and also supports the bottom. For a freestanding cabinet, add a false top that is about 1 inch larger than the cabinet on all sides.

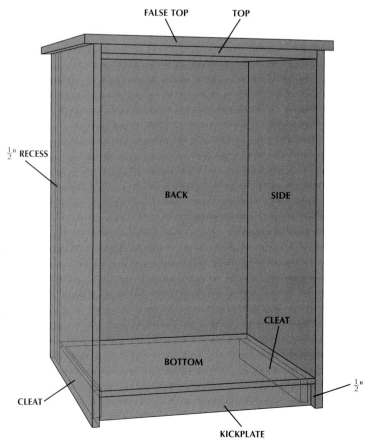

FALSE TOP   TOP

$\frac{1}{2}$" RECESS

BACK   SIDE

CLEAT

BOTTOM

CLEAT

$\frac{1}{2}$"

CLEAT

KICKPLATE

1. Making the sides.

◆ From $\frac{3}{4}$-inch plywood, cut side panels the planned height and depth of the cabinet, then finish the edges *(page 128)*. Also cut two cleats 2 inches wide and $2\frac{1}{2}$ inches shorter than the width of the sides.

◆ Lay one side panel flat, inside face up. Position the cleat flush with the bottom of the panel and set in $1\frac{1}{4}$ inches from its front edge.

◆ Drill three pilot holes for $1\frac{1}{4}$-inch No. 8 flooring screws through the cleat, one near each end and one at the center.

◆ With glue and screws, fasten the cleat to the side panel *(right)*.

◆ Attach the other cleat to the opposite side panel in the same way.

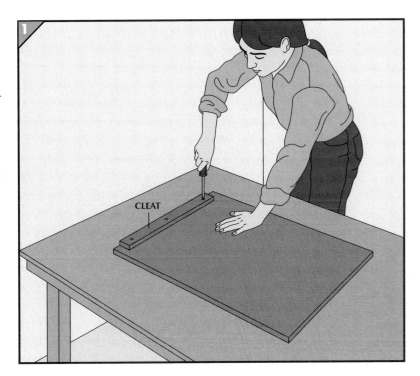

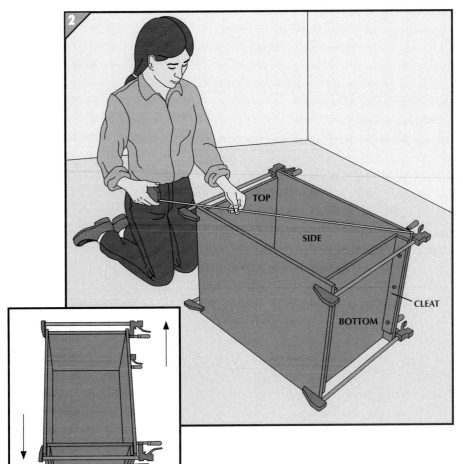

2. Squaring the carcass.

◆ Cut the top and bottom panels to size, making them $1\frac{1}{2}$ inches narrower than the width of the cabinet. For a hardboard back, make the top and bottom panels the same depth as the side panels. For an inset plywood back, cut them $1\frac{1}{4}$ inches shallower than the side panels. Finish the panel edges *(page 128)*.

◆ With a helper, set the two side pieces upright with their front edges down and slip the top and bottom pieces between them so the bottom is resting against the cleats and the top is flush with the edges of the side pieces.

◆ Secure the assembly with four bar clamps, then measure the carcass diagonally in both directions *(left)*. Identical diagonal measurements indicate that the carcass is square. If it is not, loosen the clamps slightly and slide one jaw of each clamp outward at opposite corners *(inset)*, then tighten the clamps and measure the diagonals again.

3. Marking pilot holes.

◆ Set a combination square to the distance between the bottom of the side panel and the center of the bottom panel edge.
◆ Holding the square against the bottom of the side panel, slide the head along the edge and lightly draw a line using the end of the ruler as a guide *(right)*.
◆ Mark the other side panel in the same way, then repeat the process to mark lines on the side panels in line with the top.

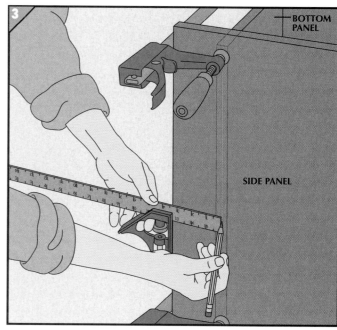

4. Drilling and fastening.

◆ At each marked line, drill pilot holes for counterbored flooring screws through the side panels and into the bottom panel, locating the holes about $1\frac{1}{2}$ inches from each end and every 6 inches in between.
◆ Drill pilot holes every 6 inches through the side panels into the top panel, then unclamp the carcass.
◆ With wood glue and screws, fasten the side panels to the top and bottom panels.
◆ Install clamps and re-check the carcass for square *(Step 2)*.
◆ Attach the back *(below or opposite)* before the glue dries completely.

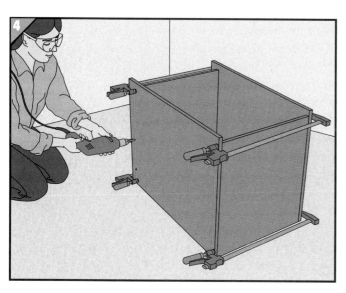

INSTALLING THE BACK

A plywood back.

◆ Cut a $\frac{3}{4}$-inch plywood back to fit between the sides and to cover the rear edges of the top and bottom.
◆ Slide the back piece into place between the two side pieces *(right)*.
◆ Mark screw-hole lines on the back in line with the edges of the other panels, as in Step 3 above.
◆ Drill pilot holes for 2-inch No. 8 flooring screws through the back and into the top and bottom panels, and through the sides into

the back panel. Space the holes $1\frac{1}{2}$ inches from each end and every 6 inches in between.
◆ With glue and screws, fasten the back to the frame.

To add a false top, first drill a clearance hole for a 1-inch screw at each corner of the cabinet top. Then center the false top over the top, and from inside the cabinet, drill pilot holes up through the clearance holes into the false top. Screw the false top in place.

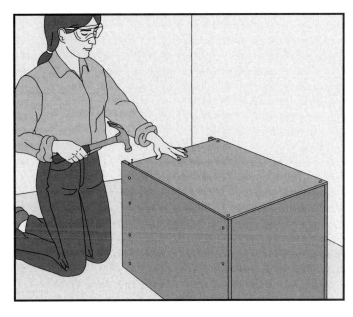

A hardboard back.

◆ Cut a piece of $\frac{1}{8}$-inch hardboard $\frac{1}{8}$ inch narrower than the cabinet and $\frac{1}{8}$ inch shorter than the distance from the top of the top panel to the bottom of the bottom panel.

◆ Set the back panel in place so it is slightly inset from the edges of the cabinet all around.

◆ Secure the back panel to one side panel with a 1-inch finishing nail driven into both corners, then add nails in the corners of the other side panel *(left)*.

◆ Drive nails every 3 inches around the perimeter of the back.

◆ Fasten the false top as described opposite *(bottom)*.

ADDING THE KICKPLATE

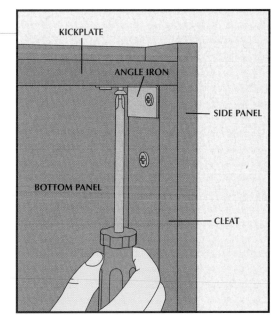

Attaching the angle irons.

◆ Turn the cabinet onto its back.

◆ Cut a kickplate from $\frac{3}{4}$-inch plywood 2 inches wide and long enough to fit between the side panels.

◆ Position the kickplate so it is resting on the ends of the cleats.

◆ With $\frac{5}{8}$-inch No. 6 wood screws, attach a 1- by 2-inch angle iron to each cleat, setting it back slightly from the ends of the cleats *(page 133)*.

◆ Holding the kickplate down with one hand, screw the angle irons to the back of the kickplate *(right)*.

◆ Add a third angle iron, fastening the middle of the kickplate to the bottom panel.

TRICKS OF THE TRADE

Keeping Everything Level

Uneven floors can make a perfectly square piece of furniture tilt or rock, but adjustable feet—consisting of a sleeve and a screw—will solve the problem. To install the feet at each corner, drill a hole in the bottom of the side panel slightly smaller than the sleeve and deep enough to accommodate the screw. To avoid splitting the wood, reinforce it with a C-clamp, protecting the surface with wood blocks. Tap the sleeve into place with a hammer *(right)*, then twist in the screw.

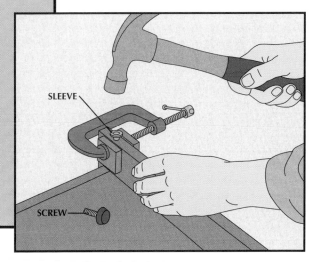

Storage space within your cabinet can be neatly organized with the addition of adjustable shelves. Putting in a vertical divider creates a separate compartment for a CPU. Building a larger cabinet and including shelves yields a bookcase.

Versatile Shelving: Installing adjustable shelves allows you to change the shelf spacing after the cabinet has been assembled. Simply drill two rows of holes into each side of the cabinet and insert shelf-support pegs or clips into the holes at the desired height. To ensure that each pair of holes is drilled at exactly the same height, use a hole-spacing jig *(below and opposite).* Cut shelves to fit between the side panels.

A Vertical Divider: Create a separate compartment for a CPU by installing a vertical divider from the bottom of the cabinet to a fixed shelf near the top *(page 140).* To prevent the CPU from overheating, the cabinet must be deep enough to allow for 3 inches of space behind the unit. Make the compartment 2 inches higher and wider than the CPU. For increased storage space, add shelves on one side of the compartment and build a drawer above it.

TOOLS

Circular saw	Combination bit
Marking gauge	C-clamps
Electric drill	Corner clamp
Stop collar	Screwdriver

MATERIALS

Plywood ($\frac{3}{4}$")	Wood glue
Shelf-support pegs	Flooring screws (1$\frac{1}{2}$" No. 8)

SAFETY TIPS

Protect your eyes with goggles when you are drilling.

INSTALLING SHELVING

1. Making a hole-spacing jig.
◆ Cut a strip of $\frac{3}{4}$-inch plywood 4 inches wide and as long as the inside height of the cabinet. Mark an arrow at one end of the jig to indicate the top.
◆ Adjust a marking gauge to half the width of the strip and mark a line down the center *(right).*
◆ Starting at the bottom, mark the centerline at 1-inch intervals and drill a hole through the jig at each mark, the same diameter as your shelf pegs.

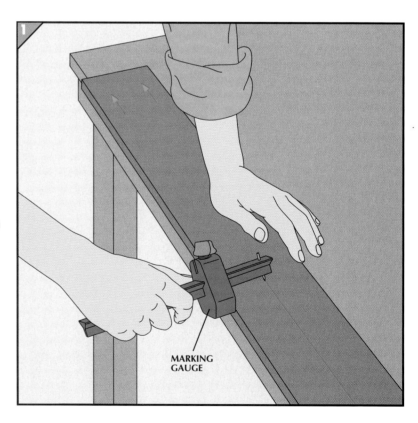

MARKING GAUGE

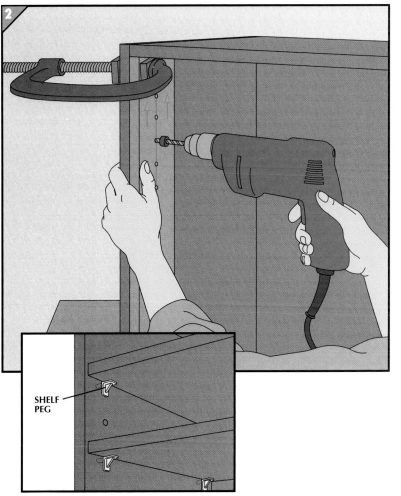

SHELF PEG

2. Drilling the holes in the cabinet sides.

◆ Add a stop collar or a piece of tape to the bit to mark the drilling depth—the thickness of the jig plus the length of the shelf-peg shafts.

◆ Clamp the jig to one side of the panel, with an edge flush against the front of the cabinet, and the correct end pointing up.

◆ Drill through each hole in the jig *(left)*.

◆ Repeat the procedure at the remaining three corners of the cabinet.

◆ From $\frac{3}{4}$-inch plywood, cut the shelves to fit between the cabinet sides; make them $\frac{1}{8}$ inch shallower than the depth of the cabinet so they will be set back from the front. Finish exposed edges *(page 128)*.

◆ Push shelf pegs into the holes at the desired height and install the shelves *(inset)*.

A COMMERCIAL HOLE-DRILLING JIG

The jig shown here will make quick work of drilling evenly spaced shelf- support holes. The wood strip is held against the front edge of a cabinet side panel, with the clear plastic template on the inside face. Starting at the bottom, holes are drilled through one of the two rows of holes in the jig. (To vary the location of the holes in relation to the cabinet edge, the wood strip can be attached to the opposite edge of the template.) When the last hole at the top has been drilled, the jig is moved up and a shelf-support peg is slipped through the appropriate-size index hole into one of the drilled holes to align the jig. The remaining holes are drilled, then the procedure is repeated at the back edge of the panel, and at both edges of the opposite side panel.

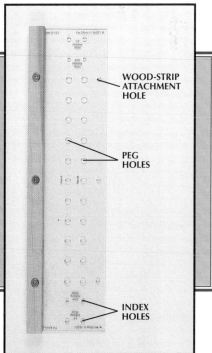

WOOD-STRIP ATTACHMENT HOLE

PEG HOLES

INDEX HOLES

A VERTICAL DIVIDER

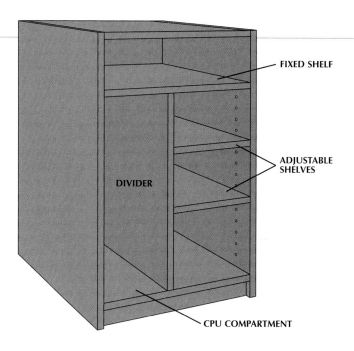

A CPU compartment.
A cabinet supporting a desktop will likely provide more than enough space to accommodate a vertical CPU. The compartment can be cut off at the top by a fixed shelf, which will allow you to use the space above the CPU as a shelf or a drawer. The cavity beside the CPU can be fitted with small adjustable shelves; be sure to drill the shelf-support holes *(pages 138-139)* in the divider before installing it.

FIXED SHELF

ADJUSTABLE SHELVES

DIVIDER

CPU COMPARTMENT

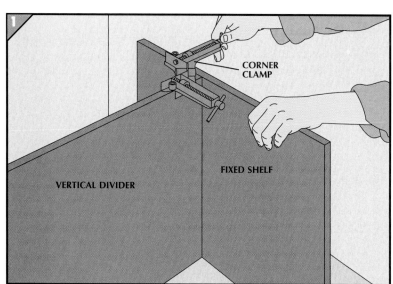

CORNER CLAMP

FIXED SHELF

VERTICAL DIVIDER

1. Joining the divider and shelf.
◆ From $\frac{3}{4}$-inch plywood, cut a shelf to fit between the sides of the cabinet, then cut the divider to fit between the bottom of the cabinet and the shelf. Finish exposed edges *(page 128)*.
◆ Set the two pieces on edge and fasten them together with a corner clamp *(left)*.
◆ Mark a line for screw holes across the shelf centered on the divider *(page 136, Step 3)*.
◆ Drill pilot holes for $1\frac{1}{2}$-inch No. 8 counterbored flooring screws through the shelf into the divider, locating the screws $1\frac{1}{2}$ inches from each edge and every 6 inches in between.
◆ With glue and screws, fasten the shelf to the divider.

2. Installing the assembly.
◆ Set the cabinet on its back and insert the shelf-and-divider assembly.
◆ Mark lines for screw holes across the sides and along the bottom, as described on page 136.
◆ Drill counterbored pilot holes through the sides of the cabinet into the fixed shelf *(right)* and through the bottom of the cabinet into the divider; locate the holes $1\frac{1}{2}$ inches from each edge and every 6 inches in between.
◆ Fasten the assembly to the cabinet with glue and screws.

Fitting a small cabinet with drawers provides storage for files and supplies. A large cabinet with shallow drawers can be used to store photographs, artwork, or blueprints.

Drawer Design: A drawer is little more than a box consisting of four sides and a bottom. In addition, the simplest drawer to make has a false front that overlaps the frame of the cabinet *(below)*, concealing any imperfections in the fit. When planning the size of desk drawers, you'll need to make them slightly narrower than the opening in the cabinet to allow for drawer glides; this clearance will vary with the type of glide used. Drawers can be made any height to accommodate the contents. File drawers and other tall drawers go at the bottom of the cabinet. To reduce weight, cut drawer sides only 6 inches high, then make a false front the height of a drawer insert *(box, page 143)*.

Making Drawers: Cut the front, back, and sides from $\frac{3}{4}$-inch plywood, and the bottom from $\frac{1}{8}$-inch hardboard. To withstand the stresses of being opened and closed, doors are typically built with stout joinery, which incorporate grooves called dadoes and rabbets. It's best to assemble the drawers *(pages 142-143)* before attaching the hardware and aligning the false fronts.

Drawer Hardware: The simplest way to install drawers in a cabinet is with commercial drawer glides. One glide is attached to the drawer, and the other fastens to the side of the cabinet; interlocking channels on the glides enable the drawer to slide smoothly. To install file drawers, use special full-extension glides. These glides consist of three telescoping channels. They allow the drawer to be pulled out far enough for you to reach the back of the drawer.

TOOLS

Tape measure	Hammer
Circular saw	Screwdriver
Table saw or router	Hand-screw
Bar clamps	clamps
Electric drill	Combination
Combination bit	square

MATERIALS

Plywood ($\frac{3}{4}$")	Flooring screws
Hardboard ($\frac{1}{8}$")	($1\frac{1}{4}$", 2" No. 8)
Drawer glides	Spiral or coated
Drawer pulls	common
Wood glue	nails (1")

SAFETY TIPS

Wear goggles when you are nailing or when using an electric drill or power saw.

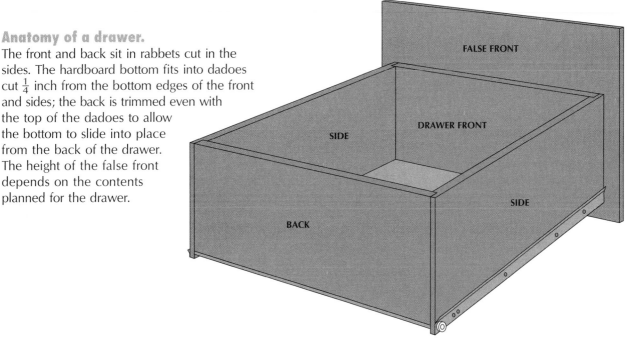

Anatomy of a drawer.
The front and back sit in rabbets cut in the sides. The hardboard bottom fits into dadoes cut $\frac{1}{4}$ inch from the bottom edges of the front and sides; the back is trimmed even with the top of the dadoes to allow the bottom to slide into place from the back of the drawer. The height of the false front depends on the contents planned for the drawer.

FALSE FRONT

DRAWER FRONT

SIDE

SIDE

BACK

Positioning the drawer glides.

◆ First, determine the number of drawers *(right)* you want in the cabinet and the height of their false fronts. Size each false front so that it extends $\frac{1}{4}$ inch below the bottom of the drawer. In addition, leave a $\frac{1}{8}$-inch gap between the fronts and a $\frac{1}{8}$-inch reveal around the cabinet frame.

◆ To mark the position of the drawer glides on the cabinet frame, start with the bottom drawer: Measure the distance from the lower edge of the glide to the screw holes, add $\frac{1}{4}$ inch, and draw a line that distance above the cabinet bottom on both interior side panels.

◆ For the second drawer, measure the height of the bottom drawer's false front and subtract $\frac{1}{2}$ inch. Draw a line that distance above the first line.

◆ To mark the glide position of all other drawers, measure the height of the false front directly below and add $\frac{1}{8}$ inch.

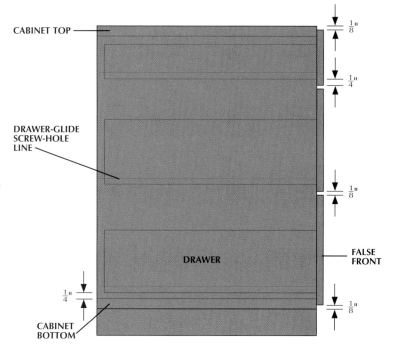

ASSEMBLING THE DRAWER

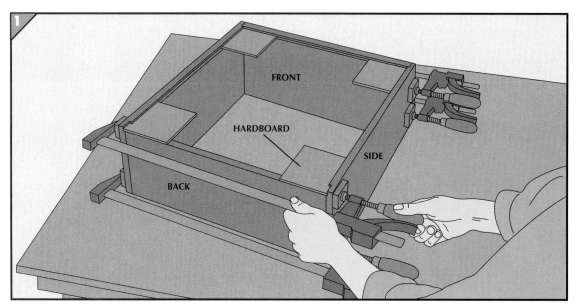

1. Clamping the pieces together.

◆ From $\frac{3}{4}$-inch plywood, cut the drawer sides the desired height and $\frac{1}{4}$ inch shorter than the depth of the cabinet.

◆ With a table saw or router, cut a rabbet at each end of the sides, $\frac{1}{8}$ inch deep and $\frac{3}{4}$ inch wide.

◆ Cut the drawer front to the same height as the side pieces, and the back piece $\frac{3}{8}$ inch narrower to allow the drawer bottom to slide in. Measure the cabinet opening, then subtract $1\frac{1}{4}$ inches (to account for the thickness of the two rabbeted side pieces) plus the clearance specified for the drawer glide. Trim both pieces to that width.

◆ Cut a dado $\frac{1}{4}$ inch deep and $\frac{1}{8}$ inch wide along the inside faces of the front and side pieces, $\frac{1}{4}$ inch from the bottom edges. Finish exposed edges *(page 128)*.

◆ Assemble the drawer upside down on a worktable, slip small squares of $\frac{1}{8}$-inch hardboard into each corner, then clamp the drawer with four bar clamps *(above)*.

◆ Drill pilot holes for 2-inch No. 8 counterbored flooring screws through the sides into the front and back pieces.

◆ With the hardboard squares in place, fasten the front, sides, and back with glue and screws.

2. Adding the bottom.
◆ Cut a piece of $\frac{1}{8}$-inch hardboard to fit in the grooves in the drawer sides and front, then slide it into place *(left)*.
◆ With 1-inch spiral or coated common nails, fasten the bottom to the edge of the drawer back, spacing the nails every 3 inches.

A SUPPORT FOR HANGING FILES

An ordinary drawer of the appropriate size can be equipped for hanging files with a commercial insert like the one shown here. Some models are adjustable to accommodate either letter- or legal-size files. For legal-size files, change the orientation of the insert, or of the files so they run from back to front instead of side to side.

INSTALLING DRAWER GLIDES

1. Attaching the cabinet hardware.
◆ Determine the location of the drawer glides *(page 142)* and mark a line for each glide across the cabinet side.
◆ Separate a drawer glide into its pieces and set the one that attaches to the cabinet against the side panel so the screw holes are centered on the marked line. Fasten it with the screws provided *(right)*.
◆ Screw the remaining glides to the cabinet side in the same way.

For a file drawer, engage the mating glides with those in the cabinet and pull them all the way out until they lock *(inset)*.

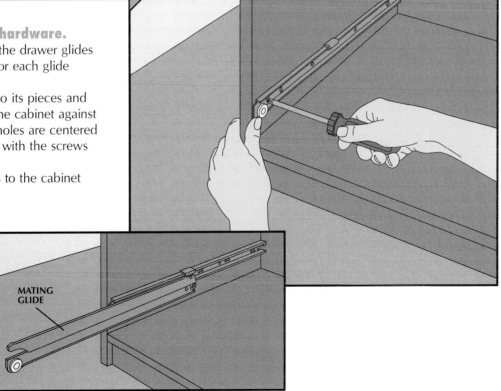

MATING GLIDE

2. Fitting glides on the drawers.

◆ Position the drawer glide on the drawer according to the manufacturer's instructions; for the model shown, the channel is positioned flush with the front of the drawer and the wheel at the back.

◆ Fasten the glide to the drawer through the oblong screw holes with the screws provided *(right)*.

◆ Test-fit the drawer in the cabinet; it should slide smoothly. If not, loosen the screws and move the channel sideways slightly.

◆ When the glides are well adjusted, drive screws through the remaining holes.

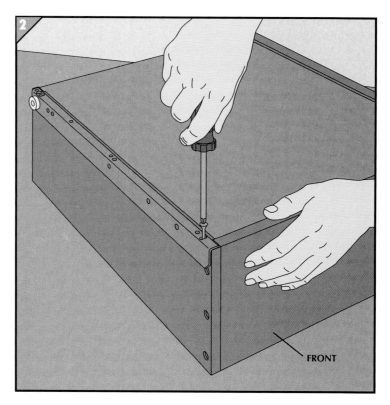

FRONT

ADDING THE FALSE FRONTS

WOOD BLOCK

1. Positioning the first piece.

◆ Cut the drawer false fronts to the desired size *(page 142)* and finish exposed edges *(page 128)*.

◆ Install the bottom drawer and pull it partway out. Set two blocks of wood cut $\frac{1}{8}$ inch higher than the top of the kick-plate installed earlier at the bottom of the cabinet.

◆ Set the false front on the blocks and, resting it against the front of the drawer, draw a line along the top of the drawer on the back of the false front *(left)*.

2. Fastening the false front.

◆ Remove the drawer and place it on the false front, centering it between the edges and aligning the top of the drawer with the marked line.
◆ Secure the pieces with hand-screw clamps.
◆ Drill pilot holes for $1\frac{1}{4}$-inch No. 8 countersunk flooring screws through the drawer front into the false front. Locate one row of holes 1 inch from the top of the drawer and another row 1 inch from the bottom, spacing the holes 1 inch from each end and every 6 inches in between.
◆ Drive the screws *(right)*.

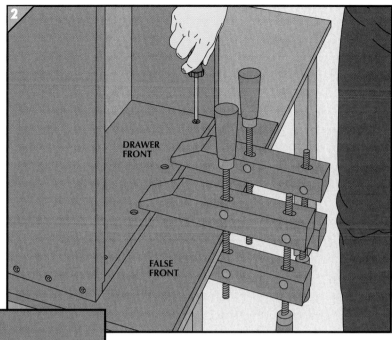

DRAWER
FRONT

FALSE
FRONT

3. Positioning the remaining pieces.

◆ Install the bottom drawer in the cabinet, then slide in the second drawer.
◆ Pull the two drawers out partway, and stack two quarters on the false front of the bottom drawer near each end, creating a $\frac{1}{8}$-inch gap between the false fronts.
◆ Set the second false front on the quarters, aligning it with the one below *(left)*, and draw a line along the top of the drawer on the back face of the false front.
◆ Fasten the second false front to the drawer *(Step 2)*.
◆ Attach the remaining false fronts in the same way.

TRICKS OF THE TRADE

Aligning the Front with Brads

To facilitate the positioning of a false front, set the drawer face up and drive two brads into the drawer front, leaving the heads protruding. (Make sure the brads are not located where the drawer handle will be installed.) Snip off the ends of the brads with pliers *(right)*. Install the drawer and position the false front *(Step 1, opposite)*, pressing it against the brads on the front of the drawer. Remove the drawer and fasten the false front *(Step 2, above)*, using the indentations left by the brads to place the false front correctly.

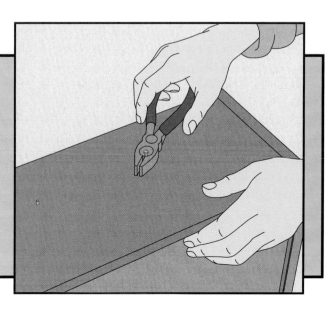

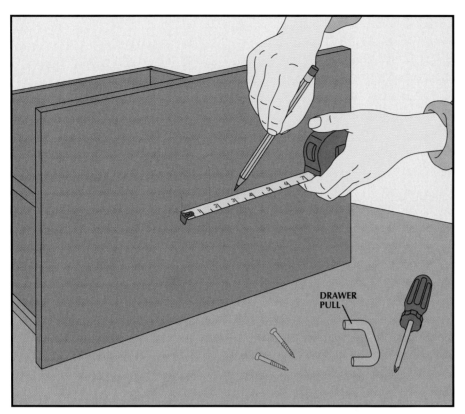

DRAWER
PULL

Placing the hardware.

◆ With a tape measure and combination square, locate and mark the center of the false drawer front with two crossing lines. If your drawer pull has a single fastener, drill a hole for it where the lines cross.

◆ For a two-fastener pull, measure the distance between the two screw holes on the drawer pull, divide the measurement by two, and mark this distance on each side of the center *(left)*.

◆ Drill a clearance hole into the false front and through the drawer front at each mark for the screws provided with the drawer pull.

◆ Holding the drawer pull in position against the false front, drive the screws from the inside to fasten the pull to the drawer.

A HIDDEN WORK SURFACE

Expand a desk's work space by including a pullout "breadboard" in the top of a cabinet supporting a desktop. The unit consists of a $\frac{3}{4}$-inch plywood rectangle cut as wide and as deep as a drawer and screwed to the top of a front tall enough for fastening a pull. A false front, cut to match the spacing of the drawer false fronts below it, conceals the seam and the top edge of the cabinet with a $\frac{1}{8}$-inch reveal. Mount the work surface in the cabinet so it clears the top by $\frac{1}{4}$ inch.

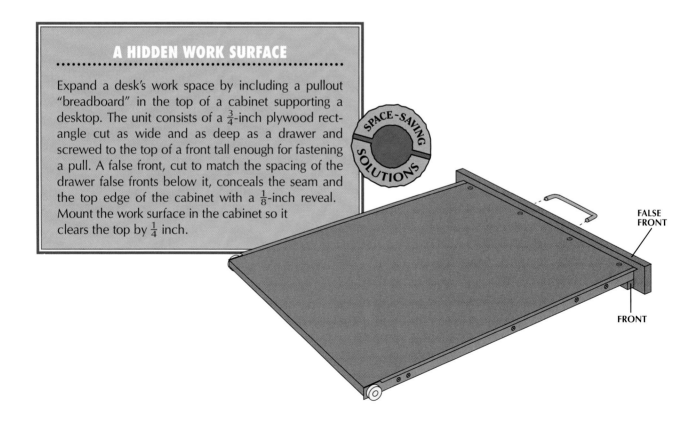

SPACE-SAVING SOLUTIONS

FALSE
FRONT

FRONT

Doors can conceal the contents of a cabinet, safeguarding supplies and hiding clutter. The simplest door to install is one that overlaps the front of the cabinet *(below)*, masking any minor errors in measurement and construction. The door can be made from the same $\frac{3}{4}$-inch plywood as the cabinet.

Types of Door Hinges: Spring-loaded hinges lock in the open position, and hold the door in place when it is closed, making a catch or latch unnecessary. A special kind of spring-loaded hinge—called a European hinge *(page 148)*—allows for easy adjustment if the door shifts or sags with time. If the cabinet will support a desktop, install the door so it opens away from you when you are seated at the desk.

Hardware Requirements: The number and size of hinges required for a door depend on its dimensions. Two rules of thumb apply: First, for a door that is taller than 2 feet, install three hinges; second, make sure the total length of the hinges equals at least one-sixth the length of the door edge. For example, if the door is 24 inches high, use two 2-inch hinges.

When only two hinges are required, place them a quarter of the way from the top and bottom of the door; with three hinges, place one in the center and the other two 4 or 5 inches from the top and bottom.

TOOLS
Circular saw
Combination
    square
Screwdriver

MATERIALS
Plywood ($\frac{3}{4}$")
Hinges
Handle

SAFETY TIPS
When drilling, protect your eyes with goggles.

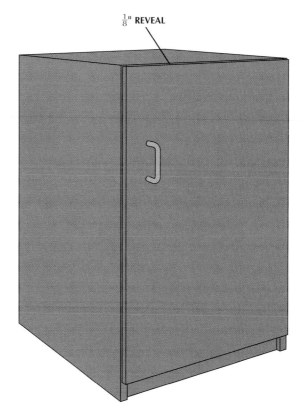

$\frac{1}{8}$" REVEAL

An overlapping door.
An overlapping door *(right)* is cut to fit over the cabinet front, inset $\frac{1}{8}$ inch from the sides, the top, and the top of the kickplate. Designed to hide small irregularities in the construction of the cabinet, this type of door is easier to fit than other styles. Its handle is attached in the same manner as a drawer pull *(page 146)*, but is positioned vertically near the un-hinged edge of the door.

1. Fastening hinges to the door.
◆ Cut a door from $\frac{3}{4}$-inch plywood, making it $\frac{1}{8}$ inch smaller all around than the front of the cabinet frame. Finish exposed edges *(page 128)*.
◆ With a combination square, mark a line along the inside face of the door, $\frac{5}{8}$ inch from the hinged edge.
◆ Position the hinges on the door along the line *(left)*.
◆ Fasten the hinges by driving the screws provided through the oblong holes.

2. Positioning the door.
◆ Set the door on wood blocks $\frac{1}{8}$ inch higher than the kickplate, and hold it partially open against the cabinet *(right)*.
◆ Have a helper open the hinges against the inside of the cabinet and mark the center of the oblong holes.
◆ Open the door completely, align the oblong holes with the marks, and drive the screws.
◆ Close the door and check its alignment. If necessary, adjust the door's position by loosening the screws attaching the hinges to the door or cabinet and adjusting the position of the hinges.
◆ When you are satisfied with the alignment, drive screws in the round holes.

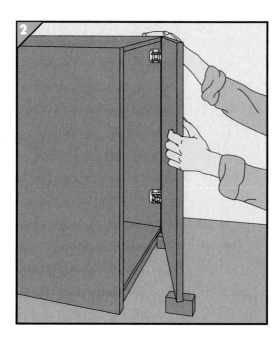

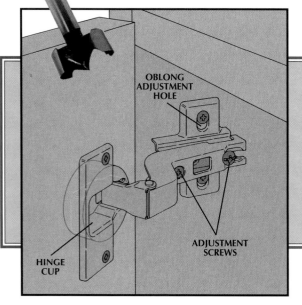

EURO-STYLE HINGES

Spring-loaded European hinges are easy to adjust in all directions. The cup on one leaf fits into a cavity drilled in the door with a Forstner bit *(photograph)*; the other leaf is screwed to the side of the cabinet. Oblong holes in the cabinet leaf allow the hinge to move up and down on its mounting screws. In-and-out adjustments are accomplished by turning two screws in the center mechanism of the hinge. You can remove the door by removing the adjustment screws and sliding the hinge leaves apart.

A cabinet on wheels can be easily stored under a desk or tucked into a corner of the room and rolled out when needed. The cabinet can be fitted with drawers—a mobile filing cabinet comes in very handy—or shelves, and is ideal for housing a printer.

The cabinet illustrated below is constructed in the same way as the one shown on pages 134 to 137, with a few exceptions. To provide a flat surface for fastening the casters, the sides are rabbeted to rest on the bottom and there is no kickplate.

Plate-style casters *(photograph)* are fastened to the bottom of the cabinet with screws. To simplify screwing the mounting plate to the cabinet, separate the plate from the wheels; if the two parts do not come apart, rotate the caster as necessary to reach the mounting screws. (Stem casters, comprising a shaft that slides into a sleeve inserted in a drilled hole, cannot be used with this piece.)

Choose casters with large wheels like those shown below rather than ones with a small rolling ball—the type with a wheel supports more weight. If you plan to store the cabinet under a desk, be sure to take into account the height of the wheels when determining the height of the cabinet.

A false top can be fastened to the top of the cabinet to serve as a work surface; be sure to include its thickness in determining the overall height of the cabinet.

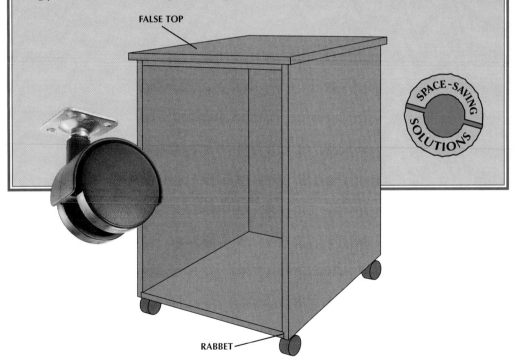

FALSE TOP

RABBET

SPACE-SAVING SOLUTIONS

Transforming a pair of small cabinets into a computer workstation calls for the addition of a desktop spanning the cabinets and a keyboard tray between them.

A standard desk work surface measures 30 by 60 inches. Make the top long enough to allow no less than 26 inches between cabinets.

Desktop Details: Depending on the material you are using and its thickness *(page 126)*, this distance may be too great for the top to span without reinforcement. You can stiffen the desktop with the rabbeted edging shown on page 128 or with a case for a keyboard tray screwed to the underside of the desktop *(page 152)*.

For an attractive look, design the top to overhang the front and sides of the cabinet. An overhang at the back leaves space behind the desk for plugging equipment into electrical receptacles.

Paths for Wires: In addition to a rear overhang, the desktop will also need openings for telephone and electrical wires, as will the back and sides of the cabinet.

The simplest solution is to cut holes through the panels and install a plastic grommet in each opening *(opposite)*. These grommets are available in a variety of sizes. You can also buy plastic clips and channels designed to guide wires along a desk or wall.

The Keyboard Tray: The tray is installed with drawer glides that lock in position when pulled all the way out. If the cabinets supporting the top are close enough together that reinforcement is not required, you can simply fasten the tray hardware to the sides of the cabinets. You can also purchase a commercial keyboard tray instead of building one yourself.

TOOLS

Electric drill	Screwdriver
Combination bit	Circular saw
Hole-saw	Bar clamps
attachment	Hand-screw
C-clamps	clamps

MATERIALS

Plywood ($\frac{3}{4}$")	Wood glue
Flooring screws	Plastic grommet
($1\frac{1}{4}$", 2" No. 8)	Drawer glides

SAFETY TIPS

Protect your eyes with goggles when you are using power tools.

MOUNTING THE WORK SURFACE

Fastening the desktop to the cabinets.
◆ Position the two cabinets parallel to each other and the correct distance apart. Remove any drawers from them.
◆ Drill a clearance hole for a No. 8 flooring screw at each corner of the cabinet tops.
◆ Cut the top from $\frac{3}{4}$-inch plywood large enough to overlap the cabinets 1 inch on each side and 2 inches in back; in front, make the overlap 1 inch, or $\frac{1}{4}$ inch past the front of any drawers or doors. Finish exposed edges *(page 128)*.
◆ With a helper, position the desktop on the cabinets *(left)* and clamp it to them.
◆ From inside the cabinets, drill pilot holes for $1\frac{1}{4}$-inch No. 8 flooring screws up through the clearance holes into the underside of the top.
◆ Drive a screw up into each pilot hole.

Drilling openings.
◆ Mark the location of holes for wires and buy plastic grommets of the appropriate size *(photograph)*.
◆ Fit an electric drill with a hole-saw bit the same size as the grommet, then cut a hole at each marked location *(right)*.
◆ Press the plastic grommet into place.

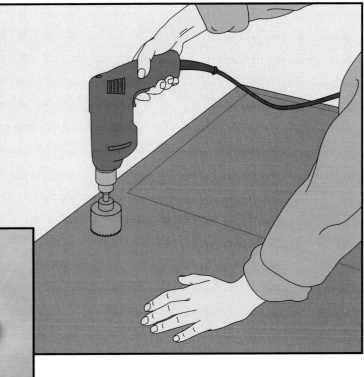

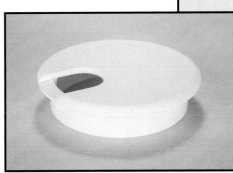

A TRACK FOR CONTROLLING CABLES

The many cables, wires, and power cords from home-office equipment can create an untidy tangle on the floor or behind a desk. This can also pose a tripping hazard. One of many commercial products for neatly routing this wiring along a desk or wall is the plastic track illustrated at right. Cut to length with a utility knife, the track is fastened to a surface with an adhesive strip attached to the back.

Avoid putting printer cables longer than 6 feet in the same track as a power cable, to prevent electrical interference.

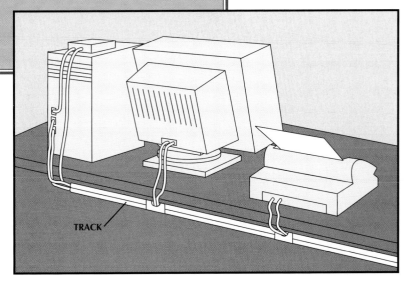

TRACK

A keyboard tray in a case.
The keyboard tray at right fits in a case—a box without a front or bottom, mounted to the underside of the desk-top and to the cabinets. Built wide enough to span the distance between the cabinets, the case is also deep enough to accept locking drawer glides.

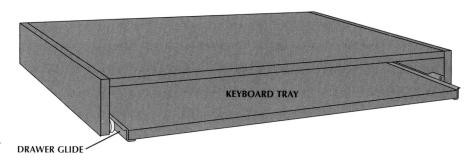

KEYBOARD TRAY

DRAWER GLIDE

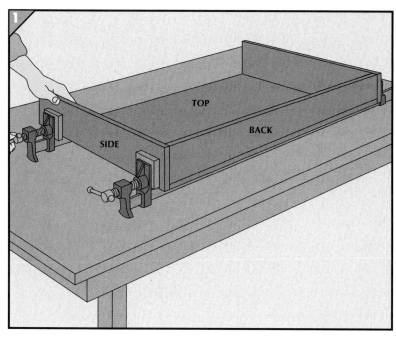

TOP

BACK

SIDE

1. Assembling the case.
◆ Cut the two side pieces from $\frac{3}{4}$-inch plywood long enough to accommodate the depth of the keyboard tray, plus 3 inches for wires, and wide enough to hold the tray the desired distance below the top.
◆ Cut the top piece to a length equal to the distance between the cabinets less $1\frac{1}{2}$ inches, and to a width matching the length of the side pieces.
◆ Cut the back piece the same length as the top and $\frac{3}{4}$ inch narrower than the side pieces. Finish exposed edges of all the pieces *(page 128)*.
◆ Assemble the pieces with bar clamps *(left)*, protecting the stock with wood pads.
◆ Drill pilot holes for 2-inch No. 8 countersunk flooring screws through the sides into the top and back, spacing them every 6 inches.
◆ Fasten the pieces together with glue and screws, then turn the assembly over and countersink screws to fasten the top to the back.

2. Mounting the case and tray.
◆ Drill clearance holes for $1\frac{1}{4}$-inch No. 8 flooring screws 1 inch from the edges and every 6 inches around the perimeter of the top of the keyboard case, and every 6 inches through the sides of the keyboard case into the sides of the cabinet.
◆ Position the case under the top and secure it there with hand-screw clamps.
◆ Drill pilot holes into the underside of the top and the cabinet sides through the clearance holes.
◆ Drive screws through all the pilot holes *(right)*.
◆ Cut the keyboard tray from $\frac{3}{4}$-inch plywood, making it the depth of the case, less 3 inches to accommodate wires, and the width of the case less the clearance required for drawer hardware. Finish the exposed edges *(page 128)*.
◆ Install locking drawer glides on the case and keyboard tray *(pages 143-144)*.
◆ Slide the keyboard tray into the drawer glides mounted in the case.

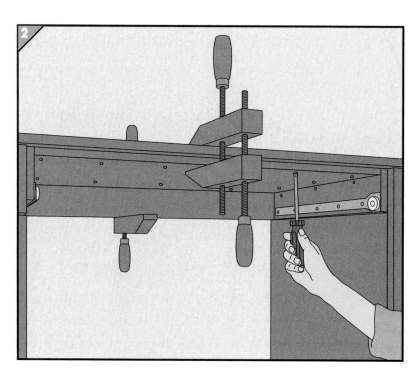

Fastening a top to a pair of cabinets is only one way to create a desk. You can also build a freestanding desk, supported by plywood legs, and design it to be rectangular or custom-made to fit into a corner. If you are planning to build more than one unit and place them side by side, ensure that the tops are all the same height and depth.

A Corner Unit: A five-sided desk unit *(below)* fits neatly into a corner, making efficient use of space in a small room. It can also be sized to fit between a pair of rectangular desks or cabinets no more than 30 inches deep and is an ideal spot for a computer monitor, freeing desk space on the other work sur-faces. The open front edge of the desk can be fitted with a keyboard tray *(page 152)*.

A Rectangular Desk: A simple four-sided desk *(page 155)* can be designed in the same way as a small cabinet; the only difference is that the desk is built without a bottom. The desk can be made any size; if built just wide enough to accommodate a keyboard tray, it can serve as a compact comput-er workstation.

Finishing Touches: Useful addi-tions to these desks include adjustable feet for leveling *(page 137)* and holes with grommets for routing wires *(page 151)*.

TOOLS

Carpenter's square
Tape measure
Circular saw
Protractor
Straightedge
C-clamps
Electric drill
Combination bit
Screwdriver

MATERIALS

Plywood ($\frac{3}{4}$")
Flooring screws (2" No. 8)
Angle irons
Wood glue

SAFETY TIPS

Put on goggles when using any power tool.

Anatomy of a corner unit.

The top of this desk is designed with two 48-inch edges that fit in a corner of a room, two short edges designed to butt against adjoining desk units, and a diagonal edge long enough to accommodate a keyboard tray. The back panels and the side panels are fastened to the edges of the top panel. For a freestanding unit, cut the false top to overhang the top panel as for the cabinet *(page 134)*. If it will abut a cabinet or desk, make the overhang dimensions the same on all the units but cut the false top flush with the side panels where the units meet. By dou-bling the thickness of the top, the false top reinforces the desk.

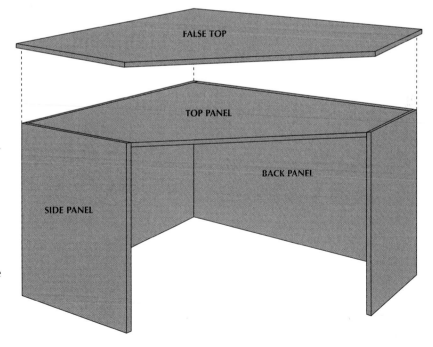

FALSE TOP

TOP PANEL

BACK PANEL

SIDE PANEL

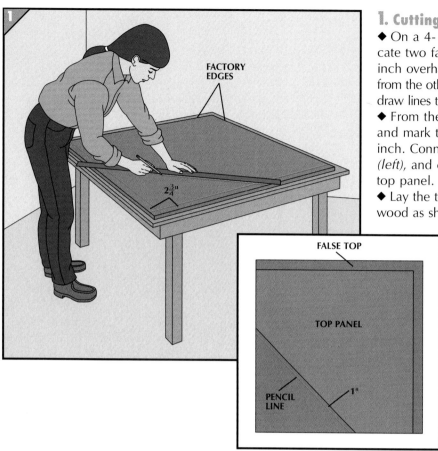

FACTORY EDGES

$2\frac{3}{4}''$

FALSE TOP

TOP PANEL

PENCIL LINE

1"

1. Cutting the desktop.

◆ On a 4- by 4-foot square of $\frac{3}{4}$-inch plywood, locate two factory edges that form a corner. For a 2-inch overhang near the wall, measure in $2\frac{3}{4}$ inches from the other two edges with a carpenter's square, and draw lines the length and width of the plywood square.

◆ From the factory edges, measure along each line and mark the depth of the adjoining units less $\frac{3}{4}$ inch. Connect these marks with a diagonal line *(left)*, and cut along all three lines to complete the top panel.

◆ Lay the top panel on another 4-foot square of plywood as shown in the inset. Measure out 1 inch—the amount of false-top overhang on the adjacent units—from the diagonal edge of the top panel and mark a parallel line on the lower plywood square.

◆ Cut along the line to complete the false top.

◆ Finish exposed edges *(page 128)*.

2. Attaching the side panels.

◆ Cut two side panels to the desired height, making their width equal to the length of the side edges of the top plus $\frac{3}{4}$ inch. Finish exposed edges *(page 128)*.

◆ Clamp the top to a work surface and have a helper hold one side panel in position against it, aligning the front edges of the two panels.

◆ Mark screw-hole lines on the side panel centered on the top panel, as shown on page 136.

◆ Drill counterbored pilot holes for 2-inch No. 8 flooring screws through the side panel into the top, locating the holes $1\frac{1}{2}$ inches from each edge and every 6 inches in between along the marked line *(right)*.

◆ Fasten the side panel to the top panel with glue and screws.

◆ Attach the opposite side panel in the same way.

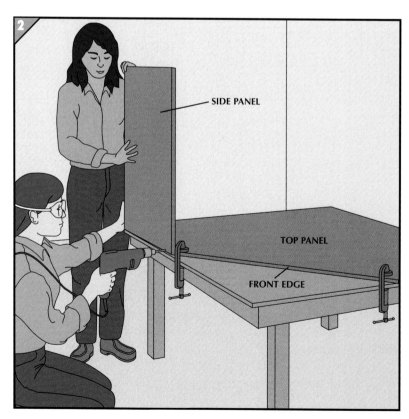

SIDE PANEL

TOP PANEL

FRONT EDGE

3. Adding the back panels.

◆ From $\frac{3}{4}$-inch plywood, cut a back panel the same height as the side panels and the width of one of the back edges of the top panel. Cut the second back panel $\frac{3}{4}$ inch wider.

◆ Working with a helper, position the wider panel against a back edge of the top panel so its edge is covered by a side panel *(right)*.

◆ Drill pilot holes and fasten the panel as you did for the side panels *(Step 2)*, driving the screws through the back panel into the top panel, and through the side panel into the back panel.

◆ Position the second back panel against the top panel between the first back panel and the side panel. Secure it to all three in the same way as the first back panel.

◆ Turn the base upright and fasten the false top to it in the manner shown on page 150.

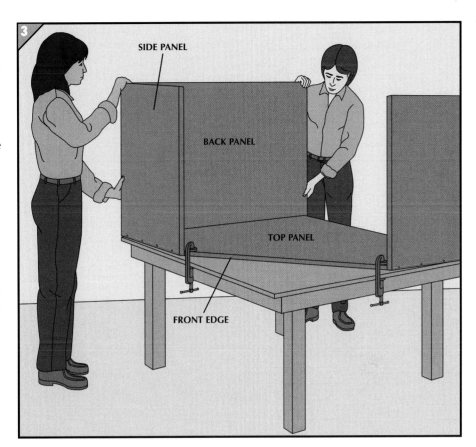

A RECTANGULAR DESK

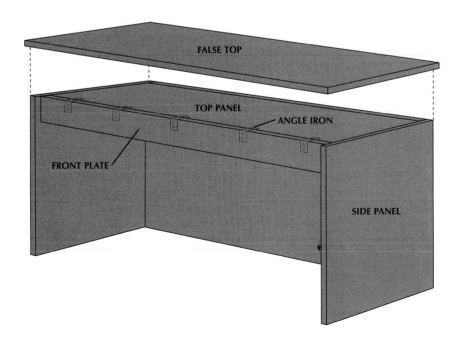

Building the piece.

A rectangular desk can be assembled in the same way as the corner unit opposite: Set the top panel on a work surface and, working with a helper to position the side panels, fasten them to the top. Cut the back panel to fit between the two side panels so that its edges are hidden. Fasten it to the top and the two side panels *(page 154, Step 2)*. A front plate reinforces the top and gives the desk a more finished appearance. Fasten the plate to the desktop with angle irons spaced every foot. A false top—with overhanging edges as described on page 150—is then fastened to the base.

Shelving on or above a desk keeps office materials organized and frees precious desk space. A custom shelving unit can either be fastened to the desktop or mounted on the wall above it.

A Desktop Unit: You can design desktop shelves with compartments for a computer monitor and other equipment such as a printer. Consider including small doors and drawers to keep supplies out of sight. Such units usually span the full length of the desk; make it deep enough to accommodate its planned contents, but not so deep as to take up too much desk space. See that no shelf exceeds the maximum span for the material you are using *(page 126)*.

A Wall Unit: Wall-mounted shelving can be firmly fastened to the studs, or even tucked in between them *(opposite)*. Vertical cubbyholes keep temporary files sorted and readily accessible. It's a good idea to size shelf compartments for letter- or legal-size files.

TOOLS

Table saw	Combination bit
Circular saw	Screwdriver
Bar clamps	Carpenter's level
Electric drill	Wallboard tools

MATERIALS

Plywood ($\frac{1}{8}$", $\frac{3}{4}$")	Wood screws
1 x 2 lumber	(3" No. 10)
Wood glue	Angle irons
Flooring screws	Wallboard patching
(2" No. 8)	materials

SAFETY TIPS

When using a power tool, protect your eyes with goggles.

DESKTOP SHELVING

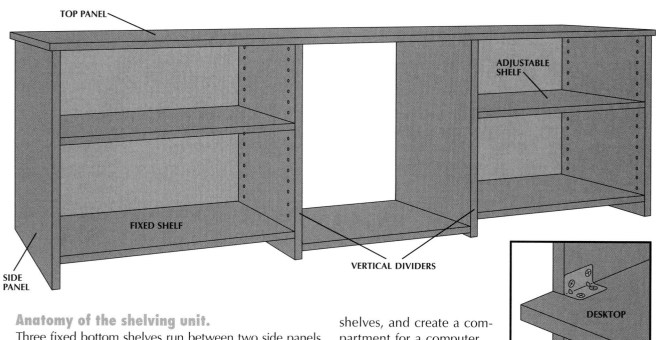

TOP PANEL

ADJUSTABLE SHELF

FIXED SHELF

VERTICAL DIVIDERS

SIDE PANEL

DESKTOP

Anatomy of the shelving unit.

Three fixed bottom shelves run between two side panels and vertical dividers, with the middle shelf positioned below the other two to allow the fastening of all these shelves to the dividers. The side panels are joined by a top panel that overlaps them at the front and sides. Two vertical dividers help support the top and the bottom shelves, and create a compartment for a computer monitor. Adjustable shelves on either side provide for storage, and a hardboard back on each side section adds rigidity to the structure. The sides of the unit are anchored to the desktop with small angle irons *(inset)*.

Assembling and hanging the unit.

◆ From $\frac{3}{4}$-inch plywood, cut the top, the bottom, the fixed shelf, and the sides *(page 135, Step 1)*. Cut a plywood back panel to fit in the frame formed by other pieces.

◆ Cut matching dadoes $\frac{1}{8}$ inch wide and $\frac{1}{4}$ inch deep at the desired intervals across the top of the fixed shelf and the underside of the top to accommodate the dividers. Finish exposed edges *(page 128)*.

◆ Clamp the pieces together and drill pilot holes for 2-inch No. 8 counterbored flooring screws, then fasten the panels together with glue and screws.

◆ With a carpenter's level, mark a level line on the wall for the bottom of the cabinet. Cut a 1-by-2 ledger the length of the cabinet and, with 3-inch No. 10 wood screws, fasten it to the studs so its top is even with the line.

◆ Have a helper hold the unit on the ledger.

◆ Near the top and middle of the unit, and every 12 inches in between, drill pilot holes for 3-inch No. 10 wood screws through the back into each stud *(right)*. Screw the unit to the wall.

◆ Cut $\frac{1}{8}$-inch plywood divider panels to fit in the dadoes and slide them into place *(inset)*.

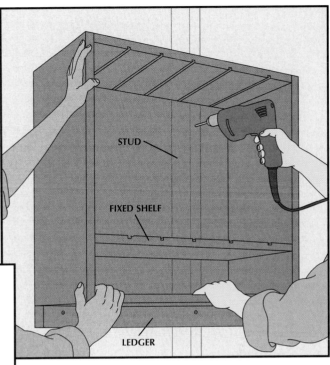

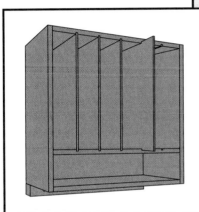

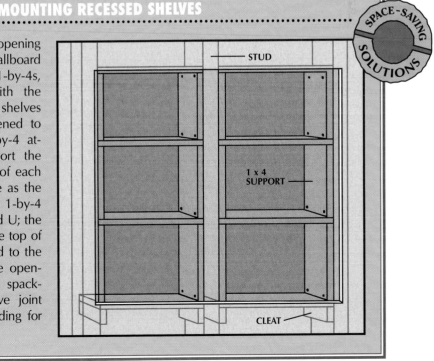

MOUNTING RECESSED SHELVES

You can fit shelves in an opening made by cutting away wallboard between studs. Built from 1-by-4s, the shelves rest flush with the studs' edges. The bottom shelves rest on 1-by-2 cleats fastened to stud faces. Lengths of 1-by-4 attached to the studs support the middle shelves. At the top of each unit, a board the same size as the shelves is nailed to two 1-by-4 supports to form an inverted U; the assembly is inserted into the top of the wall opening and nailed to the studs. The perimeter of the opening can be smoothed with spackling compound or adhesive joint tape and framed with molding for a more finished look.

SPACE-SAVING SOLUTIONS

Consider tucking a small office into a closet; if the space is not deep enough to accommodate a computer, it can still be used for desk work. To adapt a closet, you may need to widen the opening and install bifold doors *(pages 63-65)* or a pair of prehung doors. Then, install storage shelves and a work surface *(below)*. Pages 126 to 133 explain how to prepare and join the wood.

Hanging Shelves: The sturdiest and most versatile shelves are ones supported by a system of standards and brackets. To support heavy items, mount heavy-duty brackets with a pair of prongs that snap into the standard, rather than just a single prong; and choose a system where the shelves fasten to the brackets rather than just rest on them *(opposite)*. To anchor the shelving system solidly, fasten each standard to a wall stud. For the shelves, choose material that can span the 16 inches between studs without sagging *(page 126)*. Locate the bottom shelf high enough to clear any equipment you plan to install on the work surface below.

The Work Surface: If the closet is deep enough, put in a desk. If it is not, consider hanging a work surface from cleats fastened to the closet wall *(pages 160-161)*, positioning it at a comfortable height *(page 109)*.

Recovering Hidden Space: To expand a closet office, you can store a rolling cabinet under the work surface *(page 149)*, and mount light-duty shelves on the end walls or to the backs of prehung doors *(page 161)*.

TOOLS

Electronic stud finder
Electric drill
Countersink bit
Screwdriver
Carpenter's level
Circular saw
C-clamps

MATERIALS

Heavy-duty shelf standards and brackets
Plywood ($\frac{3}{4}$")
1 x 2s
1 x 3s
Wood screws ($1\frac{1}{4}$", 2" No. 8; 3" No. 10)
Wood glue

SAFETY TIPS

Put on goggles when you are using a power saw or drill.

Anatomy of a converted closet.
This closet holds a work surface supported by cleats fastened to the back and end walls. The front edge of the work surface is reinforced with an apron that interlocks with the end cleats. Enough space has been left between the front edge of the work surface and the doors for a desk chair to remain in the office when the doors are closed. A group of five standards supports two sets of shelves on brackets, which are staggered to share the center standard.

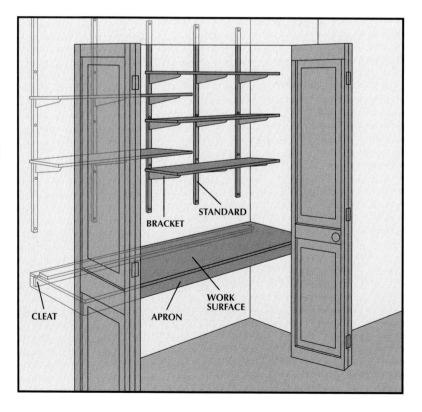

STANDARD

BRACKET

CLEAT

APRON

WORK SURFACE

1. Attaching the first standard.

◆ Locate the studs at the back of the closet with a stud finder and mark the drywall at the middle of each stud with a vertical line.
◆ Hold the first standard in position centered over a line and mark the top screwhole.
◆ Remove the standard and drill a pilot hole for one of the screws provided.
◆ Replace the standard and drive the screw almost all the way *(right)*.
◆ Allow the standard to hang plumb, then mark the remaining screw holes.
◆ Swing the standard sideways to drill pilot holes, then drive the rest of the screws.

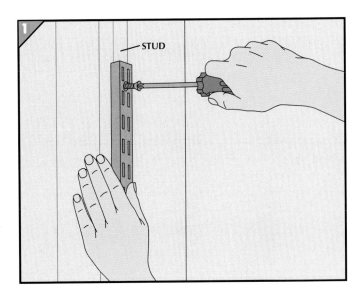

2. Fastening the remaining uprights.

◆ Insert a shelf bracket in the first standard, and another in the same position on a second standard.
◆ Place the second standard against the wall over a stud and set a level across the brackets. Adjust the height of the second standard so the brackets are level, then mark the top of the second standard on the wall *(left)*.
◆ Install the second standard as you did the first, ensuring that its top edge is in line with the mark.
◆ Repeat this procedure to install the rest of the standards.
◆ Snap the brackets into the standards at the desired height, then cut shelves at least 2 inches longer than the distance between the end brackets, finish exposed edges *(page 128)*, and mount the shelves.
◆ Fasten the shelves to the brackets with the screws provided, the longer screws in the back and the shorter ones in the front *(inset)*.

TRICKS OF THE TRADE

Supporting the Ends of Shelves

If your standard-and-bracket system does not call for fastening the shelves to the brackets, you will need to cut the shelves to overlap the brackets by a couple of inches. Doing so may be difficult if the last bracket is close to the end of the closet. To prevent the shelf from slipping off, screw two small metal plates to the end of each shelf *(right)* and hook the plates over the outside of the brackets.

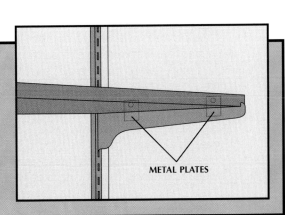

METAL PLATES

1. Preparing the cleats.

◆ For the back cleat, cut one 1-by-3 to the length of the closet and another 5 inches shorter.
◆ With C-clamps, secure the two boards to the edge of a worktable *(right)* with $2\frac{1}{2}$ inches of the longer board extending at each end. Starting 1 inch from the end, drill pilot holes for 2-inch No. 8 countersunk wood screws every 12 inches through the shorter piece into the longer one.
◆ Fasten the pieces together with glue and screws.
◆ For each 1-by-3 end cleat, cut one piece $1\frac{3}{4}$ inches shorter than the depth of the work surface and a second piece $\frac{3}{4}$ inch shorter than the first.
◆ Fasten the end cleats together with glue and screws spaced at 12-inch intervals so the longer piece extends $\frac{3}{4}$ inch past the lower one to interlock with the back cleat *(inset)*.

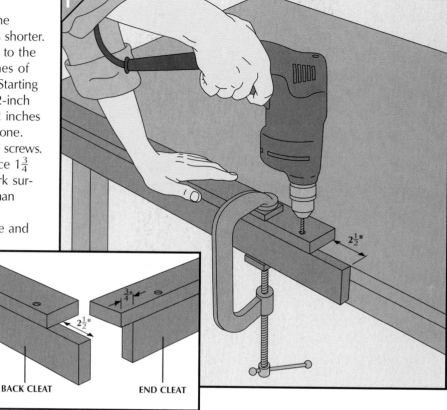

BACK CLEAT   END CLEAT

2. Mounting the cleats.

◆ Mark the back wall of the closet $\frac{3}{4}$ inch below the desired height of the work surface.
◆ With a helper, hold the back cleat against the wall with its top edge at the mark and level it.
◆ Drill a pilot hole for a 3-inch No. 10 wood screw through the cleat and into a stud near each end of the cleat *(left)*, and drive the screws. Then drive a screw into each remaining stud.
◆ Interlock an end cleat with one corner of the back cleat *(inset)*, and fasten it to the wall. Fasten the other end cleat in the same way.

BACK CLEAT   END CLEAT

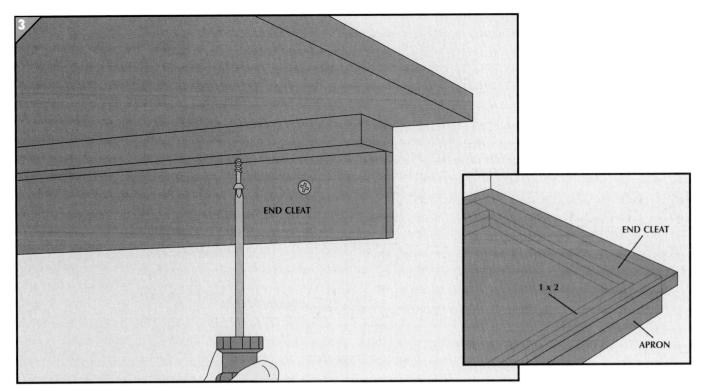

END CLEAT

END CLEAT

1 x 2

APRON

3. Adding the work surface.

◆ Cut the work surface and, after finishing the exposed edge *(page 128)*, set it on the cleats.

◆ With a helper holding the work surface down, drill pilot holes for $1\frac{1}{4}$-inch No. 8 wood screws up through the projecting part of the cleats into the work surface, locating the holes every 12 inches.

◆ Drive the screws *(above)*.

◆ For the apron that will support the work surface's front edge, cut a 1-by-3 to the length of the closet and a 1-by-2 that is 5 inches shorter.

◆ Position the 1-by-2 against the 1-by-3 face to face with their top edges flush so the 1-by-3 extends $2\frac{1}{2}$ inches past each end of the 1-by-2. Drill pilot holes for 2-inch No. 8 wood screws every 12 inches through the 1-by-2

into the 1-by-3 and glue and screw them together.

◆ Fit the apron into place, interlocking it with the end cleats *(inset)*; clamp it to the top.

◆ Drill pilot holes for 2-inch screws up through the apron's 1-by-2 and into the underside of the work surface, spacing the holes every 12 inches. Glue and screw the apron in place.

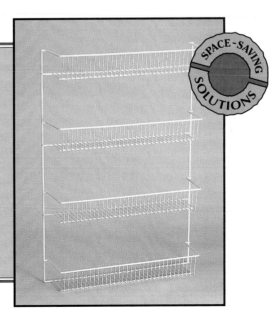

HIDDEN SPACE BEHIND A DOOR

SPACE-SAVING SOLUTIONS

The back of a prehung closet door can offer useful storage space. A wire shelf unit *(right)* can keep small office supplies at hand when the door is open; other types are available to hold large items, such as file folders. To make sure the door can close, buy shelves no deeper than the space between the front edge of the work surface and the front of the closet. Alternatively, hang the shelves high enough so they will clear the work surface when the door is closed. To hang the shelves, use hollow-wall anchors with short shanks specially designed for hollow-core doors.

When lack of space for a home office is a problem, consider building a work surface that folds against the wall. You can install such a desk in a small office, or even in an area such as the living room that is doing double duty as an office. The desk is stored out of the way against the wall, ready to be set up when needed.

Designing the Desk: Plan to install the desk at a comfortable height for working *(page 109)*. Although you can design it with a depth and length that best suits your needs, there are a couple of constraints: For the legs to fold back against the desktop, the top must be longer than the legs; and for the desk to rest flat against the wall, it must be higher than it is deep.

TOOLS
Circular saw
Electric drill
Countersink bit
Screwdriver
Table saw
Dado blade
Hacksaw
Carpenter's level
Electronic stud
 finder

MATERIALS
Plywood ($\frac{3}{4}$")
2 x 2s, 2 x 4s
Flooring screws
 ($1\frac{1}{4}$", 2" No. 8)
Wood screws
 ($\frac{5}{8}$" No. 6; 4" No. 10)
Piano hinges
Locking braces
Wood glue

SAFETY TIPS
When using power tools,
protect your eyes with goggles.

Anatomy of a folding desk.
The work surface is hinged to a 2-by-4 ledger fastened to the wall. An apron of 2-by-2s frames three sides of the desktop, lending it rigidity. When the desk is open, its front edge is supported by a pair of 2-by-4 legs. Each leg has a plywood plate set into it which is hinged to the bottom of the desktop; locking braces hold the legs open. Adjustable feet *(page 137)* help level the desktop.

To store the desk, the locking braces are released and the legs are folded up against the top *(inset)*; the table is then lowered against the wall. The apron hides the ends of the folded legs.

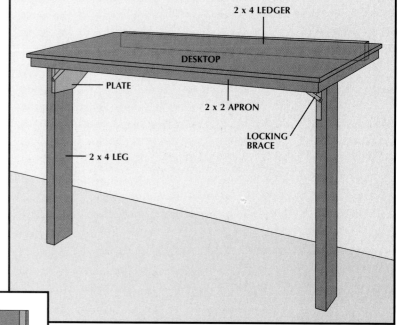

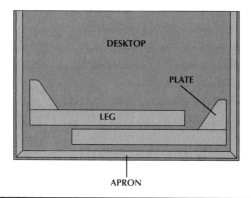

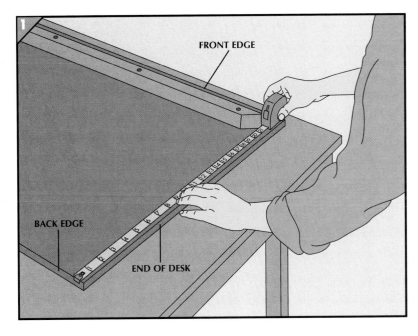

1. Attaching the apron to the top.

◆ From $\frac{3}{4}$-inch plywood, cut the desktop to the desired size and set it face down on a work surface.

◆ Cut a 2-by-2 apron piece 2 inches shorter than the top, and miter both ends to a 45-degree angle. Position the piece parallel to and 1 inch from the front edge of the top, centering it between the ends of the top.

◆ Drill pilot holes for countersunk 2-inch No. 8 flooring screws, spaced every 12 inches, and fasten the 2-by-2 to the top with glue and screws.

◆ Measure from one outside edge of the apron piece to the back edge of the top *(left)*, and cut two 2-by-2s to this length, mitering one end of each board.

◆ Fasten the 2-by-2s to the top in the same way as the first 2-by-2, parallel to and 1 inch from the edges, so the mitered ends meet those of the first 2-by-2.

2. Assembling the legs.

◆ Cut 2-by-4 legs to the desired height.

◆ With a router or a table saw and dado blade, cut a rabbet at one end of each leg $\frac{3}{4}$ inch deep and 6 inches wide.

◆ From $\frac{3}{4}$-inch plywood, cut two plates 10 inches long and 6 inches wide, tapering an edge of each piece 4 inches from one end *(inset)*.

◆ Fit a plate into the rabbet at the end of one leg. Drill four pilot holes for $1\frac{1}{4}$-inch No. 8 countersunk flooring screws and fasten the plate to the leg with glue and screws *(right)*.

◆ With a hacksaw, cut a piano hinge to a length of 10 inches. Fasten one leaf of the hinge to the plate with $\frac{5}{8}$-inch No. 6 wood screws.

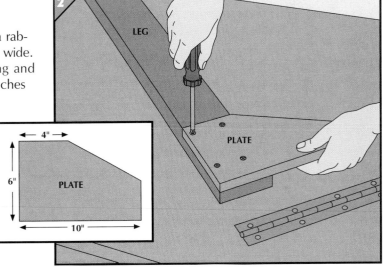

3. Attaching the legs to the top.

◆ Stand a leg in one of the corners formed by the front and side apron pieces, leaving $\frac{1}{2}$ inch between the leg and the front apron board for the locking braces you will install.

◆ Fasten the free leaf of the piano hinge to the top with $\frac{5}{8}$-inch No. 6 wood screws *(left)*.

◆ Fold the leg down against the desktop.

◆ Position the second leg so it will clear the first when folded *(inset, opposite)*, and fasten it to the desktop.

4. Bracing the legs.

◆ Open one of the locking braces all the way and position it against the leg and the top so the distances indicated as A and B in the illustration are equal.
◆ Fasten the brace to the leg and top with the screws provided, driving the screws only partway *(right)*.
◆ Check that the leg folds properly. Adjust the location of the brace if necessary and drive the screws the rest of the way.

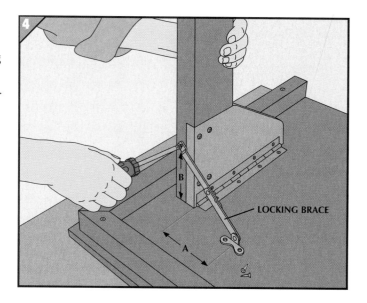

LOCKING BRACE

5. Attaching the hinge to the top.

◆ Cut a length of piano hinge to fit between the side apron pieces attached to the top.
◆ Fasten the hinge to the underside of the top, flush with the back edge, driving $\frac{5}{8}$-inch No. 6 wood screws into each end hole and every second hole in between.

6. Mounting the desk.

◆ Mark a level line on the wall at the height of the top surface of the desk. Locate and mark the studs along the line.
◆ Cut a 2-by-4 ledger to fit between the apron pieces fastened to the top. Have a helper hold the ledger with its top edge even with the line on the wall and check it for level. Then, drill pilot holes for 4-inch No. 10 countersunk wood screws through the ledger and into each stud, and fasten the ledger to the wall.
◆ Make two temporary legs by cutting two 2-by-4s to the same length as the permanent legs.
◆ Lock the permanent legs in the open position and set the desk upright with its back edge against the face of the ledger and its top surface flush with the top edge of the ledger. Prop up the back of the desk with the temporary legs.
◆ From under the desk, fasten the free leaf of the piano hinge to the ledger with $\frac{5}{8}$-inch No. 6 wood screws driven through every second screw hole *(right)*.
◆ Remove the temporary legs.

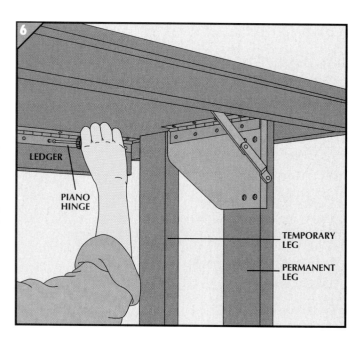

LEDGER

PIANO HINGE

TEMPORARY LEG

PERMANENT LEG

Furniture made of veneered MDF or good-quality plywood can be finished in the same way as solid-wood furniture. You can stain the wood, then apply a clear finish. On lower-quality plywood with many surface defects, use paint.

Preparing the Surface: Before finishing your furniture, sand its surfaces. Using a belt or orbital sander, or working by hand, start with 120-grit sandpaper and follow with 220-grit. Remove sanding dust with a tack rag. After sanding, repair cracks or gouges in the surface with wood filler. Even minor blemishes will show through a clear finish.

Staining: Penetrating stains soak into the wood and color the fibers, accentuating the grain. The non-penetrating variety covers the wood with a colored film and fills the wood pores, obscuring the grain. This type is a good choice for coarse-grained woods.

Stains are made with various solvents as the base, including water, oil, and alcohol. Oil-base stains are the easiest to work with; they are simply wiped on with a sponge or cheesecloth.

Before applying a stain, coat wood plugs and any other exposed end grain with sealer; use shellac for water- or oil-base stains and oil-base wood conditioner for alcohol-base products.

Applying a Clear Finish: Polyurethane varnish is ideal for surfaces that must stand up to wear because it dries to a clear, high-gloss surface that is durable and resistant to spills. This type of varnish is applied with a brush in several coats *(below)*; the more coats applied, the more lustrous the finish.

MATERIALS

Sandpaper
   (220-, 400-grit)
Tack rag
Varnish

SAFETY TIPS

When applying varnish, put on goggles and nitrile gloves.

Brushing on polyurethane varnish.

◆ Dilute the varnish as recommended by the manufacturer.
◆ Place the furniture on scrap-wood props.
◆ Dip a paintbrush into the varnish to half the length of the bristles and apply a heavy load of finish to a small area, working across the grain.
◆ Without reloading the brush, go back over the area, brushing with the grain *(right)*.
◆ To smooth the finish, lightly run the tip of a nearly dry brush over the area, holding the brush almost perpendicular to the surface and working with the grain. Cover the rest of the furniture in the same way.
◆ Let the finish dry as recommended on the label, then press your thumb against the surface and wipe the area with a soft cloth; if the thumbprint remains, more drying time is needed.
◆ With 220-grit sandpaper, rub the surface lightly and evenly, working with the grain. Remove the dust with a tack rag.
◆ Apply additional coats in the same way as the first, letting each one dry and sanding it before applying the next coat.

◆ Allow the final coat to dry for 24 hours, then if desired, polish the finish to a soft sheen with 400-grit sandpaper.

OFFICE DECORATION

When decorating your home office you don't have to be bound by what an office is supposed to look like. But there are certain things you should think about before committing to a decorating scheme. What kind of ambience is best for you? Will neutral, relaxed tones help you concentrate on business or will they put you to sleep? Bright and vibrant hues can stimulate, but also can distract. Will clients be coming to your office? What kind of message do you want your decor to convey to them?

If your office is part of another room, the contrast between living space and working space should not be too jarring. Choose colors and textures that blend well with what is already in the room. If your office is in a separate room, you have more freedom. Do you want your office decor to blend with your living space, or do you want to create a distinctive look that signals the transition from home to work when you walk through the door?

Color is your most important decorating tool. Although many studies have been done on how color affects humans, it is impossible to formulate precise rules because our reactions are largely subjective. Here is a very basic palette with a few general guidelines.

Black: sophisticated and elegant; classic, powerful. Use as an accent color.

White: also elegant and sophisticated; cool, serene, and peaceful. Be careful when painting walls pure white, it can look gray and dingy. Use a very pale off-white, or add a splash of color for an extremely subtle pastel. The result often looks "whiter."

Gray: dignified, calm, soothing. It can be very hard to match different grays.

ABOVE: On a color wheel, contrasting or complementary colors face each other, while colors that harmonize are side by side. The device can help you choose the colors for your decorating palette.

Red: passionate, warm, exciting, strong, and stimulating. Probably better used sparingly in an office.

Yellow: happy, optimistic. However, too much bright yellow can be irritating.

Blue: cool, peaceful, relaxing. Darker tones are elegant. But too much blue depresses some people.

Green: refreshing, dignified, easy on the eyes. Suggests hope and renewal.

Brown: outdoorsy, rustic, comfortable; yet can also be depressing to some people.

Light affects our perception of color; take color samples into your office to get a true idea of how they will look. The reverse is also true: color affects light. Dark colors seem to absorb light; if you have dark walls, you may need additional lighting. Paler colors reflect light and make a room look brighter. Color also affects our perception of space. A small, boxy office can be made to seem larger with pale neutral colors. Using a monochromatic color scheme for all the elements in the room—walls, window treatments, floor coverings—also helps give an illusion of space. Color can even be used to alter the perceived shape of a long, narrow room. Painting the end walls a dark color will visually shorten the room.

PAINTABLE WALLPAPER

If you need to cover wood paneling, concrete block, or any wall that is in less than perfect condition, try one of the new textured vinyl wall coverings made for this purpose. They are prepasted and washable and are applied like ordinary wallpaper. Once on the wall, you can either leave it white or paint it. If you decide to paint, let the wall covering dry for 72 hours and then give it two coats of a latex paint.

Paintable wallpaper adds textural interest to walls while covering small imperfections. It can be left bare or painted.

Covering your walls with a good quality paint is the simplest and least expensive way to add color to a room. Most types are washable, although semigloss or gloss are easiest to clean. Wallpaper offers an infinite variety of color and texture choices for your walls. Choose a paper with a washable vinyl finish for longer life. If you are looking for a wall covering that provides some acoustical and thermal insulation, try cork. Many types can be left as is, or painted. Cork is sold as adhesive-backed squares or in rolls. Another possible wall covering is wood paneling, a beautiful, but more expensive, option.

WINDOW TREATMENTS

When choosing fabrics for the windows in your home office, avoid any with frills and other embellishments—a simple treatment such as horizontal or vertical blinds or basic fabric shades is more businesslike and provides much better control over the natural light.

Horizontal blinds (also available as mini-blinds) are usually made of vinyl or aluminum. They provide excellent control over sunlight, and can often be adjusted to a wide range of angles to block light while letting in air. Vertical blinds also work well and come in a wide choice of colors and

fabrics. Fabric shades come in different varieties and combine style and elegance with practicality. There are single-pleat shades that fold up like an accordion, and cellular shades with construction resembling a honeycomb sandwiched between two sheets of fabric. Cellular shades also offer some insulation value. Another option, plastic film, adheres to the glass and helps block solar heat and glare.

MEASURING FOR WINDOW TREATMENTS

For your blind or shade to fit properly, accurate measurements are essential. Use a sturdy metal tape measure, never a cloth tape. Most windows are not perfectly square, so measure in three different places, and round your measurements off to the nearest $\frac{1}{8}$ inch. For the width, use the narrowest measurement; for the height, use the longest measurement. If you are mounting your shade or blind outside the window opening to hide an ugly frame or just to make the window look bigger, add at least $1\frac{1}{2}$ inches all around to minimize light leakage and ensure privacy. If possible, have a salesperson confirm your measurements; otherwise, measure twice and then have a friend confirm the figures. Be very careful not to mix up the height and the width, a common mistake that spells disaster.

For an inside mount, measure the height and width of the window from jamb to jamb in three different places (right). For an outside mount, determine the height and width, then add at least $1\frac{1}{2}$ inches to each side (far right).

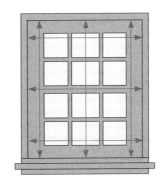

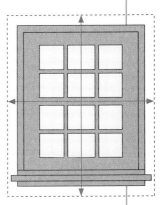

CHAPTER 5

TOOLS OF THE TRADE

A PERSONAL COMPUTER IS THE BACKBONE OF MOST HOME offices. With the right software, your computer can be secretary, accountant, and graphic designer all rolled into one. Connect a modem and add communications software, and you have a reliable receptionist and answering service. Hook up to the Internet and you have the world at your fingertips—marketing and research opportunities are limited only by your imagination.

This chapter is about choosing the technology you need and putting it to work for you. You'll learn more about what personal computers can do than how they do it. It is possible to get a system that works for you at an affordable price, but you will have to spend some time and effort in the research phase. Of course, a computer is not the only machine you will need in your office, so we have included a section on other equipment you might need to run your business efficiently.

RIGHT: Modern technology—personal computers, printers, modems, and faxes—makes it possible for a single individual to run an office.

CHOOSING COMPUTER EQUIPMENT

Your first major computer decision will be to determine what kind of machine you need. The computer world is divided into two basic camps: Macs and PCs. Macs, short for Macintosh, are made by Apple Computer Inc., and PCs, which stands for personal computers, originally were made by IBM and now are made by IBM and just about everybody else.

Which should you buy? Conventional wisdom has it that a PC is best for business applications and a Mac for work that involves graphics or desktop publishing. Mac owners will often tell you that their machines are more user-friendly; however, Macintosh computers may be losing that advantage because of Microsoft Windows, a graphic interface that makes using a PC easier—some say more like a Mac. Generally, PCs are less expensive than Macs for comparable systems, but Apple's prices are on their way down. A Mac may be easier to upgrade by adding memory, video, sound, and other peripherals, a feature that tends to give it a somewhat longer life. On the other hand, there is probably more software available for PCs.

Unless you are already a dedicated user of one type of computer—in which case, you may be better off sticking with what you know—your decision probably will be based on considerations other than the machines themselves. You should consider, for instance, what everybody else has. If you are telecommuting, what type of computer are they using in the main office? If you are self-employed, what type of com-

ABOVE: IBM-compatible PCs are considered by many users to be the best choice of personal computer for business applications. This model features a tower design in which the disk drives are in a unit separate from the monitor.

puter do most of your clients use? There are software programs that allow you to transfer data between the two platforms, but this is not always easy. So, in the absence of other, more important considerations, using the same type of computer as the people you do business with is probably an advantage.

Another factor is the type of software you will be using. If your business requires a specific program or programs, then of course you will want to buy a system that runs that software.

Now that the biggest decision is made, you can concentrate on such things as speed, performance, and capability. The following are just general guidelines—the numbers change so quickly that it is almost impossible to give specifics in a book like this. To tap into current information, consult some of the hundreds of available magazines on the subject. *PC World*, *MacWorld*, *PC Computing*, *Byte*, and *Home Office Computing* are good sources. Or ask for advice from a knowledgeable colleague or friend who understands your needs.

INSIDE THE BOX

The real workings of the computer are inside the box or tower. The central processing unit (CPU) or microprocessor is the most vital chip on the motherboard and is one of the main components controlling the speed of your computer. Don't try to save money here. Buy the fastest you can afford. Today's fastest chips, the Pentium and the PowerPC, continue to get faster all the time. The CPU can usually be upgraded when and if you need it.

Random access memory, or RAM, is the place where data and programs are stored when your computer is turned on. This is where you work, and information contained here is safe only as long as the com-

RIGHT: Floppy disks are the most common removable storage devices. Proper storage will keep them safe from dirt and dust.

puter is running. Anything you wish to keep permanently must be stored to disk. Today's software uses huge amounts of RAM; 16 megabytes (MB) is standard, but 32 MB is better. Installing extra RAM is fairly easy and prices are dropping all the time, but it is still less expensive to purchase more RAM when you buy the computer.

The hard disk drive is located deep within your computer, so you never see it. This is where data and software are stored permanently. Again, bigger is better; 3 to 5 gigabytes (GB) is recommended. Although

ABOVE: A tape drive is simple to install and use. This device is an inexpensive way to ensure that you have backups of your hard disk's contents.

it is possible to add an external hard disk or a second hard disk—if there is room inside your computer—or to upgrade your hard disk for more storage space, it is easier and cheaper to buy more at the start.

Floppy disks are the most common removable storage devices. They are usually inserted into a slot in the front of the computer. These disks (only the part inside the case is really floppy) come in two sizes, 5.25 inches in diameter and 3.5 inches in diameter, although the larger size is now nearly obsolete. They are used to ship new programs and to back up the files that are on your hard disk.

CD-ROM (Compact Disc, Read-Only Memory) drives can be either internal or external. As the name implies, these discs, which look just like audio CDs, are used to store information—pictures and sound as well as text. Most software is now shipped on CD-ROM, which is a real advantage. Because they can store huge amounts of information, you only need to insert the one CD when loading a new program instead of a number of diskettes. Their

large capacity also makes them ideal for reference software such as dictionaries and encyclopedias. The computer reads directly from the CD, so your hard disk isn't filled with information that you use only occasionally. As with all other computer components, these disk drives are getting faster all the time. As a general rule, if the programs you use involve a lot of graphics, you will need a faster CD drive, if you work mainly with text, a slower one may serve you just as well.

BACKUP DEVICES

Even more precious than your computer (it can, after all, be replaced if the house burns down—that's why you have insurance), is the data in it. Depending on your business, your most important assets may be stored on your hard disk. You should take a long hard look at just how much of your work you could afford to lose. Regularly backing up your files can keep lost data to a minimum.

At the very least, you should keep copies of important files on floppy disks, prefer- ably stored off-site. Ideally, though, you should regularly back up your entire hard disk. To do this you need a backup device that will make the whole procedure relatively painless. There are a few different options, recordable CDs (CD-Rs) and optical drives for example, but many experts still consider a tape backup drive to be the best solution. These drives are fairly inexpensive, the entire hard disk can be backed up on one tape, and you can usually set the software to work automatically. Removable cartridge drives are another option; they have the convenience of floppy disks with the speed of a hard drive. New versions of these drives are very affordable.

With a portable computer, you can pack up your office and take it on the road with you. Notebooks weigh between 6½ and 10 pounds (including necessary accessories such as power cords, AC adapters, floppy drives, carrying case); subnotebooks are somewhat smaller. Notebooks can do just about anything a desktop computer can do. They are a lot more expensive, and portable computers are more complicated than desktop models, so be prepared to spend more time choosing one. Evaluate the screen carefully to make sure you can read it in any type of light you may be working in. Try out the keyboard to see if it fits your hands and if you can work with it comfortably; there can be variations in key size, spacing, and placement. Other things to consider are pointing devices, battery life, size and weight of the AC cord, CD-ROM drive, fax and modem add-ons, and weight.

Quite possibly, you don't require all the power that a notebook offers when you travel, but if you need to keep track of

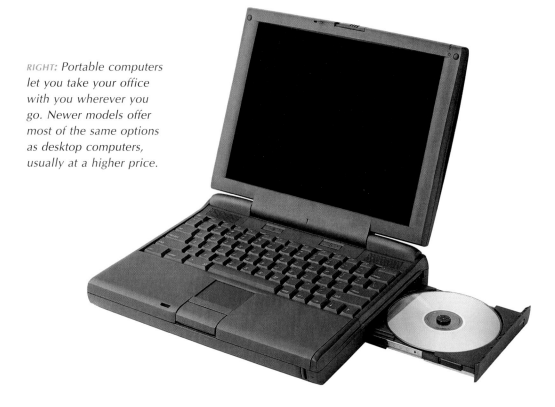

RIGHT: Portable computers let you take your office with you wherever you go. Newer models offer most of the same options as desktop computers, usually at a higher price.

640 BY 480 PIXELS

800 BY 600 PIXELS

1024 BY 768 PIXELS

1280 BY 1024 PIXELS

appointments, send e-mail, and keep your to-do lists up to date, you might consider one of the new generation of personal digital assistants (PDAs), also called organizers, palmtops, and handheld PCs (HPCs). Some of these pocket-size computers can handle a variety of business applications including word processing and spreadsheets, and can even connect to the Internet. When you get back home, data can be transferred from your PDA to your desktop computer using a special serial cable and connectivity software. They work on AA or AAA batteries and most have optional AC adapters.

MONITORS

Monitors come in a very wide range of prices. As with everything else, you get what you pay for. Here are some of the factors that affect the prices of monitors:

Screen sizes range from 13 to 21 inches (measured diagonally), with 14 to 15 inches being the standard. Prices are scaled

accordingly. If you do a lot of graphics or desktop publishing, a larger screen will allow you to see the details clearly.

Picture quality is an important consideration if you spend hours each day staring at your monitor. There are several factors that determine the quality of the picture. The image on the screen is made up of dots and space. Dot pitch refers to the space—measured in millimeters—between the dots on the screen. The more space, the less dots, and the poorer the quality of the picture. Don't buy any monitor with a dot pitch over .28 mm.

Without getting too technical, a "fast refresh rate" means the screen will flicker less, which is easier on your eyes. The minimum acceptable refresh rate is 70 Hz. While we're on the subject of flickering, a "noninterlaced" monitor has a more stable image than an "interlaced" one; it is also more expensive but, again, it's worth it.

Resolution is the number of horizontal pixels by the number of vertical pixels. The higher the resolution, the more objects you see on screen. But more is not necessarily better. Since the screen size remains the same, what you see is correspondingly smaller. On a small monitor, high resolution may make text unreadable. Generally, a resolution of 800 by 600 is the most you'll want on a 14- or 15-inch screen.

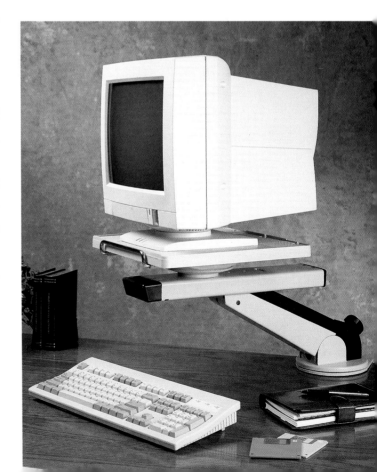

BELOW: Ergonomic keyboards are designed to fit your hands' natural positioning. By reducing strain on your hands, wrists, and forearms, they can help prevent repetitive stress injuries such as carpal tunnel syndrome.

Most monitors allow you to adjust brightness and contrast, but there should also be controls to allow you to change the picture height and width and to move the picture vertically and horizontally. Other controls allow you to correct distortions in the picture. All the knobs and buttons should be front-mounted so that they are easy to reach.

No matter how much care you have taken when choosing a monitor, long hours in front of it are bound to take a toll. To

LEFT: Platforms that let a monitor float above your work surface give you more space on your desktop. Many include a rack for storing the keyboard when it is not in use.

help relieve strain on your neck and shoulders, position the monitor so that the top line of the display is at eye level. There are many devices on the market that allow you to change the position of your monitor—from simple boxes or wedges to adjustable arms. Be kind to your eyes: Use an antiglare filter for your computer and clean the screen regularly. The contrast and brightness should be adjusted to a comfortable level.

For more hints on saving your eyes, see page 95. The jury is still out on the dangers of the radiation your monitor gives off; different studies have come up with conflicting conclusions. To be on the safe side, don't sit any closer to the monitor than you have to, and especially avoid sitting near the sides or back.

INPUT DEVICES

With a typewriter the keyboard was an integral part of the machine; with a computer you have the luxury of finding a keyboard that suits your personal tastes and work habits. Keyboards have different feels.

BELOW: Pressurized air, available in aerosol-spray cans, will blow dust, lint, and other debris out from under the keys of a computer keyboard.

Some have a crisp, sharp feel while others are soft and mushy. Visit a computer store and try out several models. What does the keyboard sound like? Oddly enough, many people dislike a silent keyboard; a slight clicking sound provides satisfactory feedback, particularly for individuals who are used to the sounds of a typewriter.

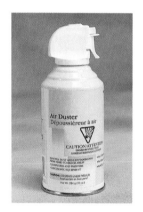

The layout of the keyboard can vary, also. The most common is the "QWERTY" layout, which was developed to prevent key jams on typewriters. If you were trained or learned to type on a typewriter, this is the layout you are familiar with. The "DVORAK" layout places the most frequently used letters on the home row to minimize finger movement. If you like this arrangement, you can buy a specially designed keyboard, or you can use software to make the changes and then relabel the keys yourself.

There can be other variations to keyboard layout, for example, large L-shaped enter keys, a thumb-activated backspace key, or a Delete key that is double the width of other keys. Some keyboards even allow you to swap keys to suit your personal taste. And then there are keyboards with input devices, such as a trackball, mouse, or touchpad built right in. Choosing the right keyboard will improve productivity, and can also help to prevent painful repetitive stress injuries.

CLEANING THE KEYBOARD

Keep your keyboard clean. An accumulation of dirt under the keys can interfere with the mechanisms. If your keys are sticking or otherwise not responding properly, turn the computer off, disconnect the keyboard, turn it upside down and shake it. Buy a can of pressurized air from an office supply store and use it to blow the dust out from under the keys. If the keys look dirty, again, unplug the keyboard and use a cloth dampened with water or glass cleaner (make sure it is damp, not wet) to wipe the keys. Let them dry completely before reconnecting the keyboard.

The best way to avoid spilling anything on your keyboard is never to eat or drink near your computer. If you do spill something, unplug the keyboard immediately, drain it, and wait until it is completely dry before plugging it back in.

Cover your keyboard when it is not in use. A simple clean cloth is adequate, or buy a plastic keyboard cover from an office supply store.

POINTING DEVICES

These days all personal computers come equipped with a mouse. A Macintosh won't work without one, and the same is almost as true for most applications run under Microsoft Windows on a PC. The Mac mouse has one button; a PC mouse usually has two buttons, although it can have three. As the mouse moves and its buttons are clicked, it generates signals that are sent to the computer. The software driver that came with the mouse then interprets these signals so the computer knows how to respond. Depending on your point of view, a mouse either simplifies life by eliminating the need to memorize key functions or complicates it unnecessarily by interrupting your typing pattern and slowing you down every time you have to reach for the mechanical rodent. As with everything else, try out a few in the store to see how they feel and how much pressure is needed to click the buttons.

ABOVE: This handy storage device will keep a computer mouse from getting in the way when it isn't being used.

Repetitive stress injuries (RSI) are common among office workers. Carpal tunnel syndrome (CTS), in particular, is a very real danger for computer keyboard users. Repetitive motions of the hands and fingers cause the flexor tendons to rub against the sides of the tunnel made by the wrist bones and the transverse carpal ligament, irritating the tendons and causing them to swell. Symptoms include tingling or numbness in the hand, sharp pains shooting up the arm from the wrist (especially at night), burning sensation in the fingers, and inability to grasp objects firmly or to make a fist. If you suffer from any of these symptoms, don't ignore them. With early detection and treatment, CTS need not be debilitating. Even more important, with proper work habits you need never suffer. The following advice will help you avoid such problems.

■ Your seat and work surface should be at the proper height *(see pages 108-109).*

■ Keep your wrists in a neutral position (forearms, wrists, and hands in a straight line), if your keyboard is so thick that you have to bend your wrists upward to reach the keys, invest in a padded wrist rest.

■ Never rest elbow, forearm, or wrist on a hard surface.

■ Use minimum force to strike the keys.

■ Alternate between activities during the day; you should take a 10-minute break from keyboarding every hour or so.

■ Check out an ergonomic keyboard *(see page 179).* These strange-looking boards are designed to reduce the strain on hands and wrists. See if one works for you.

Mouse problems

A mouse or trackball can also cause RSIs. To minimize the damage, follow these pointers:

■ Keep the mouse at the same level as your keyboard, and keep your wrist in a neutral position.

■ Don't grip the mouse too tightly.

■ Move the mouse from the shoulder, don't make your wrist do all the work.

■ Don't click too forcefully.

Desktop workout

Simple stretches can help improve circulation. Here are a couple of exercises that can help hands and arms recover from long periods at the keyboard:

■ Make a fist and hold for a couple of seconds; then, stretch out your fingers and hold for five seconds. Do several repetitions.

■ Stretch your arms out in front of you and raise and lower your wrists 5 to 10 times.

■ Squeeze a tennis ball.

If you have any of the symptoms of carpal tunnel syndrome, consult a doctor.

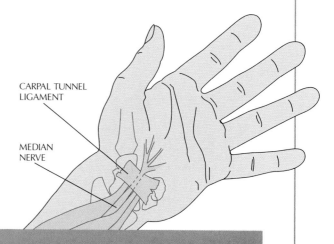

CARPAL TUNNEL
LIGAMENT

MEDIAN
NERVE

Carpal tunnel syndrome is caused by compression of the median nerve in the tunnel formed by the bones of the wrist. If present, this painful condition should be treated immediately to avoid permanent problems.

Your mouse will work better if it is clean: Close open files, turn the mouse upside down and remove the plate over the ball. Gently wipe the rollers with a cotton swab dipped in alcohol. Wash the ball with soapy water—never an alcohol- or ammonia-base cleaner—and dry it well before reassembling. Using a mouse pad helps reduce the accumulation of dirt and dust on the roller.

A trackball is like an upside-down mouse. However, because the device stays put and you roll the little ball with your fingers, it requires less space on your work surface for its operation. With a touchpad you move the cursor by sliding your fingertip across the surface of the pad. Tapping on the pad has the same effect as clicking the buttons on a mouse.

ABOVE: This printer/fax/copier/scanner is one of a new breed of machines developed especially for small offices. They save space and make it possible to set up an office in any corner of a home.

SCANNERS

A scanner is a device that allows you turn whole pages of text or pictures into digital images that can be stored on your computer's hard disk. Sounds great if you have mountains of text that you want to enter in a hurry, but there is a catch. Scanners enter the text as a graphic image that thereafter can't be edited by your word processor. If you are scanning text that you will want to edit, you will need an optical character recognition (OCR) program that converts the graphic image back into text your word processor can recognize. This is not an easy thing to do. Think how similar "o," "e," and "c" look. Before you buy, check out the OCR's accuracy rate by having a salesperson demonstrate how the scanner works with the sort of document you will actually be scanning.

There are three main types of scanner. Handheld scanners are moved over the document's surface manually. They cover only a few inches at a time, so you would have to make two or three passes to scan an average-size page. To make them work properly, you need a steady hand. With a sheet-fed scanner you feed sheets of paper into the machine. On some models you can detach the scanning head in order to scroll bound material. Flatbed scanners look a bit like photocopiers. They usually give a better quality image, and can handle books and other bound material.

PRINTERS

If you need to share the results of your work with others, chances are you will need a printer. There are three main types of printers: laser printers, ink jets, and dot-matrix printers. Make sure that the printer you choose will work with the rest of your system and your software applications. When comparing the prices of different printers, remember to add in the price of consumables—ink cartridges, ribbons, or toner. A low selling price may not be a bargain if you end up spending much more for supplies than you would for another, slightly more expensive, model. Ask the salesperson about the price of supplies, their availability, and the estimated cost per page.

Laser printers are the most expensive type of printer but they give excellent print quality. The images created by the laser printer are made up of hundreds of tiny dots of toner that are fused to the paper's surface. The resolution determines the quality of the print. Resolution is measured in dots per inch (dpi): the more dots, the less space, and the better the product. These are also the fastest printers.

Ink-jet printers have tiny nozzles in their print heads that print images by squirting dots of ink onto the paper. As with laser printers, higher resolutions deliver better quality images. Ink jets are less expensive than laser printers and quite a bit slower, but the print quality is almost as good. These printers offer an affordable way to

ABOVE: Dot-matrix printers are an attractive option in terms of price, but the quality may not be good enough for your business purposes.

print good quality color pictures, but check the output of a color printer carefully before you buy. Some models create blacks by mixing colors and you may not like the result. Purchase only paper that is recommended for use with an ink jet; the ink will bleed into some papers resulting in fuzzy edges. Cost per page may be higher than for a laser printer.

The least expensive printer is the dot-matrix. These printers produce images by impact. They come with 9-, 18-, or 24-pin

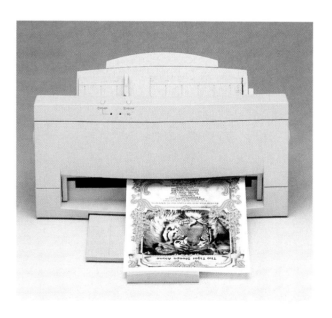

ABOVE: Ink-jet printers deliver high-quality black and white output. They also offer an affordable way to print excellent color pictures. Some models will print on paper, film, transparencies, and fabric.

heads that pound an inked ribbon onto the paper's surface—a very noisy process. Again, the more dots, the clearer the image; however, the result is not nearly as good as even the cheapest ink-jet printer. Although there are dot-matrix printers that claim to produce "near letter quality" (NLQ) results, these are not suitable for business correspondence. They do, however, do two things that the more expensive printers can't handle. Because they are the only printers to print by impact, they are the only printers that can handle multipart forms. They will also print banners on continuous-feed paper.

MODEMS

A modem takes the digital signals from your computer and turns them into audio signals that can be sent over the same lines your telephone uses. This is no longer an optional piece of equipment for the home office. It opens up a world of possibilities since it offers you Internet access and voice and e-mail capabilities. With the right software, a modem allows your computer to

RIGHT: An external modem attaches to a serial port in a computer with a cable. With a modem, one computer can share data, fax, and voice information with many others.

serve as an answering machine. It can also turn your computer into a fax machine. Instead of printing pages onto paper and then sending them through a stand-alone fax, you can transmit them directly from your hard disk to another computer or to a fax machine. Incoming faxes can be viewed before printing them out; and the faxes you do print will last longer than those printed on thermal fax paper.

Modems come in two varieties. An internal modem costs less, but installing it means you will have to open up your computer and play with its insides. You also need to have an empty expansion slot. External modems are more expensive because you are paying for the case and a separate power supply. This type of modem attaches to a serial port in the computer with a cable, and can be easily switched from your desktop computer to your notebook. Some of the newer models feature call display and can double as a speaker phone, even when the computer is off.

Speed is measured in bits per second (bps), and every letter, space, and punc-

tuation mark takes eight bits. Faster modems will save you time and money on long distance and online service charges; 33.6 bps is the minimum you should buy. Modems are designed so that a fast modem can slow down enough to allow it to communicate with a slower one.

MULTIMEDIA

Multimedia takes your computer beyond simple text and graphics and gives it sound and video capabilities. This can be a highly effective way of getting your audience's attention when you make a presentation—and of course games are fun when you have these options.

A growing number of companies are selling complete multimedia computing systems with the sound card, speakers, video card, microphone, and CD-ROM drive included in the package. Many also come with a wide variety of preloaded software applications that include all the extras. If you have an older system, you can either retrofit it yourself with a pre-assembled multimedia kit or have it done for you by a

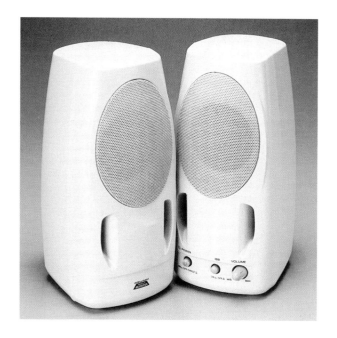

competent technician. Although the components may be purchased separately, they are often more expensive that way, and when buying a kit, you know that the various components that make up the system will work together once installed.

BUYING A COMPUTER

There are several purchase options when buying a new computer. Small stores that specialize in computer sales usually have more knowledgeable personnel. In a smaller store, though, the selection may be limited and prices may be somewhat higher. On the positive side, if you find what you are looking for, you will probably get better ser-

vice and that is worth paying for, especially if you are a computer novice. However, computer stores may be more interested in selling in volume to large companies than selling a single computer to an individual buyer. The only way to find out is to see how they treat you when you visit the store.

Computer superstores have much more variety than small shops and prices are usually quite competitive. There is less service than at a smaller store, but that gives you the chance to wander the aisles and look over the many systems that are available. When you are ready to do business, increase your chances of finding help by shopping during off-peak hours.

Office supply stores are another possibility. These stores are used to catering to small and home business needs. Prices vary, so shop around.

Electronics stores also sell computers, but as part of a wide array of other electronics equipment. Finding knowledgeable sales staff may be difficult, but if you already know what

RIGHT: Microphones enable you to input sound into a computer as digital information, transforming a computer with sound-editing software into a ministudio.

- Only you know what you need to run your business; define your needs clearly and put them in writing. Be sure to include a list of any software you might need for your business.
- Do some research before you go shopping. Salespeople are there to sell their product; if you want an objective opinion read the product reviews in the major computer magazines.
- Find a salesperson who is willing to answer your questions. If the first person you speak to can't give you the information you need, find someone else or go to another store.
- Don't attempt to get the "ultimate" computer. Whatever model you choose, there will be something bigger, better, and faster out next week, and it will cost less, too. Select something that will serve your needs for the next two to five years and accept the fact that it will eventually be necessary to upgrade. Remember: a computer purchase is a business deduction for tax purposes.
- Don't forget the old saying, "If it sounds too good to be true, it probably is." Everyone wants to get a good deal, but prices that are dramatically lower than those of the competition may mean something's wrong with the computer or the company.
- Ask about technical support. Who provides it? What is the availability? Is there any charge?
- If something goes wrong with the system, who will service it and where?
- Will the repairperson come to you or will you have to take the computer in? Must you keep the original packaging?
- Take a close look at the warranties. Who is covering service, the manufacturer or the retailer? Are you buying an extended service program? What does it cover and for how long? Is this already covered by the manufacturer's warranty?
- Do you have all the manuals for all the system's components?
- Negotiate. You can usually get something for the price of asking.

you need, this option may be the answer for you, and prices are usually good.

Although mail-order houses often offer very attractive prices, this is not necessarily so. Check prices carefully before you buy. If you choose to go this route, ask about servicing arrangements when and if something goes wrong with the computer. Can it be serviced locally, or will you have to send it back to the manufacturer? Ask about the company's return policy. Do they charge a "re-stocking" fee for returned merchandise?

Clones or locally assembled systems are another way to go. These are systems put together by small local companies and they are made up of the same quality components as many of the brand-name systems. They are usually less expensive because the smaller company has less overhead. One argument against buying this sort of system is the absence of the around-the-clock technical support that you have at your fingertips with a large company. You may find, though, that the personalized attention you do receive during business hours is worth the wait. Look for a well-established company and make sure that it has a good reputation.

LEASING YOUR COMPUTER

Many home businesses decide to lease their computers instead of buying them outright. The first step involves choosing your system at a store or from a mail-order house. Then you set the terms of the lease either directly with the retailer or with a leasing company. The company will buy your system and then you pay them back—plus interest. In the end you will have paid quite a bit more than the original purchase price of the computer and at the end of the lease you will own nothing. In order to keep the computer, you will have to pay the leasing company an additional amount, which is typically the "fair market value" of your equipment.

Leasing does makes sense if you need a new system but don't want to tie up your cash or lines of credit, or get a bank loan to finance your purchase. There could also be tax advantages to this arrangement.

There are various kinds of power problems that can affect your computer's performance or even destroy it. Here are some of the bad things that can happen to good computers:

■ **Blackout:** total loss of power that can be caused by lightning storms, excessive demand on the power grid, or various kinds of damage to the power lines. A blackout will cause the loss of current work and may even cause the hard disk to crash, resulting in the loss of the file allocation table and all the data on the disk drive.

■ **Spike:** an instantaneous, dramatic increase in voltage that can be caused by lightning or when power is restored after a problem on the line. A spike can damage or completely destroy hardware.

■ **Surge:** a short-term increase in voltage usually lasting a fraction of a second when nearby high-powered electrical motors switch off and the extra energy is dissipated through the power lines. Prolonged multiple stressing can cause premature failure of the chips.

■ **Sags or brownouts:** short-term decreases in voltage levels caused by the start-up demands of other electrical devices. Deprives the computer of power and can cause the keyboard to freeze or the system to crash unexpectedly, resulting in lost or corrupted data.

■ **Electro-Magnetic Interference (EMI) or noise:** electrical noise can be caused by generators, radio transmitters, mechanical ringer phones, lightning, and other factors. It can introduce errors into executable programs and data files.

What you can do

Protect your system and your data by investing in a power strip with surge suppression. Underwriters Laboratories specification 1449 gauges the maximum surge power that the suppressor will let through to your equipment. Choose a surge suppressor with a UL 1449 rating of 330 volts. If there are a lot of electrical storms in your area, you may want a suppressor that allows you to plug in your phone to protect your phone lines against surges. Some suppressors also indicate when the wiring in your office is faulty. This should be corrected by a qualified electrician as faulty wiring can stop the suppressor from working properly.

Surge suppressors wear out like everything else; look for one that indicates when it is no longer performing adequately. To be on the safe side, buy one from a company that promises to pay for repairs or replacement of equipment damaged while plugged into its suppressor. An uninterruptible power supply offers added protection against power problems *(page 71)*.

Surge suppressors protect sensitive equipment and data from all kinds of electrical problems; invest in a good one. The model shown at left also serves telephone lines.

SOFTWARE SELECTION

Without software a computer is little more than a glorified typewriter wired to a video screen. Most computers come with basic pre-installed software programs—an operating system, for example—that are automatically loaded into the computer's memory when the disk drive is switched on. These programs prepare the computer so that you can load in other software programs that will enable you to write letters and proposals, publish newsletters, print graphs and pie charts, send e-mail, or balance your books.

When you buy a new computer system, some of these word processing, graphics, communications, and accounting programs may be bundled (or included) with the hardware. In some cases, the programs may suit your needs exactly. However, depending on the nature of your business, you may need more specialized packages, or ones with more features and capabilities than the software that comes with the computer. In such a case, you will need to purchase separate software packages. Some programs can run to several hundred dollars, so it's worth determining precisely what you need before buying.

Consider software with secure password protection if your computer files will contain confidential information.

WORD PROCESSING SOFTWARE

Word processors are the most commonly used type of software. Whatever business you are in, chances are you will be writing letters or putting together proposals or reports for clients. Word processing software packages range from the extremely simple to the very complex, and are priced accordingly. Even the simplest ones will offer some basic editing and formatting features that allow you to center, indent, boldface, and underline text, move text around in a document, change text by inserting or deleting, and set such things as margins, tabs, line lengths, and number of lines per page. With more sophisticated programs, you have all the tools you need to turn out a variety of professional-looking documents. These features typically include the choice of several fonts, or type styles—even within the same document. You can also usually produce documents in outline form or insert page breaks at any point.

Most programs are shipped ready to use. The default settings allow you to start working without having to worry about setting margins and tabs or choosing a typeface. But you don't have to stop there. Almost anything can be changed to suit your needs or whims. Text can be centered on the page or justified to the left or right. With justified text, the ends of lines in a column of text align vertically, rather than being ragged—as would be the case with a typewriter. The program achieves this by automatically adjusting the spacing left between words and letters.

You can also use double or single line spacing. Add emphasis with boldface, italics, or underlining. Use columns to enhance readability of newsletters. Change the size of the type or change the font. Making these changes is easy. With most programs, none of these operations takes more than a couple of keystrokes or clicks.

Here are some other features offered by all better-quality word processors:

■ Typically, text can be moved or copied simply by selecting or highlighting it, placing the cursor at the point in the document where you wish to insert the text, then pasting the text into place with the appropriate command. In most cases, you can be working on two documents at the same time, and move text from one document to the other.

■ You can add headers or footers to documents. Page numbers can be centered or placed on the right or left, top or bottom, or suppressed altogether.

■ The footnote feature automatically numbers footnotes and keeps track of any changes you make to them so the final arrangement is correct.

■ The search and replace feature can be used to automatically find and replace one, several, or every occurrence of a word or phrase in a document that needs to be changed. In most cases, the search can be initiated from any point in a document and can proceed either forward or backward.

- Most programs allow you to insert graphics and tables into a document.

- The built-in thesaurus can enhance your vocabulary and save time looking up words in the printed version of this writing tool.

- The spell checker will help catch typos as well as genuine spelling mistakes. However, it won't point out incorrectly used homonyms—"there" instead of "their," for example—so relying on a spell checker is not a substitute for proofreading. These tools can usually be used in one of two ways: You can either set up a spell checker so that the computer will immediately emit a sound when you make a typing mistake; or, you can run it when you have finished a document—the spell checker will review the document from beginning to end and point out the typos. A good spell checker can be customized. It is useful to be able to add uncommon words you use regularly—proper names, for instance—into the spell checker's inventory.

- Grammar checkers are available, but they still have a long way to go before they will be useful.

- Most word processing programs allow you to save time and keystrokes with tools known as macros. A macro allows you to record into memory a series of commands, or text and commands, that you can then recall as needed with one or two keystrokes, saving you from having to key in the entire series each time you need to insert it into a document. Use macros to enter items such as letter closings, frequently used headings, and anything else you type on a regular basis.

- People who regularly write longer documents will find the outline feature a real help in organizing their thoughts. Headings and subheadings are automatically numbered or tabbed as you enter them. And they are automatically renumbered or retabbed if you change them around. The outline can be used to create a table of contents for the finished document.

- A preview feature or layout view lets you see your document in its finished form before you print it so that you can fix any formatting errors, add page breaks, or add or subtract text.

BELOW: Most word processing programs make it easy to produce outlines like this one. A single mouse click automatically assigns a unique tab position and font to each level of information, organizing them into a neat hierarchy.

TITLE LINE

FIRST MAIN TOPIC
ITEM 1
ITEM 2
ITEM 3
ITEM 4
ITEM 5

SECOND MAIN TOPIC
ITEM 1
ITEM 2
SUB-ITEM 1
SUB-ITEM 2
ITEM 3
ITEM 4

THIRD MAIN TOPIC
ITEM 1
SUB-ITEM 1
SUB-ITEM 2
ITEM 2
SUB-ITEM 1
SUB-ITEM 2
SUB-ITEM 3
ITEM 3
SUB-ITEM 1
SUB-ITEM 2
SUB-ITEM 3
SUB-ITEM 4

FOURTH MAIN TOPIC
ITEM 1
ITEM 2
SUB-ITEM 1
SUB-ITEM 2
POINT A
POINT B
POINT C
ITEM 3
ITEM 4
ITEM 5
ITEM 6

FIFTH MAIN TOPIC
ITEM 1
SUB-ITEM 1
SUB-ITEM 2
ITEM 2

SIXTH MAIN TOPIC
ITEM 1
ITEM 2
ITEM 3
SUB-ITEM 1
SUB-ITEM 2
POINT A
POINT B
POINT C
SUB-ITEM 3

CONCLUSION

BELOW: This page from a recipe booklet is just one example of how text and photographs can be brought together in a custom-made layout using a desktop publishing program.

SALSIFY

Salsify is an autumn root vegetable, often called the "oyster plant" because of its taste. Its long, thin shape is similar to the parsnip. There are two kinds of salsify; true salsify is whitish and thick, with rootlets, while black salsify is longer, lacks rootlets, and is more tapered. When choosing salsify, look for ones which are firm, unblemished, and heavy for their size. Black salsify is the easier one to peel; use a vegetable peeler and treat it like a carrot. It's best to wear gloves and peel them under cold running water because the raw flesh is very sticky and, unless you work very quickly, it will stain your skin.

RACK OF PORK WITH ROASTED GARLIC AND SALSIFY

Garlic becomes so sweet and tender when roasted slowly as in this recipe that it makes a surprisingly delicious—though still quite fragrant—spread.

Preparation Time: 20 minutes
Cooking Time: 2 hours

1 rack of pork (with at least 1 chop per person, about 4 ½ pounds)
Salt & freshly ground black pepper
3 medium carrots, peeled and diced
2 ribs celery with leaves, diced
3 large heads of garlic, halved horizontally
1 large onion, quartered
3 tablespoons olive oil
1 cup fresh sage, plus some leaves for garnish

2 cups apple juice
2 tablespoons apple jelly
1 teaspoon Chinese mustard
12 black salsifies, peeled, rinsed, and cut in 2-inch pieces
Juice of 1 lemon

1. Preheat oven to 425°F.
2. Season the pork with salt and pepper. Place carrots and celery in a large roasting pan and lay the pork on top. Surround with the garlic and onions. Brush the pork and vegetables generously with olive oil and scatter the sage leaves on top. Roast for 10 minutes.
3. Reduce heat to 350°F and cover loosely with foil, shiny side down. Continue to roast for 1 hour and

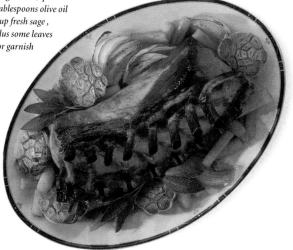

20

DESKTOP PUBLISHING

Desktop publishing software allows you to combine text from your word processing package with illustrations, charts, graphs, and photographs to create the complex layouts necessary for professional-looking newsletters, reports, brochures, manuals, and books. All desktop publishing software enables you to manipulate graphics and text, and gives you precise typographic control over the textual elements. These programs also feature indexing and cross-referencing features superior to those you'll find in most word processing programs. The more expensive, high-end professional page-layout packages will allow you to produce some very sophisticated designs and handle book-length publishing projects, but to get the best results from these programs, you will need to have your documents printed professionally. Unless desktop publishing is a significant part of what you do each day, you can probably manage quite well with one of the low-end programs. They are a bit easier to learn and much less expensive.

PRESENTATION SOFTWARE

If your business involves presenting concepts or products in front of groups of potential clients, presentation software can be a worthwhile investment. This variety of software will help you create visual displays that your audience will remember long after you have stopped speaking. Whether you want to put together a few simple graphs or charts or present a full-scale multimedia show, you can find a program that will help you pull it off.

Presentation software programs come with sets of predesigned slides that allow you to coordinate color schemes, backgrounds, fonts, and layouts—you simply substitute your material for the placeholders. Customize your slides by adding your company logo, or add your choice of graphics, animations, video, and sound effects. Even if you can't draw a straight line, you can produce creative results with most of these programs. Packages typically come with a selection of clip art. For a truly stunning on-screen presentation, many programs can combine special

BELOW: A bar graph is a striking yet simple way to present information graphically. Presentation software helps you design the visuals, which can then be displayed in a number of ways.

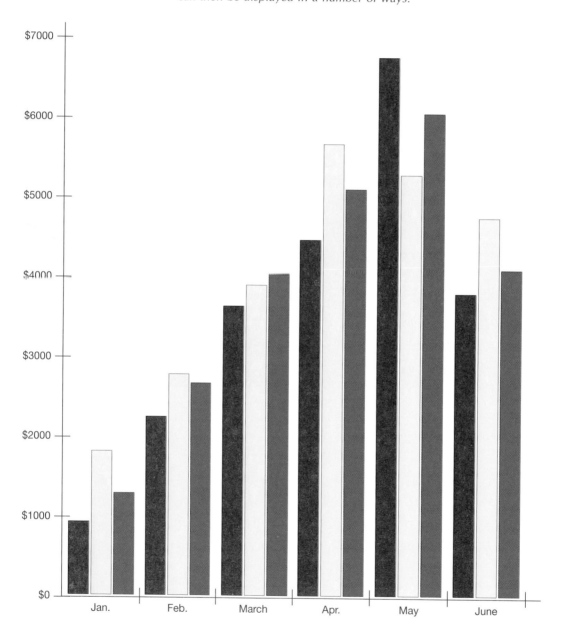

effects such as fades and dissolves to change from one slide to another.

Once you've put your presentation together, you have a choice of several output options: on-screen presentations, color transparencies, flip charts, 35 mm slides, videotape, and recordable CD. You can also prepare audience handouts to remind potential customers of your message after the presentation is over.

GRAPHICS SOFTWARE

Whatever the nature of your business, appearance is important. With graphics software, you have the capability to produce graphs, charts, and illustrations to add visual interest to your printed work. There are two basic types of graphics programs: draw programs and paint programs.

When you create a picture in a draw program, also known as vector graphics, your illustration or drawing is stored on disk as a mathematical formula, which makes it easy to change the size of the image. Altering the geometry of the artwork changes its appearance. This type of program gives illustrators, designers, and other graphics professionals precise control over their creative work.

A paint program is more free-flow. You use different on-screen tools to paint designs on the screen, and the resulting picture is stored on disk as a series of dots. Changing the size or shape of this type of image, called a bit-mapped picture, is more difficult because it is composed of a random collection of dots with no inherent design that the computer can recognize to hold them together.

Before you invest a lot of time and money in either type of software program, check out the graphics capabilities of your word processing, database, and spreadsheet programs—one of them may offer some graphic possibilities for turning numbers into charts.

Clip art is another type of graphics software that provides a simple way to add pizzazz to your work. These are collections of ready-to-use, royalty-free graphics that can be utilized for your publications once you've purchased the program. There are

BELOW: A small selection of the thousands of examples of clip art is shown here. Clip art is ideal for livening up or personalizing business cards, advertising flyers, stationery, memos, or fax cover sheets.

hundreds of collections on the market, and they are available in different resolutions; the packages that contain artwork with lower resolutions are fine for on-screen presen-tations, but higher-resolution packages are better for printed output.

Basically, spreadsheets are the numerical equivalent of word processing programs. These packages will perform a variety of mathematical, statistical, and financial calculations using computerized, on-screen worksheets. Spreadsheets can balance your budget or checkbook, calculate your expenses, or allow you to explore "what if" scenarios for your business.

The typical worksheet is made up of rows that run from side to side and columns that run up and down. Rows are identified by numbers along the worksheet's left edge, and columns are identified by letters across the top edge. The boxes created by the intersection of the columns and rows are called cells. Cells contain either data or formulas. Once you learn how to create formulas, you can use a worksheet to add numbers, calculate sales tax, find the rate of return on an investment, and much more. When you change the information in a cell, the spreadsheet immediately does all the new calculations, saving you hours of work. You can save formulas with the spreadsheet. Most spreadsheets have macros that allow you to automate repetitive operations.

There are formatting tools that let you print worksheets to include in reports. Some software allows you to turn data into graphs and charts.

DATABASES

Database programs or database managers are applications that allow you to store, organize, access, and analyze information. Data is entered into files that organize information in rows and columns. Fields are columns that hold a specific type of information. For example, you can have one field for first names, another for last names, a third for area codes, and so on. The database automatically will file things

BELOW: A wide range of accounting programs is available, from very basic ones designed to help you organize expenses to others that allow more complex calculations and business projections; but all contain the ubiquitous spreadsheet, such as this one.

ANNUAL EXPENSES

	Jan.	Feb.	March	Apr.	May	June	July
PRODUCTION							
Graphic artist	$	$	$	$	$	$	$
Photography	$	$	$	$	$	$	$
Printing	$	$	$	$	$	$	$
Paper	$	$	$	$	$	$	$
subtotal	$	$	$	$	$	$	$
ADMINISTRATION							
Telephone	$	$	$	$	$	$	$
Utilities	$	$	$	$	$	$	$
Maintenance	$	$	$	$	$	$	$
Postage	$	$	$	$	$	$	$
Deliveries	$	$	$	$	$	$	$
subtotal	$	$	$	$	$	$	$
MARKETING							
Travel	$	$	$	$	$	$	$
Promotion	$	$	$	$	$	$	$
Advertising	$	$	$	$	$	$	$
Business cards	$	$	$	$	$	$	$
subtotal	$	$	$	$	$	$	$
TOTAL	$	$	$	$	$	$	$

BELOW: Entering information about clients, business contacts, or even friends in a database provides you with a convenient way to retrieve the information. The sample shown shows typical fields—categories of information—but you can add any to suit your purpose.

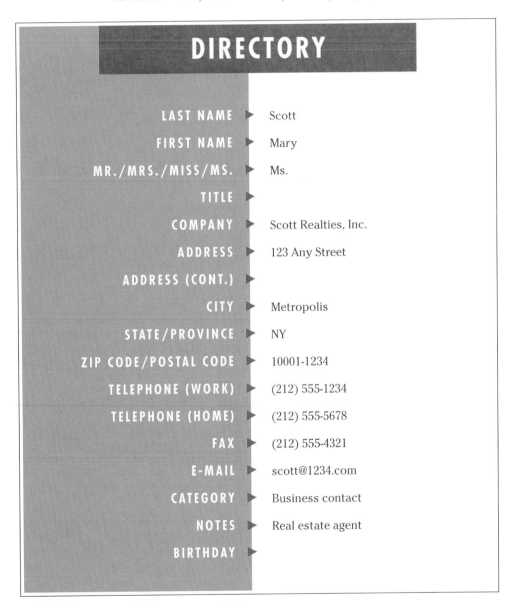

DIRECTORY

LAST NAME ▸	Scott
FIRST NAME ▸	Mary
MR./MRS./MISS/MS. ▸	Ms.
TITLE ▸	
COMPANY ▸	Scott Realties, Inc.
ADDRESS ▸	123 Any Street
ADDRESS (CONT.) ▸	
CITY ▸	Metropolis
STATE/PROVINCE ▸	NY
ZIP CODE/POSTAL CODE ▸	10001-1234
TELEPHONE (WORK) ▸	(212) 555-1234
TELEPHONE (HOME) ▸	(212) 555-5678
FAX ▸	(212) 555-4321
E-MAIL ▸	scott@1234.com
CATEGORY ▸	Business contact
NOTES ▸	Real estate agent
BIRTHDAY ▸	

for you—all you have to do is enter the information and choose the way you want it filed—alphabetically, numerically, or chronologically, for example.

Information can be sorted and viewed in a variety of ways. Form view allows you to see one record—all the information pertaining to one person, place, or thing—at a time. Or, you can access information according to specific needs. For example, you may want to send a mailing to all your customers who own dogs or who live in a specific area; if the appropriate information has been entered into the database, the program can easily enumerate the people who belong on the list.

INTEGRATED SOFTWARE PACKAGES

Integrated software packages combine several different programs, usually a word processor, a database, a spreadsheet, and a communications program. Sometimes, graphics software and other programs are also included. Because these programs are designed to work together, they use the same menus and commands, which makes them much easier to learn. Integrated programs have several other advantages: They allow data to be moved easily from one program to another; they use less disk space than a number of individual programs (an important consideration for a notebook computer, which may not require all the power of a separate program); they are less expensive; and they are often included in the price of a new computer.

None of these programs has all the features of programs that are available separately, but for most needs, they may be more than adequate. If a software package comes with your new computer, check out all of its capabilities before you invest in other programs.

"Suites" are another form of bundled software. Like integrated software packages with four or five different types of software, these are specially priced packages of full-scale programs. You can even buy special versions available for the home office. Purchasing software this way can result in substantial savings over buying programs separately.

UTILITY PROGRAMS

Often sold as collections, utility programs are small programs that assist with disk management and make your work faster and easier. The following are some of the more useful and popular:

Disk defragmenters: When you save a file onto a computer's hard disk, the information is stored in small segments wherever there is room. Data from a single file, especially a large one, may be stored all over the disk. As more and more files are saved and deleted, the more fragmented the data on a hard disk becomes. A fragmented disk can slow down a computer's performance. A defragmenter reconstructs files so that all the data from each one is in the same sector of the disk. This not only helps speed up a computer, but also reduces wear and tear on the hard disk.

Recovery tools: These allow you to retrieve any files that you might have erased by accident.

Backup software: This automatically backs up—or saves to the hard disk—your work as you go.

File encryption: This allows you to set passwords to prevent unauthorized access to your files.

Diagnostic tools: These check for both hardware and software problems.

VOICE-RECOGNITION SOFTWARE

Voice-recognition software is designed to enable the user to talk into a microphone connected to a computer, and issue commands or dictate text instead of pointing and clicking with a mouse or keying in information. Unfortunately, many of these programs don't work very well. With some, a lot of time must be spent "training" the software to recognize the user's speech patterns by reading a set list of words into the microphone. All programs require the user to pause between words, which slows dictation speeds down considerably. Accuracy rates are improving with each new version of these programs; and while they might be too slow for people who are able to type, they can be invaluable for people who must work on a computer despite disabilities that leave them unable to type.

OFFICE MACHINES AND SUPPLIES

PHOTOCOPIERS

If you find yourself frequently interrupting your workday with side trips to the local photocopy shop, it might be time to consider getting your own copier. Most major manufacturers of this equipment offer a line of machines especially designed for the small or home office. Features vary depending on the model, so it is vitally important to shop around and compare the various offerings in your price range. Remember, price is not always an accurate indication of what you are getting for the money.

Most copiers in the small- or home-office category can make reductions or enlargements, but very few have automatic sheet feeders. For trouble-free copying, shop for a machine that has multilevel contrast controls, power-saver settings, toner-saver modes, and that has reliable technical support and service. Not all models make copies at the same speed, but in most cases, performance is in the range of 8 to 12 pages per minute.

If your copy needs are very modest, you might be happy with an entry-level personal copier. But bear in mind that these small table-top machines have relatively slow copy speeds and generally only produce copies that measure $8\frac{1}{2}$ by 11 inches.

Here are a few additional points to consider when looking for a photocopier:

How often does the toner cartridge have to be changed? How is toner added? What settings and features can be adjusted without a service call? What is the maximum size original the copier can handle? How is the machine cleaned and maintained? Can the machine handle duplex copying

RIGHT: Multifunctional units consist of a fax machine, printer, scanner, and copier all rolled into one machine. These are ideal in offices where space is at a premium.

(copying on both sides of the sheet without transferring toner to the machine's mechanisms)? How much will consumables such as paper and toner cost?

FAX MACHINES

Late-model personal computers are generally equipped with a fax-modem that will allow you to transmit text files directly from the computer over a phone line to another computer or to a fax machine. If your system lacks this feature, you can hook up an external fax-modem to the computer and send faxes through it. Some of these external models have voice-mail capabilities, and so do double duty as phone answering machines. Even if you can send a fax from your computer, there are bound to be times when you need to transmit papers directly; for this, you will need a conventional fax machine.

There are two basic types: thermal fax machines and plain-paper fax models. Thermal fax machines cost less and generally are less expensive to maintain. There is no need to buy replacement ink cartridges because these machines use heat to print words and images on the paper. However, thermal paper is not designed for long-term storage: Light and heat can cause it to darken, and even under the best of circumstances, the print will fade.

Plain-paper fax machines not only cost more to buy, but they also cost more to run. These machines may be worth the investment, though. Plain paper is easier to read from, and faxes printed on it can be filed away for lengthy periods of time without worrying that the ink will fade. These machines can double as photocopiers if your copying needs are very modest. When comparing models, be sure to investigate the price of the ink cartridge each machine uses.

Here are some features to consider when shopping for a fax machine:

- Out-of-paper reception. This feature

BELOW: *Paper shredders help you dispose of sensitive papers without worrying about breaches of confidentiality.*

stores an incoming message in its memory in case the machine runs out of paper before the end of the incoming transmission. The rest of the fax can then be printed once the paper is restocked.

• A document feeder handles your original document automatically so you don't have to stand at the machine putting the pages in one at a time.

• An auto-redial feature will redial a busy line until it makes a connection.

• If you are considering a thermal fax machine, check that it has a paper cutter. This feature cuts each page off the roll of paper as it is printed out.

MULTIFUNCTION MACHINES

Many manufacturers are now producing machines that perform a variety of tasks that used to require several separate pieces of equipment. Multifunction units contain printers, copiers, fax machines and scanners, all in one. Compared to stand-alone machines that perform the same functions these machines can represent significant savings in both money and space. Before

purchasing a multifunction unit, check it out carefully to be certain that its level of quality is the same as that of individual machines. Also, consider what you would do if one component broke down. Let's say your scanner stopped working. How long could you operate without your printer and fax while the scanner was being serviced?

PAPER SHREDDERS

Until the paperless office becomes a reality, disposing of unwanted paper will remain a concern. For many businesses, putting documents such as business records, canceled checks, and credit card records out with the garbage, or in a recycling bin, could lead to a breach of confidentiality. A paper shredder is a simple, economical solution to this problem.

There are both straight-cut and cross-cut shredders, and machines in each category come in a wide variety of sizes and

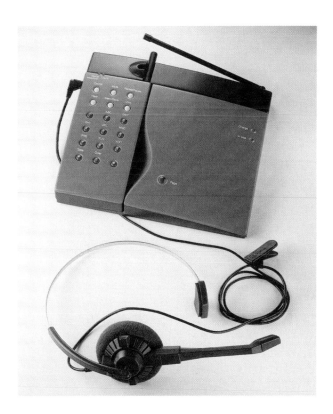

with a range of capabilities. Some models stand alone; others fit over the top of a wastebasket. When selecting a shredder, keep in mind the volume and type of paper you will need to dispose of. Features to consider include an automatic on/off switch, a reverse switch, and a safety cut-off. Also find out whether the machine can handle staples; what size shreds it produces; how easy it is to empty; and how many pages it can handle at once.

TELEPHONES

While many office machines are specialized and may be optional for your business, the telephone is arguably the one indispensable device every office—home or otherwise—will need. Today's telephones come with a wide variety of options, and many of these features can greatly simplify the operation of a home office.

If you spend many hours on the phone each day, or need to use your hands for other tasks while you are speaking over the phone, a hands-free telephone can be a real plus. Speaker-phones—devices that allow you to carry on a phone conversation a few feet away from the receiver—give you freedom of movement, but they compromise privacy, and sound quality with most models can be poor. Many phone units offer a hands-free or speaker-phone feature that is activated by the touch of a button. Generally, a speaker phone is best reserved for calls in which one end of a conversation involves a group of people. For one-on-one hands-free conversations, a headset is a better choice.

Both hard-wired and remote headsets are available. Hard-wired models are attached to a unit you can leave on a desk, while a remote headset is operated by a battery-powered receiver that clips to your belt. If you choose a hard-wired headset, make sure the wire is long enough to allow you to move easily around your office.

A cordless phone is another handy item for the home office. With this device, you can move easily from room to room and never miss an important business call.

If your business involves a lot of traveling, you may want to invest in a cellular phone so that you can stay in touch while you are on the go. Although there were problems with reliability and call security with the first generation of portable phones, the newest models employ digital technology that offers greater security, longer battery life, and other convenient features. Models and services vary widely, so discuss your needs carefully with your service provider before signing a contract.

A pager or beeper is a much less expensive way to keep yourself available. Various types are available for sale or rent. Some models signal the user with a silent vibration rather than a loud buzz. Others can display the number you should call, or even a short message.

TELEPHONE-ANSWERING DEVICES

A telephone-answering device (TAD) records phone messages for you when you are not in the office. A TAD can be a separate machine or a built-in component of your telephone; some external fax-modems that connect to computers have TAD capabilities. As well as recording messages,

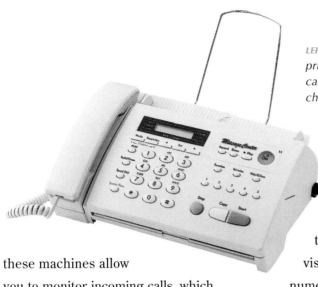

LEFT: *This telephone comprises a ring selector and can function as a fax machine, copier, and printer.*

these machines allow you to monitor incoming calls, which can be a plus for the home worker who wants to avoid taking personal calls during office hours. Some TADs also keep track of the time your calls came in. A remote access feature is handy, as it enables you to pick up messages when you are away from your office.

RING SELECTORS

If you use the distinctive-ring service offered by many phone companies *(page 223)*, you will need a ring selector. This device ensures that only the selected ringing sequence passes to the phone to which it is connected.

CALCULATORS

Whatever the type of calculations you need to make, there is a calculator on the market designed to help you figure it out. You can buy specialized scientific and business calculators—some models even feature graph functions that provide you with a visual representation of the numerical results. Pocket-size calculators and desktop models are also available. Some models run on batteries, others are solar-powered, and still others come with an AC cord. Certain calculators, both desktop and handheld, can print out the results of your calculations.

When choosing a calculator, make sure that the buttons are large enough for you to use comfortably and that you can clearly see the numbers on the display screen. If you need a calculator that produces a printout, compare the prices of consumables such as paper and ink before deciding which model to buy.

LABEL PRINTERS

Labels are used to identify files, personal property, video and audio tapes, and various other items. Many businesses use labels when addressing parcels and envelopes. Labels can often be prepared on a computer or typewriter, but if you use labels frequently, it may be faster and more convenient—and more professional-looking—to use a label printer. Some of these printers work alone, whereas others connect to a computer and use special software to produce personalized labels. The more sophisticated machines can print logos, graphics, and bar codes as well as text, and they also can print on different kinds of tape. The number of lines that can be printed for an individual label varies with the printer.

ELECTRONIC ORGANIZERS AND OTHER GADGETS

Personal electronic organizers can help you keep track of appointments, manage expenses, keep your to-do list, and store all your important phone numbers. Most include a calendar and scheduler, and a clock with an alarm. Many organizers also have a built-in calculator. If privacy is a concern, select a model that allows you to choose a password. Anyone who uses the device will then have to key in the password to access the data.

Other electronic gadgets that streamline the operation of a home office include: spell checkers; thesauruses to improve your vocabulary; dictionaries to check the meaning of unknown words; speaking dictionaries that will also give you correct pronunciation; and foreign language dictionaries and translators. These products vary in quality, usefulness, and price, so check them out carefully before buying. Some word-processing programs include spellers, dictionaries, and thesauruses.

OFFICE SUPPLIES

For an office to run efficiently, you need to have ample amounts of basic supplies on hand. Buying in quantity saves both money and the aggravation of having to go shopping in the middle of the workday

START-UP SUPPLIES

Although individual needs vary depending on the business, here is a list of items you will probably need on your desktop:

- Calendar
- Clock
- Copy holder
- Date stamp
- File rack for current files
- In tray and out tray
- Ink pad
- Letter opener
- Pencil sharpener
- Rolodex or address book
- Ruler
- Scissors
- Stapler and staple remover
- Tape dispenser

You will need a supply of consumables, including the following:

- Business cards
- Business forms—invoices, statements
- Correction fluid
- Diskettes and a box for filing them
- Envelopes—assorted types and sizes, including padded envelopes
- Erasers
- Felt-tip pens
- File folders

- Highlighters, including dry highlighters if you have an ink-jet printer—the wet kind smear printouts
- Index cards
- Ink cartridges for the printer and the plain-paper fax
- Labels—assorted types for file folders and addressing mail
- Markers
- Pads—assorted types and sizes for memos, notes, rough drafts, messages
- Paper—computer or typing paper, copier paper, fax paper, paper for calculators, etc.
- Paper clips—assorted sizes
- Pencils
- Pens
- Post-it™ Notes—including the type specially designed to be attached to a fax instead of a cover page. This saves transmittal time, paper, and possible long distance charges.
- Rubber bands
- Stamps
- Staples
- Stationery
- Toner for photocopier (the correct type for your model)
- Transparent tape

when you run out of something unexpectedly. If your office is short on storage space, keep a week's supply of needed items close by and store the rest elsewhere in the house.

The box on page 213 lists a wide array of desktop accessories. Although few of these items are high-tech, they can make your office life considerably easier. Many of them can be attractive as well as functional, so you will likely find accessories that complement your office decor.

The box also lists the consumables that any business typically requires in order to run smoothly. It's important to maintain a running inventory of the supplies you have on hand, especially if these items are out of sight, stored in areas of the house outside your office. Keep your inventory list close by and remember to check and update it regularly. You should restock whenever you open the last or next-to-last container of each supply.

The items shown at right are more specialized, but might be very useful, depending on the nature of your work.

This in/out basket allows you to keep current files and desktop supplies organized and out of the way.

A punch allows you align perforations with ease. Heavy-duty models can perforate several sheets at a time.

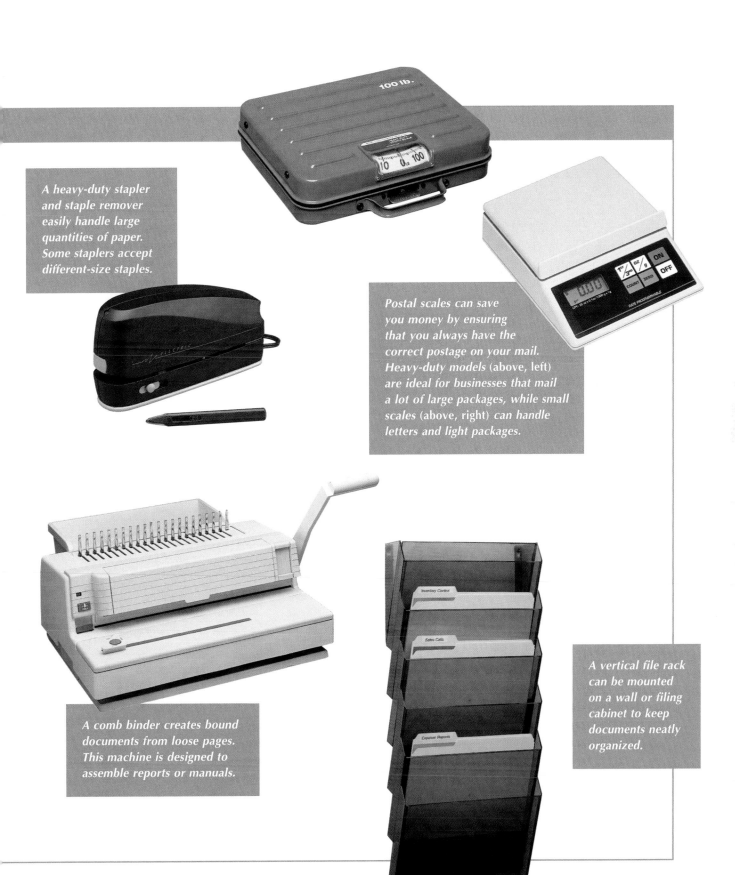

A heavy-duty stapler and staple remover easily handle large quantities of paper. Some staplers accept different-size staples.

Postal scales can save you money by ensuring that you always have the correct postage on your mail. Heavy-duty models (above, left) are ideal for businesses that mail a lot of large packages, while small scales (above, right) can handle letters and light packages.

A comb binder creates bound documents from loose pages. This machine is designed to assemble reports or manuals.

A vertical file rack can be mounted on a wall or filing cabinet to keep documents neatly organized.

BASIC OFFICE
REFERENCE LIBRARY

A dictionary is the one indispensable reference book. Dictionaries not only define words; they help you pronounce and spell them. A good dictionary will give usage examples to clarify definitions, and include added features such as abbreviations, foreign words and phrases, legal and scientific terms, information on weights and measurements, and information on foreign currencies. Foreign language and bilingual dictionaries and specialized dictionaries are also available.

A good general encyclopedia is a handy addition to any library. An encyclopedia offers concise summaries of information on almost any subject. Many encyclopedias are now available on CD-ROM. Some reference works on CD-ROM include an encyclopedia, dictionary, thesaurus, atlas, and almanac all in one package.

Office handbooks offer advice on business practices, language, document formatting, and other subjects. Books on language usage and style are also helpful.

Other reference books that can prove helpful are business directories, atlases, biographical references, financial references, current telephone directories, a ZIP code directory, and a current catalog from your office supply store.

SUGGESTED REFERENCE BOOKS AND SOFTWARE

Dictionaries:
- *Merriam Webster's Collegiate Dictionary, 10th Edition*
- *Webster's New World College Dictionary, 3rd Edition*
- *The American Heritage Dictionary*
- *Random House Dictionary of the English Language*
- *Gage Canadian Dictionary* (Canadian English)

Books on Language and Style:
- *The Merriam-Webster Dictionary of English Usage*
- *Elements of Style*, by William Strunk and E.B. White
- *Chicago Manual of Style*, University of Chicago Press

Encyclopedias:
- *Encyclopedia Americana*
- *Encyclopedia Britannica*
- *Columbia Encyclopedia* (one-volume work)
- *The New York Public Library Desk Reference* (a good source of general information)

Encyclopedias on CD-ROM:
- *Grolier's Encyclopedia*
- *Compton's Encyclopedia*
- *The Microsoft Encarta Encyclopedia*

GLOSSARY OF
COMPUTER TERMS

Application: a software program with a user interface designed to perform a specific function, such as word processing packages, desktop publishing software, spreadsheets, and graphics programs.

ASCII: an acronym for American Standard Code for Information Interchange. The international standard for turning characters into binary code.

Auto answer: a setting that enables modems to answer incoming calls over the telephone network.

Backup: copies of information stored on a hard disk to protect against lost or damaged data. Information can also be backed up on floppy disks or written onto recordable CD-ROMs.

Baud rate: the number of bits a modem can transmit each second; the speed with which a modem is able to receive or transmit information is usually expressed as a baud rate.

Binary: a numerical system used by computers, in which information is represented by combinations of two symbols such as ones and zeros; all data must be changed to binary code before a computer can use it.

Bit: the smallest unit of computer information; the word "bit" is a contraction of "binary digit."

Bit-mapped (fonts or graphics): characters or images stored in a computer as a collection of dots.

BPS: bits per second. The speed at which a modem transmits or receives data.

Bug: a mistake made in producing software that can cause it to fail.

Byte: a sequence of eight bits treated as a unit for computation or storage; the standard unit for measuring disk storage and memory capacity.

CAD: an acronym for Computer-Aided Design.

CD-ROM: an acronym for Compact Disk Read-Only Memory. CD-ROMs can be used for permanent storage of information.

Character: any letter, number, punctuation mark, or symbol.

Clip art: drawings or other images that can be used in a computer document without paying a royalty.

Clock speed: the speed of a computer's CPU; expressed in megahertz.

CPU: acronym for Central Processing Unit, the heart of a computer.

Crash: a serious malfunction that, at the very least, results in the loss of any data not saved to disk. In some cases, a crash can also result in the loss of everything on the hard disk.

CRT: Cathode Ray Tube, a computer monitor's picture tube.

Cursor: the small flashing line or rectangle that indicates the point at which a computer user is located in a document.

Database program: a program that allows the user to store information in fields and records, and to subsequently retrieve it using queries and reports.

Default: factory settings; what a computer does if the user does not choose a different option.

Directory: related files on a hard disk; also called folders.

Disk: a round plate, generally made of plastic, metal, or glass, for storing data either magnetically or optically.

DOS: Disk Operating System, a basic, pre-installed program that prepares a computer for application software.

Dot pitch: a way to measure the sharpness of a computer monitor by indicating the space between the phosphor dots on the display screen.

E-mail: electronic mail that can be transmitted from one computer to another.

Expansion slot: a space inside a computer's casing where expansion cards can be inserted, providing a computer with additional capability (such as sound).

File: the basic unit of stored information.

Function key: one of the keys, usually 12, at the top of the keyboard used to perform specific functions.

Gigabyte: equal to 1,024 megabytes.

Glitch: a minor problem with computer software or hardware.

GUI: acronym for Graphical User Interface; a way to operate a computer by using a pointing device such as a mouse to click on icons and menus instead of typing in commands on a keyboard.

Hard copy: a printed paper copy.

Hardware: the physical apparatus of a computer system, including the CPU, monitor, keyboard, and printer.

Icon: a small picture that represents programs or files in a graphical user interface.

Interlaced: refers to a computer monitor that paints one set of horizontal lines on the screen, then fills in lines between those of the first set, resulting in a barely visible flicker that is very tiring to the eyes.

Kilobyte: equal to 1,024 bytes.

LAN: an acronym for Local Area Network; a group of computers connected together so that they can exchange files, programs, and data. They can also share peripherals such as printers, modems, and hard disks.

Megabyte: equal to 1,024 kilobytes.

Megahertz: one million cycles per second.

Modem: an acronym for MOdulator/DEModulator. This device enables a computer to transmit and receive data over the telephone network.

Numeric keypad: the number keys at the right-hand side of a computer keyboard, arranged in the same way as the keys of an adding machine.

Piracy: the making or sale of illegal copies of computer software.

Pixel: short for picture element, the phosphor dots that create the picture on a computer screen.

RAM: an acronym for Random Access Memory, where a computer stores programs and data while its power is on.

ROM: an acronym for Read-Only Memory, which contains information a computer must have to operate. This information cannot be changed.

Software: programs designed to perform specific tasks.

Spreadsheet: a program that performs a variety of mathematical, financial, statistical, and logical calculations.

Virus: a program that can damage files on a computer's hard disk.

Word processor: a program that enables the user to outline, write, edit, and print out documents.

WYSIWYG: stands for "what you see is what you get." Indicates that what is visible on screen approximates what will be produced in print.

CHAPTER 6

MAKING YOUR OFFICE WORK FOR YOU

So, BY NOW YOU'VE FOUND YOUR SPECIAL SPOT, PAINTED IT, decorated it, moved in your furniture, and chosen your equipment. In this last chapter, we will give you some guidelines on how to make your home office work.

Projecting a professional image means more than just getting the job done; you have to be able to sell your ability to do the job in the first place. Effective communications skills go a long way in proving your professionalism. Learn the best way to use the phone and the phone company's services. See how the Internet can keep you up to date with the latest technologies, market trends, and your customers' needs. And don't underestimate the importance of knowing how to write a good, old-fashioned letter.

Efficiency and productivity go hand in hand, especially for the home office worker who has to take care of all the office tasks alone. Set up office systems that work for you—and then use them.

RIGHT: Functional furnishings and up-to-date equipment are invaluable mainstays for a home office, but the most important variable is how well your surroundings suit your work habits and style.

USING THE TELEPHONE

Telephones are such an all-pervasive part of our lives that we rarely even think about them. There are some very important decisions to be made, though, that will affect the vital workings of your home office.

HOW MANY LINES?

The telephone is the home office worker's main connection to the outside world. The first thing to consider is how many lines you will need to keep your business running efficiently. Many home-based workers seem to manage quite well with just one line for both home and office. However, there are good reasons for having at least one separate line for your business. You need to have access to the phone during business hours; you don't want to be competing with other family members for calling time or run the risk of having a young child answer business calls. Incoming personal calls, or calls for other family members during business hours, can be distracting. Having a separate phone line for the office helps keep your business and your personal lives separate. And don't

forget that both the installation charges and the monthly bill for a business line are legitimate tax deductions.

Now that you have decided on a dedicated phone line for your office, are you sure that you don't need more than one line? This will depend on how often you use your fax machine and modem, and how much time you spend on the Internet. If you are just starting out in business, you

ANSWERING PROFESSIONALLY

- Decide how you will answer the phone. Will you use your name, your business name, or just a simple "hello"?
- Speak clearly and distinctly; ask friends to evaluate the tone and volume of your voice on the phone.
- Use a pleasant, warm tone of voice. It really does help to smile while you're talking.
- Try to answer each phone call promptly.
- When making outgoing calls, know what you want to say and accomplish before dialing.
- When recording an outgoing message keep it short and to the point; avoid using anything cute or gimmicky.
- When leaving a message on someone else's machine, leave your number as well as your name; stick to the point, and speak clearly.

might want to try working with one line for a while to see what your needs are. Just remember, each time you change your phone lines, you will probably have to make changes to any printed materials your business uses.

PHONE SERVICES AND PRODUCTS

Phone companies offer a variety of services that simplify working from home. The following are a few of the features you may want to consider for your office. Contact your local phone company to determine what is available in your area.

The distinctive-ring feature allows you to have up to three numbers on the same phone line. This is the service you need if you can't afford—or don't receive enough calls to justify—a second phone line. You can use one number for personal calls, another for business, and a third for a fax machine. Each number has its own distinctive ring so you know how to answer each call. Using this service with a ring selector *(page 211)* ensures that only the selected ringing sequence passes to the

phone to which it is connected. However, you still have only one phone line, so only one call can take place at a time.

Call waiting enables you to receive a second call when you are already on the phone, so you can use your line even when waiting for an important call. A soft beep lets you know another caller is trying to get through. However, this feature can play havoc with fax and data transmissions unless you deactivate it by dialing *70 before sending or receiving data, or while on the Internet.

The call-display feature requires a special telephone with a display screen that shows you who is calling before you answer the phone; this enables you to decide whether you want to answer the call. A variation of this feature combines with the call-waiting service to let you see who is calling while you are already on the phone with someone else.

Voice mail is an alternative to telephone-answering devices. This service takes messages when you are out of the office or on the phone, or receiving a fax. Your messages can be retrieved when you are away from the office by using a special code.

Call forwarding automatically reroutes calls to any telephone number you specify, letting you stay in touch wherever you are.

Conference calls allow you to set up calls with three or more people at once.

Three-way calling is like having a second phone line: Add a third person to a call already in progress, or simply call and consult a third party while on the phone with someone else.

Integrated Services Digital Network (ISDN) is a digital telephone service that works over existing copper wiring. Basic Rate Interface (BRI), the most common type of ISDN, has two B channels that transmit data and one D channel that sets up and tears down the calls. The two B channels allow you to make two calls, or voice or data transmissions simultaneously. This feature also enables high-speed data transmission. ISDN is more expensive than regular phone service, requiring some specialized equipment. It is not available in all areas.

LONG-DISTANCE DIALING

Direct dialing is the quickest and least expensive way to dial long distance. To place a long-distance call in North America, dial 1, the area code, and then the number.

If you need to speak to a specific person, you can place a person-to-person call. This type of call is much more expensive, but you are charged only if you reach the person you have specified. To place a person-to-person call, dial 0, the area code, and the number. When the operator comes on the line, give the name of the person you are calling.

To call collect or to bill the call to a third number, dial 0, the area code, and the number. When the operator answers, specify either "collect" or "bill to" and then provide the information that is requested. In some places, you may be prompted for the necessary information by an automated voice system.

For long-distance directory assistance in North America, dial 1, the area code, and then 555-1212. The operator will answer, and ask for the name and address of the person you want to reach. To find out a toll-free number, dial 1-800-555-1212.

Overseas calls can also be direct-dialed. You must dial 011, then the country code, the city code, and the local number. Your local telephone directory has up-to-date listings of country and city codes. If the country you wish to call is not included, dial 0 and ask the long-distance operator for the correct code. If you also need to make the call person-to-person, collect, or if you want it billed to a third number, dial 01, the country code, the city code, and the local number. When the operator answers, request the service you want and provide the appropriate information.

If direct dialing is not possible, or if you need help placing your call, dial 0 for the overseas operator.

It is also possible to make long-distance calls to ships and boats or to motor vehicles. To call ships or boats, dial 0 and ask for the marine operator. For cars and trucks with manual mobile telephone service, dial 0 and ask for the mobile telephone operator.

INTERNATIONAL TIME ZONES

Before making long-distance calls, be sure to check the time differences. Don't forget about daylight-savings time during summer months. Here are some examples of the differences:

At noon Eastern Standard Time it is:

- 3 a.m. the next day in Sydney, Australia
- 6 p.m. in Austria
- 11 p.m. in Bangladesh
- 6 p.m. in Belgium
- 2 p.m. in Brazil
- 1:30 p.m. in Newfoundland, Canada
- 9 a.m. in Vancouver, Canada
- 1 a.m. the next day in China
- 8 p.m. in Moscow, Commonwealth of Independent States (CIS)
- 6 p.m. in the Czech Republic
- 6 p.m. in Denmark
- 7 p.m. in Egypt
- 6 p.m. in France
- 6 p.m. in Germany
- 7 p.m. in Greece
- 1 a.m. the next day in Hong Kong
- 5 p.m. in Ireland
- 7 p.m. in Israel
- 6 p.m. in Italy
- 2 a.m. the next day in Japan
- 5 a.m. the next day in New Zealand
- 6 p.m. in Nigeria
- 10 p.m. in Pakistan
- 1 a.m. the next day in the Philippines
- 12:30 a.m. the next day in Singapore
- 5 p.m. in the United Kingdom
- 11 a.m. in Chicago, USA
- 9 a.m. in San Francisco, USA

This map indicates time zones and area codes for North America. To the right of the map is a list of area codes in numerical order.

907
ALASKA

867
YUKON

867
NORTHWEST TERRITORIES

PACIFIC
TIME ZONE

MOUNTAIN
TIME ZONE

CENTRAL
TIME ZONE

250
BRITISH
COLUMBIA

403
ALBERTA

306
SASKATCHEWAN

204
MANITOBA

807
ONTARIO

250

604

206/253/425

WASHINGTON

360   509

503

541
OREGON

406
MONTANA

701
NORTH DAKOTA

218
MINNESOTA

906

612
320

715
WISCONSIN

208
IDAHO

605
SOUTH DAKOTA

507

414
608   920

707

530/916

CALIFORNIA

307
WYOMING

308

712   515
IOWA

319

312
773

309   815

510/925
OAKLAND

702
NEVADA

NEBRASKA

402

217
ILLINOIS

415/650
SAN FRANCISCO

209

801

435
UTAH

303
DENVER

970

COLORADO

816
/660   314

785
KANSAS

913   MISSOURI

618

408
831

719

316

417

573

805

818

760

602
PHOENIX

405
OKLAHOMA

918

501
ARKANSAS

90

626

909

520
ARIZONA

505
NEW MEXICO

806

228

213/310/323
LOS ANGELES

714/949

254
817
940

214
972

903

870

601

409   318
MISSISSIF

619
SAN DIEGO

TEXAS

915

830

210

512

504

281/713   LOUISIANA

956

ONLINE SERVICES

The Internet is essentially a network of interconnected computer networks. It is a communications tool used to transport electronic information. The Internet had its beginnings in the late 1960s and early 1970s, and was originally designed to connect various government mainframe computer networks together. In its early days, the Internet was used primarily as a means of providing an electronic link between research centers. Today, however, with the increasing popularity of the personal computer, the Internet is rapidly becoming an important business tool. With a computer and Internet access, even the smallest home business can make and maintain global connections.

E-mail (electronic mail) is one of the most important services offered by the Internet. E-mail combines the immediacy of the telephone with the accuracy of the printed word. And surprisingly, it costs very little. You can send messages around the world every day and probably still pay no more than the monthly cost of your basic e-mail account.

The World Wide Web (WWW) is probably what comes to mind when people think of the Internet. But the two are not the same thing. The World Wide Web is a software system operating on the Internet that conveys information to users by means of text, graphics, video, and sound. Sites are linked one to another and Website visitors can jump from one site to another by using the mouse to click on a link. The Web not only allows you to view electronic documents, but it also lets you interact with them. Businesses can use the Web to give customers the latest product information, and—combined with e-mail—the Web can allow customers to place orders, ask questions, receive support, and much more. With an Internet presence, your business is available to customers all over the world, 24 hours a day, every day.

In addition to this, the Internet is one of the most important sources of current information on almost every imaginable topic. Along with numerous online journals, newspapers, and magazines from around the world, it is also possible to

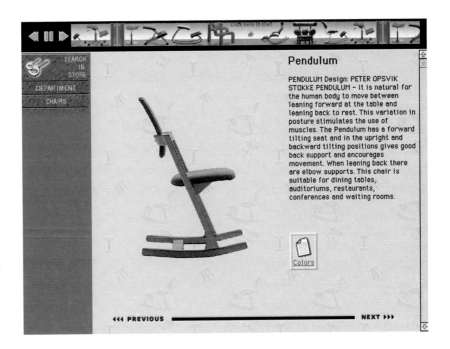

PENDULUM Design: PETER OPSVIK
STOKKE PENDULUM - It is natural for the human body to move between leaning forward at the table and leaning back to rest. This variation in posture stimulates the use of muscles. The Pendulum has a forward tilting seat and in the upright and backward tilting positions gives good back support and encourages movement. When leaning back there are elbow supports. This chair is suitable for dining tables, auditoriums, restaurants, conferences and waiting rooms.

*RIGHT: This profession-
ally produced Web
page, an example of
an on-screen catalog,
shows how the Internet
can serve to showcase
products. By clicking
on the underlined
word, known as a hy-
perlink, the viewer
goes to another screen
with more detail—in
this example, the range
of colors available.*

access libraries, government agencies and departments, and various educational institutions. If your business depends on accurate, up-to-date information, maybe it's time to get online.

GETTING ON THE INTERNET

To access the Internet, you need some basic equipment: a computer with a modem *(page 186)* and telephone service. Although ISDN lines are available in many areas *(page 224)*, the most common type of Internet connection for home offices is made over standard telephone lines. Cable technology, using the same wiring as cable television, is now becoming available in some areas to transmit digital data at very high speeds. Next, you need to choose a company that provides Internet access; the

company should supply you with the necessary software and instructions that will allow you to make your Internet connection. This software will include a Web browser, which is the application you need to navigate on the Web. The software is usually available at a nominal cost and may even be offered free as part of an Internet subscription package.

There are two main types of companies providing Internet connections: Internet service providers (ISP) and commercial online services. An ISP will take care of your e-mail account, provide full Internet access, and, if you want, set up a Website for your business. Some ISPs offer flat-rate monthly fees for unlimited access. Other plans let you pay for blocks of connection time and then charge an hourly rate for any

Electronic mail is a quick and reliable way to send written communications across town or around the world. A message can be sent to several destinations simultaneously and stored electronically until the recipient is ready to read it. It is an efficient tool for keeping telecommuters and other home-office workers in touch with their colleagues and clients.

Although messages are transmitted quickly, they should not be dashed off and sent quickly. To make the best impression on the reader, e-mail should be prepared with as much care as standard correspondence. Here are some things to remember:

- Take care with spelling and punctuation; mistakes make you look sloppy and inattentive to detail.
- Keep messages short and to the point.
- Be professional and polite.
- Privacy cannot be guaranteed with electronic communications; like writing a postcard, don't say anything you wouldn't want a third party to read.
- Check for e-mail regularly throughout the day.
- After reading messages, file any that need to be kept in the appropriate directory or folder on your hard disk; delete the rest to avoid clutter.
- Respond promptly to any messages requiring a reply.

additional time used over the course of the month. Or, you can simply pay an hourly fee. Whenever possible, choose an ISP that has a local access number—otherwise, you will have to add long-distance charges to your access fees. Many users feel that local companies also provide better service and technical support than the larger national companies. ISPs provide fast access to the Internet and are the best way to go if you intend to use the Internet extensively.

Commercial online services started out as closed information systems without Internet access. They offer information from a wide variety of sources: online versions of magazines and newspapers as well as online news feeds from organizations such as Associated Press; financial information including stock market reports; and reference materials. Today, however, most also offer full Internet access, with software packages that make navigating online a simple matter even for computer novices. If you travel a lot, this kind of connection does offer an advantage: You can connect from locations all over the world. However, these services can get relatively expensive, and sometimes the high volume of users means having to wait to connect or to get technical support.

Here are some questions to ask before choosing a service provider:

- Does the service provide the software you need and an instruction manual as part of its introductory package?
- How is connection time sold?
- Is 24-hour technical support available, either by phone or e-mail?
- Can you get technical support for the type of computer you own?
- Are calls for technical support toll-free?
- What costs are involved with setting up your own Web page?
- Do they support connections up to at least 28.8 kpbs?
- What is their user-to-modem ratio? The industry standard is one line for 10 customers. Less is even better.

You get what you pay for. If a company is charging considerably less than the competition, find out why. The savings may not be worth the frustration of first having to wait to get online and then having another delay as data trickles in.

CREATING A WEB PAGE

Like an electronic storefront that welcomes visitors 24 hours a day, 7 days a week, whether you are there or not, a Web page can help you market your product and services. A Website-creation program makes it easy to produce a personalized Internet presence. Features vary from program to program, so shop around to make sure the software you buy is the one that best suits your needs.

Once your design is finished, your page must be uploaded to your Internet service provider. Contact your ISP for instructions on how to do this. Monthly fees for storing Web pages vary, but many ISPs offer some free space with high-end accounts. Four megabytes is usually enough for a standard Website. This will allow you to introduce your business and provide product information, prices, and an e-mail address for customers to contact you. Depending on how many people visit your site, there may be additional charges for high traffic, or you may have to pay for a commercial account.

WRITING LETTERS

Any letter you send represents you and your company. Whatever the purpose of the letter, it will make a better impression if it is clear, concise, polite, and easy to read. First, it's a good idea to print a supply of letterhead, with your name, company name, and contact information—most business letters are written on preprinted letterhead. You can also include the same logo and design features that appear on your business cards *(page 242)*. To make a letter flow smoothly and progress logically, decide what you want it to accomplish, and plan what you want to say before you start writing; you may want to jot down an outline. Proofread letters carefully for mistakes in grammar, spelling, and punctuation that might make you appear slop-

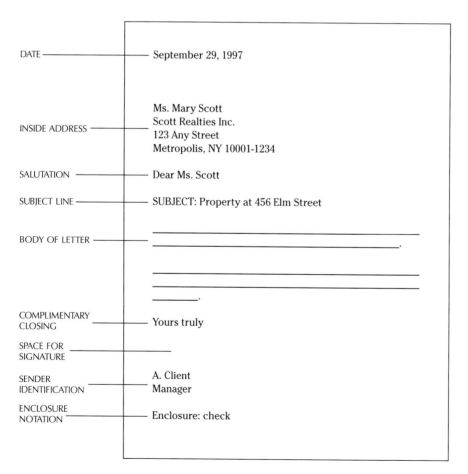

DATE —————————— September 29, 1997

INSIDE ADDRESS ——————— Ms. Mary Scott
Scott Realties Inc.
123 Any Street
Metropolis, NY 10001-1234

SALUTATION —————— Dear Ms. Scott

SUBJECT LINE —————— SUBJECT: Property at 456 Elm Street

BODY OF LETTER ——————

COMPLIMENTARY
CLOSING ————————— Yours truly

SPACE FOR
SIGNATURE

SENDER
IDENTIFICATION ————— A. Client
Manager

ENCLOSURE
NOTATION ————————— Enclosure: check

LEFT: An example of a business letter in standard block style—all lines begin at the left margin. Open punctuation has been used, meaning there is no punctuation except in the body of the letter.

py or careless. Word processors usually come with utilities such as spell checkers as well as templates for laying out business letters. If one of the templates suits your needs, use it to simplify and standardize the task of letter-writing.

There are three basic formatting styles for modern business letters. Using an accepted format makes your letter easy to type and to read. Choose the format you prefer and use it consistently.

In the block-style letter *(opposite)*, every line starts at the left margin. Paragraphs are not indented. Omitting the tab stops makes this style of letter very rapid and easy to type.

The modified-block style letter *(below)* starts the date and the complimentary clos-

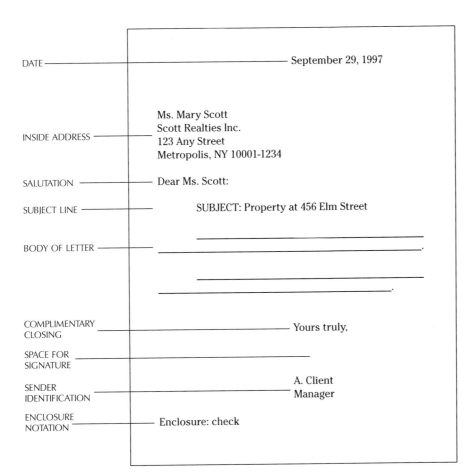

LEFT: A modified-block style business letter, in which the date, complimentary closing, and sender identification lines are centered. The subject line and the first line of each paragraph of the body may be indented, as shown, or not. The colon after the salutation and the comma following the complimentary closing are the hallmarks of mixed punctuation.

ing in the center of the page. Paragraphs usually start flush at the left margin, although they may be indented, if you prefer, or when you are writing a short, double-spaced letter so that the paragraph breaks will be evident.

The simplified letter style *(below)* is similar to the block style, but it omits the salutation and the complimentary closing. This is the quickest style to write, as no time is spent determining the appropriate salutation and closing. You will need to use a variation on the block-style letter when you automatically generate envelopes from the address on the actual letter. The U.S. Postal Service has a preferred format for addressing envelopes *(page 236)*; use this style for the inside address of your letter also.

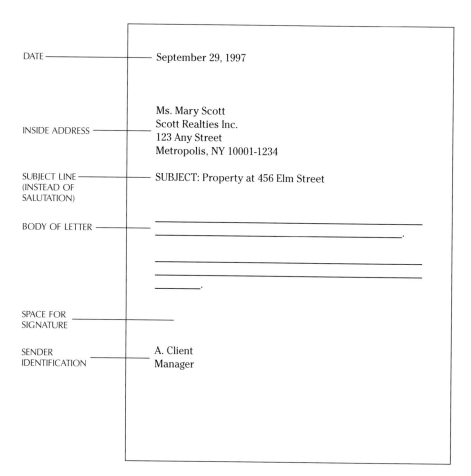

DATE ———————— September 29, 1997

INSIDE ADDRESS ————— Ms. Mary Scott
Scott Realties Inc.
123 Any Street
Metropolis, NY 10001-1234

SUBJECT LINE ———— SUBJECT: Property at 456 Elm Street
(INSTEAD OF
SALUTATION)

BODY OF LETTER ————

SPACE FOR
SIGNATURE

SENDER ———————— A. Client
IDENTIFICATION Manager

LEFT: A simplified business letter is set up like the block style, except that the salutation is replaced by a subject line, and the complimentary closing is omitted.

There are two accepted styles of punctuation for business letters. The open punctuation style uses no punctuation after the date, inside address, salutation, complimentary closing, or identification—unless they contain abbreviations. The mixed punctuation style uses a colon after the salutation and a comma after the complimentary closing.

PARTS OF A LETTER

Date: Preferred style: September 29, 1997.

Inside address: Be sure to include the person's name, his or her title, the company name, street address, city, state or province, country (if necessary), and the ZIP code or postal code. If you do not know the person's name, then use their business title; for example:

Attention Personnel Manager.

Salutation: Capitalize the first word and all nouns, for example:

- Dear Ms. Smith
- Dear Lee Smith (if gender is unknown)
- Ladies and Gentlemen
- Your Honor

Subject line: The preferred style is to start the subject line from the left margin, although it can be centered; in modified-block style it may be indented.

Body of the letter: Single-spaced with double spaces between paragraphs. Very short letters may be double-spaced. If you double-space the body of the letter, you should indent all the paragraphs.

Complimentary closing: Capitalize the first word, for example:

Yours truly.

Sender identification line: Your title (if you use one) can appear beside your name or below it. Leave at least four spaces above this line for your signature; if the letter is very short, space the identification line further down the page.

Enclosure notation: Use this to indicate that something is being included with the letter.

For multiple page letters, the second and all subsequent pages should be typed on plain paper of the same type and color as the letterhead page. Use a heading, a page number, and the date to identify each page.

HALF OF LENGTH OF ENVELOPE

ONE-THIRD
OF HEIGHT
OF ENVELOPE

RETURN ADDRESS

ADDRESS (FOLLOWING FORMAT-
TING GUIDE, OPPOSITE PAGE)

$\frac{1}{2}$"
MIN.

$\frac{1}{2}$"
MIN.

$\frac{5}{8}$"

POSTAL SERVICES

Despite the many innovations in communications technology, the postal service remains one of the most important and least expensive ways to exchange information. The U.S. Postal Service offers six classes of domestic mail with different rates depending on the destination, type of service, size of the package, and other factors. These rates, of course, are subject to frequent change.

DIFFERENT CLASSES OF MAIL

Express Mail: This is the fastest service available, offering guaranteed overnight delivery 365 days a year for both envelopes and packages.

Priority Mail: This service offers preferential handling, but is not quite as fast as Express Mail. Maximum weight accepted is 70 pounds.

First-Class Mail: This is the service for letters, postcards, greeting cards, and similar items. Any First-Class item weighing more than 11 ounces should be sent as Priority Mail. Delivery is within one to three days.

Periodicals: Periodicals mailing rates are granted only to publishers and approved news agents.

Standard Mail (A): This service is used mainly by retailers and other advertisers to promote their products and services, but can also be used by individuals to send parcels weighing less than 1 pound.

Standard Mail B (Parcels): This is the service for sending parcels weighing 1 pound or more.

Your local post office can give you more details about these services.

ADDRESSING ENVELOPES CORRECTLY

The U.S. Postal Service uses machines to scan and sort the mail. Following a few simple guidelines when addressing letter-sized mail will help ensure that your mail is correctly delivered in as short a time as possible. Letter-sized mail includes folded self-mailers, postcards, and other letter-sized pieces enclosed on four sides, as well as actual letters.

FORMATTING GUIDE

- Capitalize the entire address.
- Leave a clear vertical space between each character and word, and a clear horizontal space between each line.
- Use the two-letter state or provincial abbreviations approved by the U.S.P.S. (*box, page 238*).
- Do not use punctuation except to insert a hyphen in the ZIP+4 code.
- Use addressing abbreviations approved by the U.S.P.S. (*box, page 239*).
- Make sure ZIP codes and ZIP+4 codes are correct and complete.
- Place endorsements for special services above the delivery address or below the return address.

In the Destination Address include:

- The recipient's name and/or the name of the company.

U.S. POSTAL SERVICE SPECIAL MAILING SERVICES

Here is a list of some of the special services offered by the U.S.P.S.:

- **Certificate of Mailing:** Purchased at the time of mailing, this is a receipt to show the item was mailed. The post office does not keep a record and there is no proof of receipt.
- **Certified Mail:** With this service, the post office keeps a record to show proof of delivery.
- **Collect on Delivery (COD):** This service allows the mailer to collect payment for merchandise when it is delivered. The merchandise must have been ordered by the addressee.
- **Insurance:** Coverage can be purchased for most items; contact your post office for information.

- **Registered Mail:** Mail sent this way is placed under tight security from mailing to delivery.
- **Return Receipt:** This provides proof of delivery and is available for mail sent COD, Express Mail, registered mail, or mail insured for a minimum of $50.00.
- **Return Receipt for Merchandise:** This service provides a mailing receipt, return receipt, and record of delivery.
- **Special Delivery:** This service provides for daily delivery—even on Sundays and holidays—and is available for all types of mail, except Express Mail and bulk Standard Mail (A).
- **Special Handling:** This service is available for any parcel with unusual contents requiring special care. This does not include Special Delivery service.

ABBREVIATIONS OF STATES AND PROVINCES

These are the two-letter state abbreviations (including Washington, D.C.) used by the U.S. Postal Service:

		Maine	ME	Utah	UT
		Maryland	MD	Vermont	VT
		Massachusetts	MA	Virginia	VA
		Michigan	MI	Washington	WA
		Minnesota	MN	West Virginia	WV
		Mississippi	MS	Wisconsin	WI
Alabama	AL	Missouri	MO	Wyoming	WY
Alaska	AK	Montana	MT		
Arizona	AZ	Nebraska	NE		
Arkansas	AR	Nevada	NV		
California	CA	New Hampshire	NH		
Colorado	CO	New Jersey	NJ		
Connecticut	CT	New Mexico	NM		
Delaware	DE	New York	NY	Alberta	AB
District of Columbia	DC	North Carolina	NC	British Columbia	BC
Florida	FL	North Dakota	ND	Manitoba	MB
Georgia	GA	Ohio	OH	New Brunswick	NB
Hawaii	HI	Oklahoma	OK	Newfoundland	NF
Idaho	ID	Oregon	OR	Northwest Territories	NT
Illinois	IL	Pennsylvania	PA	Nova Scotia	NS
Indiana	IN	Rhode Island	RI	Ontario	ON
Iowa	IA	South Carolina	SC	Prince Edward Island	PE
Kansas	KS	South Dakota	SD	Quebec	QC
Kentucky	KY	Tennessee	TN	Saskatchewan	SK
Louisiana	LA	Texas	TX	Yukon Territory	YT

When mailing to Canada, use these two-letter abbreviations for the provinces and territories:

- Street address, post office box number, rural route number and box number, or the highway contract route number and box number.
- City, state, ZIP code or ZIP+4 code.
- For international mail only, include the country name in capital letters on the last line of the address.

Return Address:
- Place in the upper left corner and include the same information as above.
- When both a post office box number and a street address are used, the place where you want the mail delivered should appear on the line directly above the city, state, and ZIP code line.

ABBREVIATIONS FOR SECONDARY ADDRESS UNITS

Apartment	APT	Lower	LOWR	Terrace	TER
Avenue	AVE	Office	OFC	Trailer	TRLR
Basement	BSMT	Penthouse	PH	Unit	UNIT
Boulevard	BLVD	Pier	PIER	Upper	UPPR
Building	BLDG	Place	PL		
Department	DEPT	Rear	REAR	**Directions**	
Drive	DR	Road	RD	North	N
Floor	FL	Room	RM	East	E
Front	FRNT	Side	SIDE	South	S
Gardens	GDNS	Slip	SLIP	West	W
Hangar	HNGR	Space	SPC	Northeast	NE
Harbor	HBR	Station	STA	Southeast	SE
Lobby	LBBY	Street	ST	Southwest	SW
Lot	LOT	Suite	STE	Northwest	NW

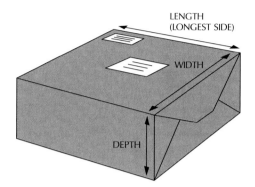

BELOW: Parcels must be measured before being mailed; oversize items won't be accepted for delivery.

LENGTH
(LONGEST SIDE)

WIDTH

DEPTH

ZIP CODES

The numbers in the ZIP code identify the state, city, and post office of a particular address, and they help to expedite automated mail processing and delivery. ZIP code directories are available at your local post office.

The ZIP+4 code is composed of the five-digit ZIP code with a four-digit add-on that identifies geographic segments within the five-digit delivery area. Using this code reduces the number of times a piece of mail must be handled. It also reduces the possibility of human error and misdelivery of mail. For information on ZIP+4 codes, contact your local postmaster or visit the Postal Service Website, located on the Internet at http://www.usps.gov.

MAILING PARCELS

Parcels may weigh up to 70 pounds and measure up to 108 inches in length, width, and depth combined. Package them properly to prevent damage. Seal the container with reinforced tape; avoid wrapping paper, string, masking tape, or cellophane tape.

Place a copy of the address information inside the container, and once it is wrapped, print the address in block letters on one side of the package. Write the return address in smaller print to the upper left of the delivery address.

Various types of packaging products are on sale at your local post office, including boxes, padded envelopes, mailing tubes, cushioning material, and tape.

Parcels Size Requirements:

- Height: minimum $3\frac{1}{2}$ inches; maximum $6\frac{1}{8}$ inches.
- Length: minimum 5 inches; maximum $11\frac{1}{2}$ inches.
- Thickness: minimum 0.007 inches; maximum 0.25 inches.

INTERNATIONAL MAIL

Letters and packages can be sent to foreign countries by airmail or surface mail.

BELOW: *Correct centering of an address on a mailing label.*

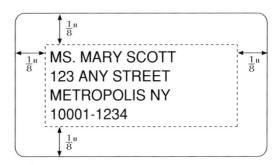

There are two special services for high-priority or urgently needed items: Express Mail International Service and Global Priority Mail. Contact your local post office for rates and information about services in the country to which you are mailing.

ALTERNATIVES TO THE POST OFFICE

There are many commercial delivery services and express services available that provide an alternative to the postal system for delivering envelopes and parcels. Although most of these services operate only within their own city, there are several national and international companies. To find out what services operate in your area, check the Yellow Pages under headings such as "Couriers," "Delivery Services," and "Messengers."

MAILING LABELS

Address labels save time, so, especially for large mailings, you may want to use them for letter-sized mail as well as for large envelopes and packages. There are several types and styles of labels available. You can use clear labels to let the color of your envelope show through, or light-colored or white labels to make your address more easily visible on a dark envelope.

If you have a label printer *(page 211)*, purchase labels designed specifically for it. Some leading office products companies have designed software that works with most popular word-processing programs to let you produce printed labels easily on your computer.

When using labels, make sure they adhere securely to the item being mailed. Follow the guidelines presented above for addressing envelopes *(pages 236-240)* and make sure to position the address in the center of the label. When attaching the label to the envelope, the label edge should be parallel to the bottom edge of the envelope and should be placed within the area the scanner will look for the address.

STATIONERY AND
BUSINESS CARDS

If you want to be treated professionally, it is vital to present a professional image. It doesn't matter how important or interesting your message is, if it isn't packaged properly, it stands a good chance of being ignored. Letterhead stationery printed on good-quality paper will get the kind of attention that plain type on inexpensive paper just can't command.

The design of your business cards should convey something of your personality and business style. What is the message you want to send? Formal and traditional? Casual and fun? Or something in between? A well-designed logo can do a lot to get your message across.

As for content, business cards should contain sufficient information to tell people what you do and how to contact you. However, avoid cluttering the card with too much information—the essentials should be readable. Decide what is important; for

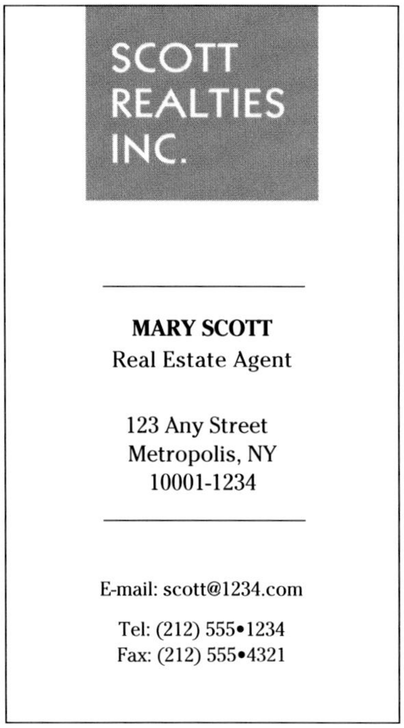

SCOTT REALTIES INC.

MARY SCOTT
Real Estate Agent

123 Any Street
Metropolis, NY
10001-1234

E-mail: scott@1234.com

Tel: (212) 555•1234
Fax: (212) 555•4321

SCOTT REALTIES INC.

MARY SCOTT
Real Estate Agent

123 Any Street
Metropolis, NY
10001-1234

E-mail: scott@1234.com

Tel: (212) 555•1234
Fax: (212) 555•4321

ABOVE: A business card should grab the reader's attention without obscuring or overwhelming the essentials of what you do and how you can be contacted. The samples shown contain the same information in both a vertical and horizontal design.

example, do you really need to list all your phone numbers? You could simply include just your office number, and use call forwarding *(page 224)* or let your machine take a message when you are out. Do you have more than one business? If so, maybe one card can't do it all.

If putting all this into a space measuring 2 inches by $3\frac{1}{2}$ inches seems an impossible task, then consider hiring a graphic designer to help you do the job.

Once you've decided on the basic look of your business card, and whether you do it yourself or hire a designer, use the same design elements to create a letterhead for your stationery and a cover page for your faxes. Obviously some adjustments will have to be made, but you should aim for a uniform look in everything that carries your company's name—including such items as invoices and statements. This will help you build a profile.

DESIGNING YOUR OWN BUSINESS CARD

If you have a creative flair or are looking to save some money, there are several software programs on the market that can help you design your own business cards. These cards are printed on perforated business card stock made for either laser or ink-jet printers. One big advantage to the do-it-yourself approach is its flexibility: You can change the design of your card or the information on it to suit any situation, and then print only the number of cards you need.

Features vary with these programs, so shop carefully. Do you want to use predesigned layouts—a good choice if you are uncertain about your creative abilities —or create your own? How easy is it to edit text? Can you print cards vertically as well as horizontally? Most programs allow you to add clip art *(page 199)*. If you already have your own logo that you want to use, make sure you can import images into the program.

The look of the finished product will be greatly affected by the quality of your printer, so consider this before deciding to print your own cards. You can always choose a program that will allow you to save the finished design and bring it to a professional printer.

FILING SYSTEMS

There is no shortcut to getting organized, but there are some tools that can make the process easier. The best filing system is the one that works for you; no matter what the experts say, if *you* can't use it, it's no good.

Businesses everywhere are inundated with paper. The first step to a good filing system is knowing what to keep and what to throw out. Each time you handle a piece of paper, ask yourself if you will need it again. If the answer is no, get rid of it.

Once you have decided what to keep, you need to be able to file it so that you can find it again quickly. Files can be grouped in various ways, but the easiest systems for use in a small home office are: alphabetical, by subject, by geographic location, or by name. If you have trouble remembering the heading under which you have placed something, you may want to make cross-references between file folders. Then, set aside regular times to deal with incoming paper. Find a routine you are comfortable with, perhaps a few minutes each day, or an hour or so each week.

Storing active files in a box like this makes it easy to move them from place to place. This can be helpful if your storage area is not in the same place as your work area.

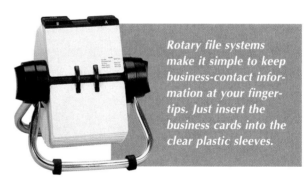

Rotary file systems make it simple to keep business-contact information at your fingertips. Just insert the business cards into the clear plastic sleeves.

A flat tray card file is a good way to keep business contact information organized.

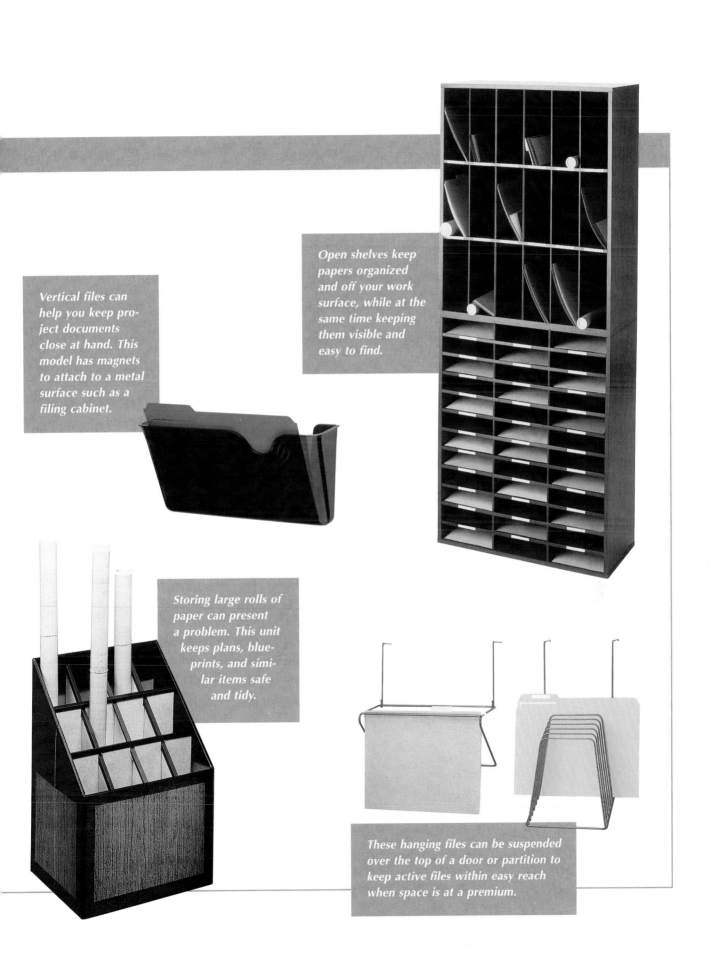

Vertical files can help you keep project documents close at hand. This model has magnets to attach to a metal surface such as a filing cabinet.

Open shelves keep papers organized and off your work surface, while at the same time keeping them visible and easy to find.

Storing large rolls of paper can present a problem. This unit keeps plans, blueprints, and similar items safe and tidy.

These hanging files can be suspended over the top of a door or partition to keep active files within easy reach when space is at a premium.

There are also different ways to file business contact information. Here again, you may wish to work out a system of cross-referencing, so that if you forget a new contact's name, but remember the business, you will still be able to put your hands on the information. An old-fashioned card address directory such as Rolodex is one of the easiest and best-known filing systems, but don't forget to check out contact-management software. These computer programs can keep track of people, meetings, messages, and to-do lists, as well as file information. If your computer has a fax modem and the appropriate software, you can use your contact manager program to automatically send a fax to a whole group of contacts at the same time.

FILING TIPS

- Find a filing system that fits with your work style and be sure to use it.
- If you use a card address directory for business contact information, decide on a standard format for each card; finding information will be much easier.
- Set aside time at regular intervals to take care of filing tasks—put things away and get rid of files that are no longer needed.
- Use specific headings; you will never find anything that has been filed under miscellaneous.
- Use headings you will remember and use cross-references if a paper could be filed under more than one heading.

- Create an index of all of your file names and keep it close at hand.
- File papers in chronological order, with the most recent in front.
- Color-code to distinguish between different categories of files (active/inactive, clients/suppliers, etc.).
- Label the drawers of your filing cabinet.
- Throw things out when they are no longer needed.

In spite of all these tips, don't sacrifice productivity for neatness. When you are running the whole show by yourself, you may not have the time to be compulsive about filing. Set priorities.

WORKING AT HOME

One of the biggest problems home workers face during their working day is getting started in the morning. How do you shun the siren lure of that extra cup of coffee and the day's paper, or ignore that pile of laundry by the basement stairs? How can you sit in front of the computer when the sun is shining and the first buds of spring are beginning to open?

When going to work means changing activities—not changing places—you have to find new ways to trigger creativity and productiveness. Discipline, while important, is only part of the solution. What you must do is find a work style that is right for you. When you dispense with the corporate clothes and the morning commute, you need a new set of switches to get yourself going in the morning. For instance, seeing the children off to school, or your spouse off to work, may be your cue to start work. Other people find it necessary to dress the part before they can settle down to work. You may find that a second cup of coffee and the daily paper are just the transition you need to take you from

family to work. After all, isn't flexibility one of the reasons for working at home in the first place?

Another problem facing home workers is knowing when to stop working. Without a definite signal to end the workday, it is easy to keep going, especially if you are working on something you enjoy, or if you are full of insecurities about your ability to make a go of a home-based business. While working hard for long hours is certainly not a bad thing and will be necessary occasionally, excessive work on a regular basis will tend to undermine your relationships with family and friends and, if taken to extremes, can compromise your health. It is important to set a time when your workday ends. Again, use something that works for you. Choose a specific time of day or use a regular event such as the return of the rest of the family. If you need to, you can always go back to work after taking a break.

Another challenge confronting home-based workers that deserves to be mentioned is loneliness. If the kind of work you

ABOVE: One of the biggest challenges of working at home is ignoring all the distractions and getting started in the morning. It helps to develop a routine that signals the start of your working day.

do leaves you on your own for long stretches of time, you may eventually find yourself sinking into loneliness and possibly depression. Even if things never get that bad, you may still find that you miss interaction with other people during the course of your working day. There are various strategies you can use to combat this problem: Get together with other home-based workers for coffee or lunch on a regular basis; go to your local library to keep up with periodicals you can't afford to subscribe to; join a local business organization; take a breather by enjoying a daily walk around the neighborhood where you can interact with people.

TIPS FOR WORKING EFFECTIVELY

Let people know that, even though you are at home, you are working. Learn to say "no" to family members or neighbors who ask favors simply because you are available during the day. However, be flexible. Remember the "home" in home office; sometimes family or friends have to come first.

- Cut down on personal phone calls by having separate numbers for home and work or using an answering machine to screen calls.

- When you reply to answering-machine messages left outside of your working hours, tell people what your working hours are.

- Be realistic about what you can accomplish each day.

- Take regular breaks throughout the day; if most of your day involves sitting, do some physical activity.

- Develop a network of people who can help you when you are swamped: colleagues or employees who can do some of the work, or family members who can take on more household responsibilities.

- If you have preschool-age children, you may need to find childcare outside of the house for at least part of the time you are working.

- Follow ergonomic guidelines in setting up and running your office. Take care of yourself—you are your own most valuable resource.

- Avoid long periods of repetitive activity; alternate tasks whenever possible.

- Eat well; skipping meals may seem to save time, but in the long run will interfere with productivity.

- Get sufficient sleep.

USEFUL REFERENCES AND ADDRESSES

FURTHER READING

Here are some other sources you can consult for more information:

The Best Home Businesses for the 90s: The Inside Information You Need to Know to Select a Home-Based Business That's Right for You
by Sarah and Paul Edwards
The Putnam Publishing Group

Jane Applegate's Strategies for Small Business Success
by Jane Applegate
Penguin Books USA Inc.

The Macintosh Bible
Peachpit Press

The PC Bible
Peachpit Press

Stephanie Winston's Best Organizing Tips
A Fireside Book published by
Simon and Schuster

Taming the Paper Tiger
by Barbara Hemphill
Kiplinger Books

Of the many magazines you can consult to stay up to date on developments with computers and software, many have online versions. Here are a few of the most popular, with their World-Wide-Web sites for further details, and their addresses and telephone numbers for any subscription inquiries you may have:

Home Office Computing
http://www.smalloffice.com
Subscription information:
P.O. Box 53561
Boulder, CO 80322
800-288-7812 or 303-604-1464

MacUser
http://www.macuser.com
Subscription information:
P.O. Box 56986
Boulder, CO 80322-6986

Macworld
http://www.macworld.com
Subscription information:
P.O. Box 54529
Boulder, CO 80328-4529
800-288-6848 or 303-604-1465

PC Magazine
http://www.pcmag.com
Subscription information:
P. O. Box 54093
Boulder, CO 80322-4093
303-665-8930

PC World
http://www.pcworld.com
Subscription information:
P. O. Box 55029
Boulder, CO 80322-5029
800-234-3498 or 303-604-1465

ORGANIZATIONS
US Small Business Administration
409 Third Street SW
Washington, DC 20416
202-205-6605

For the address and phone number of your local Small Business Administration office, call: 1-800-U-ASK-SBA (1-800-827-5722); or visit the SBA Website: http://www.sbaonline.sba.gov

Home Office Association
of America Inc.
909 Third Ave., Suite 990
New York, NY 10022
800-809-4622; Fax.: 800-315-4622
http://www.hoaa.com

Department of Treasury
Internal Revenue Service
1111 Constitution Avenue NW
Washington, DC 20224
800-829-1040 or 202-622-5000

United States Postal Services
http://www.usps.gov

Strategis, Industry Canada
Information on starting a home business:
http://strategis.ic.gc.ca

INDEX

Time-Life Books is a division of
TIME LIFE INC.

TIME-LIFE CUSTOM PUBLISHING
VICE PRESIDENT and PUBLISHER:
Terry Newell

Associate Publisher: Teresa Hartnett

Vice President of Sales and Marketing: Neil Levin

Project Manager: Jennifer M. Lee

Director of Special Sales: Liz Ziehl

Managing Editor: Donia Ann Steele

Director of Design: Christopher M. Register

Production Manager: Carolyn Clark

Quality Assurance Manager: James D. King
Produced by ST. REMY MULTIMEDIA

ST. REMY MULTIMEDIA INC.
President and Chief Executive Officer:
  Fernand Lecoq
President and Chief Operating Officer:
  Pierre Léveillé
Vice President, Finance: Natalie Watanabe
Managing Editor: Carolyn Jackson
Managing Art Director: Diane Denoncourt
Production Manager: Michelle Turbide

Staff for *The Ultimate Home Office*

Senior Editors: Marc Cassini, Heather Mills
Art Director: Chantal Bilodeau
Assistant Editor: Rebecca Smollett
Writer: Linda Jarosiewicz
Photo Researcher: Jennifer Meltzer
Designers: Jean-Guy Doiron, Robert Labelle
Photographer: Robert Chartier
Editorial Assistants: Liane Keightley,
  James Piecowye
Coordinator: Dominique Gagné
Copy Editor: Judy Yelon
Indexer: Linda Cardella Cournoyer
Systems Director: Edward Renaud
Technical Support: Jean Sirois
Other Staff: Éric Beaulieu, Hélène Dion,
  Lorraine Doré, Geneviève Dubé,
  Anne-Marie Lemay, Maryo Proulx

PICTURE CREDITS
Illustrators: Jack Arthur, Frederic F. Bigio, Lazlo Bodrogi, Adolph E. Brotman, François Daxhelet, Roger C. Essley, Nicholas Fasciano, Charles Forsythe, William J. Hennessy Jr., Walter Hilmers Jr., Fred Holz, Dick Lee, Judy Lineberger, John Martinez, Peter McGinn, Joan S. McGurren, W. F. McWilliam, Jacques Perrault, Raymond Skibinski, Ian Sproull, Vantage Art, Inc., Vicki Vebell, Whitman Studio Inc.

Photographers: 2 **(upper):** Bill Rothschild; 2 **(center):** Nick Merrick, ©Hedrich-Blessing (Herman Miller, Inc.); 2 **(lower):** Luxo Corp.; 3 **(upper):** Nick Merrick, ©Hedrich-Blessing (Herman Miller, Inc.); 3 **(center):** Apple Canada Inc.; 3 **(lower),** 5: Tim Street-Porter; 7: Sligh Furniture Co.; 14 **(upper):** Nick Merrick, ©Hedrich-Blessing (Herman Miller, Inc.); 14 **(lower left and right):** Sauder Woodworking Co.; 15: Crandall & Crandall; 26 **(upper):** Global Upholstery Co., Inc.; 26 **(lower):** Nick Merrick, ©Hedrich-Blessing (Herman Miller, Inc.); 27 **(right):** Crandall & Crandall (Knopf home/Design: Cathy Morehead & Associates); 28: Crandall & Crandall (Niemann home/Design: Cathy Niemann); 29 **(upper):** Nick Merrick, ©Hedrich-Blessing (Herman Miller, Inc.); 29 **(lower):** Bill Rothschild; 30 **(both):** Tim Street-Porter; 31: Crandall & Crandall (Pallette home/Design: Scott Brownell, AIA); 32: Bill Rothschild; 33 **(right):** Crandall & Crandall (Pallette home/Design: Scott Brownell, AIA); 34 **(upper and lower left):** Bill Rothschild; 34-35, 37: Tim Street-Porter; 46: Design Shoji; 47: Pier 1 Imports; 59: Renée Comet; 62: Robert Chartier; 64: Renée Comet; 66: Dodge-Regupol Inc.; 69: Michael Jensen; 71: SL Waber Inc.; 79: Renée Comet; 84: Photographie Glenn Moores; 90: Tim Street-Porter; 92, 93 **(upper):** Luxo Corp.; 93 **(lower):** Tim Street-Porter; 94: Luxo Corp.; 101: Robert Chartier; 103: Photographie Glenn Moores; 107: Sligh Furniture Co.; 110, 111 **(both):** Sauder Woodworking Co.; 112: Ergonomic Logic, Inc.; 113 **(left):** Sauder Woodworking Co.; 113 **(right),** 114: Global Upholstery Co., Inc.; 115: Nick Merrick, ©Hedrich-Blessing (Herman Miller, Inc.); 116, 117 **(both):** Global Upholstery Co., Inc.; 118 **(left):** Obus Forme Ltd.; 118 **(right):** Nick Merrick, ©Hedrich-Blessing (Herman Miller, Inc.); 119: Newell Office Products Inc.; 120: Crandall & Crandall (Bukow home/Design: Lana Barth, ASID); 121 **(left):** Global Upholstery Co., Inc.; 121 **(right):** Windquest Cos., Inc.; 128, 129, 130, 139: Photographie Glenn Moores; 143: Sopa Inc.; 148, 149, 151, 161: Photographie Glenn Moores; 167: Sunworthy Wallcoverings; 168, 169: Levelor Home Fashions Canada; 171: Tim Street-Porter; 172: Sony Electronics Inc.; 173: Apple Canada Inc.; 174 **(upper):** Newell Office Products Inc.; 174 **(lower),** 175: Iomega Corp.; 176: Apple Canada Inc.; 177: Adrien Duey; 178 **(both):** Newell Office Products Inc.; 179, 180, 181: Fellowes Manufacturing of Canada Ltd.; 183, 184: Hewlett-Packard Co.; 185: Balt, Inc.; 186: Canon Canada Inc.; 187: 3 Com; 188 **(upper):** Sony Electronics Inc.; 188 **(lower):** Koss Corp.; 191: Photographie Glenn Moores; 196 **(both):** Adrien Duey; 206, 207: Canon Canada Inc.; 208: Quartet Manufacturing Co.; 209: Plantronics, Inc.; 211: Brother International Corp. (Canada) Ltd.; 212: Texas Instruments Canada Ltd.; 214 **(upper):** Acco Canada Inc.; 214 **(lower):** Quartet Manufacturing Co.; 215 **(top center and upper right):** Pelouze Scale Co.; 215 **(upper and lower left):** Quartet Manufacturing Co.; 215 **(lower right):** Newell Office Products Inc.; 221: Bill Rothschild; 244 **(upper and lower):** Newell Office Products Inc.; 244 **(center):** Quartet Manufacturing Co.; 245 **(upper left):** Newell Office Products Inc.; 245 **(upper right, lower left and right):** Fellowes Manufacturing of Canada Ltd.; 248: Tim Street-Porter

ACKNOWLEDGMENTS
The editors wish to thank the following individuals and institutions: Acco Canada Inc., Willowdale, Ont.; Apple Canada Inc., Markham, Ont.; Jon Arno, Troy, MI; Arrow Fastener Co., Saddle Brook, NJ; Balt Inc., Cameron, TX; L.T. Bowden Jr., Manassas Park, VA; Brother International Corp. (Canada) Ltd., D.D.O., Que.; Canon Canada Inc., Mississauga, Ont.; Design Shoji, Ukiah, CA; Dodge-Regupol Inc., Lancaster, PA; Jon Eakes, Montreal, Que.; Ergonomic Logic Inc., Sparks, NV; Fellowes Manufacturing of Canada Ltd., Markham, Ont.; Global Upholstery Co. Inc., Concord, Ont.; Herman Miller Inc., Zeeland, MI; Hewlett-Packard Co., Palo Alto, CA; Home Tech Solutions, Cupertino, CA; Hunter Douglas Canada Inc., Mississauga, Ont.; Incotel Ltd., Montreal, Que.; Iomega Corp., Roy, UT; Sheryl Johnston, Design Essentials, Pointe Claire, Que.; Koss Corp., Milwaukee, WI; Levelor Home Fashions, Toronto, Ont.; Luxo Corp., Port Chester, NY; Paul McGoldrick, Pianoforte, Montreal, Que.; NCS, St. Laurent, Que.; Newell Office Products, Maryville, TN; NuTone Inc., Cincinnati, OH; Obus Forme Ltd., Toronto, Ont.; Occupational Safety and Health Administration, Washington, DC;. Peca Products, Janesville, WI; Pelouze Scale Co., Bridgeview, IL; Pier 1 Imports, Fort Worth, TX; Plantronics Inc., Santa Cruz, CA; Quartet Manufacturing Co., Laval, Que.; Sauder Woodworking Co., Archbold, OH; Micho Schumann, TotalNet, Montreal, Que.; Bernard Shalinsky, Ergon Associates, Montreal, Que.; Ira Shapiro, Architect, Redding CT; Sligh Furniture Co., Holland, MI; SL Waber, Mount Laurel, NJ; Peter Smollett, Toronto, Ont.; Sony Electronics Inc., San Jose, CA; Sopa Inc., Laval, Que.; Stanley Tools (Division of Stanley Canada), Burlington, Ont.; Francois St-Pierre, Lac Megantic, Que.; Sunworthy Wallcoverings (Division of Borden Decorative Products Inc.), Columbus, OH; Joe Teets, Fairfax County Public Schools, Centerville, VA; Texas Instruments Canada Ltd., North York, Ont.; Thomas & Betts, Rosemont, Que.; Thomas Lighting Accent Division, Los Angeles, CA; 3 Com, Skokie, IL; Tyfu Data Inc., Montreal, Que.; Windquest Cos. Inc., Holland, MI; Woods Industries Inc., Carmel, IN; The Woodworker's Store, Medina, MN; World Floorcovering Association, Anaheim, CA

First printing, Printed in Canada

Time-Life is a trademark
of Time Warner Inc. U.S.A.

Library of Congress Cataloging-in-Publication Data
THE ULTIMATE HOME OFFICE: designing, planning, and creating the perfect workspace for your home or apartment.
      p.   cm.
   Includes bibliographical references and index.
   ISBN 0-7835-4948-2
   1. Home offices—United States—Design.
   2. Office decoration—United States.
   I. Time-Life Books.
NK2195.04U45 1997   97-16864
747.7'9—dc21   CIP